India's Nuclear Proliferation Policy

This book examines India's nuclear program, and it shows how secrecy inhibits learning in states and corrodes the capacity of decision-makers to generate optimal policy choices.

Focusing on clandestine Indian nuclear proliferation during 1980–2010, the book argues that efficient decision-making is dependent on strongly established knowledge actors, high information turnover and the capacity of leaders to effectively monitor their agents. When secrecy concerns prevent states from institutionalizing these processes, leaders tend to rely more on heuristics and less on rational thought processes in choices involving matters of great political uncertainty and technical complexity. Conversely, decision-making improves as secrecy declines and policy choices become subject to higher levels of scrutiny and contestation. The arguments in this book draw on compelling evidence gathered from interviews conducted by the author, with interviewees including individuals who were involved in nuclear planning in India from 1980 to 2010, such as former cabinet and defence secretaries, the principal secretary to the prime minister, national security advisors, secretaries to the department of atomic energy, military chiefs of staff and their principal staff officers, and commanders of India's strategic (nuclear) forces.

This book will be of much interest to students of nuclear proliferation, Asian politics, strategic studies and International Relations.

Gaurav Kampani is Assistant Professor of Political Science at the University of Tulsa, USA.

Asian Security Studies

Series Editors:
Sumit Ganguly, *Indiana University, Bloomington*
Andrew Scobell, *Research and Development (RAND) Corporation, Santa Monica*
Joseph Chinyong Liow, *Nanyang Technological University, Singapore*

Few regions of the world are fraught with as many security questions as Asia. Within this region it is possible to study great power rivalries, irredentist conflicts, nuclear and ballistic missile proliferation, secessionist movements, ethnoreligious conflicts and inter-state wars. This book series publishes the best possible scholarship on the security issues affecting the region, and includes detailed empirical studies, theoretically oriented case studies and policy-relevant analyses as well as more general works.

Indonesia's Foreign Policy and Grand Strategy in the 21st Century
Rise of an Indo-Pacific Power
Vibhanshu Shekhar

Hizbut Tahrir Indonesia and Political Islam
Identity, Ideology and Religio-Political Mobilization
Mohamed Nawab Mohamed Osman

China and International Nuclear Weapons Proliferation
Strategic Assistance
Henrik Stålhane Hiim

Reshaping the Chinese Military
The PLA's Roles and Missions in the Xi Jinping Era
Edited by Richard A. Bitzinger and James Char

India's Nuclear Proliferation Policy
The Impact of Secrecy on Decision Making, 1980–2010
Gaurav Kampani

For more information about this series, please visit:
www.routledge.com/Asian-Security-Studies/book-series/ASS

India's Nuclear Proliferation Policy

The Impact of Secrecy on Decision Making, 1980–2010

Gaurav Kampani

Routledge
Taylor & Francis Group

LONDON AND NEW YORK

First published 2020
by Routledge
2 Park Square, Milton Park, Abingdon, Oxon OX14 4RN

and by Routledge
52 Vanderbilt Avenue, New York, NY 10017

Routledge is an imprint of the Taylor & Francis Group, an informa business

First issued in paperback 2021

© 2020 Gaurav Kampani

The right of Gaurav Kampani to be identified as author of this work has been asserted by him in accordance with sections 77 and 78 of the Copyright, Designs and Patents Act 1988.

All rights reserved. No part of this book may be reprinted or reproduced or utilised in any form or by any electronic, mechanical, or other means, now known or hereafter invented, including photocopying and recording, or in any information storage or retrieval system, without permission in writing from the publishers.

Trademark notice: Product or corporate names may be trademarks or registered trademarks, and are used only for identification and explanation without intent to infringe.

British Library Cataloguing-in-Publication Data
A catalogue record for this book is available from the British Library

Library of Congress Cataloging-in-Publication Data
Names: Kampani, Gaurav, 1969- author.
Title: India's nuclear proliferation policy : the impact of secrecy on decision making, 1980-2010 / Gaurav Kampani.
Other titles: Impact of secrecy on decision making, 1980-2010
Description: New York, NY : Routledge, 2020. | Series: Asian security studies | Includes bibliographical references and index.
Identifiers: LCCN 2019030655 (print) | LCCN 2019030656 (ebook) | ISBN 9780367356286 (hardback) | ISBN 9780429340734 (ebook)
Subjects: LCSH: Nuclear weapons--India. | India--Military policy.
Classification: LCC UA840 .K245 2020 (print) | LCC UA840 (ebook) | DDC 327.1/747095409045--dc23
LC record available at https://lccn.loc.gov/2019030655
LC ebook record available at https://lccn.loc.gov/2019030656

ISBN: 978-0-367-35628-6 (hbk)
ISBN: 978-1-03-208467-1 (pbk)
ISBN: 978-0-429-34073-4 (ebk)

Typeset in Times New Roman
by SPi Technologies India Private Limited

Contents

List of illustrations	vi
Acknowledgments	vii
List of abbreviations	x
1 The oddities of Indian nuclear behavior	1
2 Secrecy and state learning	9
3 A disaggregated nuclear weapons option (1980–1989)	49
4 Behind the veil of nuclear opacity (1989–1998)	83
5 The challenges of nuclear operationalization (1999–2010)	112
6 Conclusion: variations in practices of secrecy and its impact on nuclear outcomes	144
References	167
Index	178

Illustrations

Figures

3.1	Imagined organizational schematic of optimal decision-making	55
3.2	Organizational schematic of actual Indian decision-making (1970–1998)	55
5.1	Organizational chart of India's higher defense management	117

Tables

2.1	Epistemic actors and state learning	18
2.2	Rational optimization in closed and centralized versus open and decentralized decision-making systems	22
2.3	Agent monitoring in closed versus open decision-making systems	25
3.1	Indian ballistic missile programs (1970–1990)	56
6.1	Variations in institutions of secrecy	147

Acknowledgments

Books are long in the making and mine is no different. Ten years have passed from the time when I first started developing ideas that have become a part of this work. Before starting graduate school, I had a relatively benign notion of what it took to produce a work of this scale and magnitude. But after a 10-year slog, I have turned sensitive and appreciative of data, evidence and what it takes to construct an original argument. As my advisor Peter Katzenstein once wryly remarked: graduate students are a perpetually dissatisfied lot in the classroom except when it is time for them to produce their own work.

This book is my intellectual work. Yet it is a collective endeavor involving many. I owe primary thanks to my dissertation committee members: Peter Katzenstein, Matthew Evangelista, Christopher Way and Sumit Ganguly. In a sense, Peter Katzenstein is the architect of this project. It was Peter who pushed me on a field trip to India to try and collect data, which until then I had thought was impossible to obtain. When external funders declined to fund my research citing precisely those data concerns, Peter found money internally within Cornell, without my active knowledge of what it took for him to do so. When I despaired that my data might not add up, he reminded me that research was a quest for what might exist, not what we suppose exists. Through all these years, he has been unwavering in his intellectual and emotional support, answering every email I wrote him, returning chapter drafts in record time and providing feedback that was exquisite in its attention for detail. The treatment I received from him is probably no different from that received by dozens of students he has shepherded over the years. Through him I learnt the institutional significance of having a first-rate academic advisor in graduate school.

All committee members were remarkably generous with their support, time and attention. In the starting phases of the project Matt Evangelista as the director of the Judith Reppy Institute for Peace and Conflict Studies was instrumental in providing me seed money to get my research off the ground. I owe him special thanks for his magical ability to conjure up literature that spoke to my research, to scrutinize my arguments with meticulous care for inconsistencies and flaws, and for catching every typo and spelling mistake in my writing. Whenever I ran into an ice field that threatened to trap the vessel of my arguments, Matt helped me find a way that in retrospect seemed obvious. Chris Way played the "bad cop" on the committee subjecting my arguments to withering criticism, which to an observer unschooled in the traditions of academe might even appear hostile. However, Chris's criticisms were directed with the best intellectual intentions. They cut through the background noise and identified with precision what was valuable, unique and how what was useful could benefit from further amplification. From him I learnt the art of executing what I had heard before but not understood fully: that arrived simplicity is truly the greatest form of complexity. Finally, I owe thanks to Sumit Ganguly, who graciously sat as an external member on my committee. It was Sumit who performed the prodigious task of vetting the complex historical data that is central to my argument. Eagle eyed in spotting anomalies, Sumit was unrelenting when he differed. Yet, he was gracious in finding ways to bridge intellectual disagreements and generous in accepting new arguments when supported by data. More significant, Sumit later played an instrumental role in helping me with the publication process.

I also owe thanks to Scott Sagan who arranged for me to spend an entire year at the Center for International Security and Cooperation (CISAC), Stanford as a pre-doctoral fellow. After spending 12 months doing field work in India, I was awash and confused with all the data I had collected. My year at Stanford helped me make sense of it all and more importantly develop a multidisciplinary framework to fit my arguments. In this regard, Lynn Eden who was then director of research at CISAC, helped me through the early stages of argument construction. She was instrumental in helping me appreciate the scale of the arguments I had constructed, which proved crucial in taking the writing project to its next level.

Academic support, however, is only the spear tip of a graduate school campaign. Such endeavors, like their military equivalents, fail and succeed on the logistical and social support they receive. In this regard, I was particularly lucky to have help from Tina Slater, Judy Virgilio and Laurie Coon at the department. Tina is literally the department's administrative keystone. Forever smiling, accommodating and juggling the furiously competing demands on her time, she was the one who saw me through all the administrative thickets of graduate school safely. I doubt I would be graduating in her absence. Outside the department, I owe deep gratitude to Elaine Scott. She was the constant gardener who tilled the soil of award money paperwork at the Reppy Center to ensure that my research would flower.

Above all, it was the support I received from family and friends that saw me through graduate school. My friend Scott turned out to be an angel investor in this endeavor.

LeBron, my then partner, gave up his wonderful apartment downtown in Ithaca so that we could set up home together, sparing me the trouble of putting everything in storage before heading to India for field work. Miserable in the first few days in Delhi, my first instinct was to take the next flight back to New York. It was the daily Skype call with LeBron and his reassurance of home and continuity that helped me overcome my homesickness. In India, my mother took care of me so that I could focus on research without bothering with the logistical details of setting up house. Back in California, the place I truly consider home, my friends He Seon, Chris, Duane and Sangeeta always kept an open home so that I could get away from the grey of Ithaca, which someone described as "the place where clouds come to die." My colleague Sree and her husband Dhanu shared thousands of air miles generously to fly me several times between India and the US. Finally, I owe special thanks to my bro "Barry" who is always a phone call away, cheering me on and doing everything he can possibly do to help me on my way.

Abbreviations

AEC	Atomic Energy Commission
BARC	Bhabha Atomic Research Centre
CCS	Cabinet Committee on Security
CDS	Chief of Defence Staff
CEA	Commisariat a l'Energie Atomique
C-in-C	Commander-in-Chief
CoSC	Chiefs of Staff Committee
DAE	Department of Atomic Energy
DE	damage expectancy
DND	Draft Nuclear Doctrine
DNSA	Deputy National Security Advisor
DRDL	Defense Research & Development Laboratory
DRDO	Defense Research & Development Organization
EMIS	Electromagnetic Isotope Separation
ERL	Engineering Research Laboratories
GoM	Group of Ministers
IAEA	International Atomic Energy Agency
IAEC	Iraqi Atomic Energy Commission
IAEC	Israel Atomic Energy Commission
IAF	Indian Air Force
ICBM	inter-continental ballistic missile
IDS	Integrated Defence Staff
IDSA	Institute of Defence Studies & Analyses
IGMDP	Integrated Guided Missile Development Program
ISRO	Indian Space Research Organization
JIC	Joint Intelligence Committee
LEU	low-enriched uranium
LWR	light water reactor
MIRV	Multiple Independently Targetable Re-entry Vehicle
NBC	nuclear biological & chemical
NCA	National Command Authority

NFU	no-first-use
NSA	National Security Advisor
PAEC	Pakistan Atomic Energy Commission
PAF	Pakistan Air Force
PIG	Penning Ionization Gauge
PMO	Prime Minister's Office
PNE	Peaceful Nuclear Explosion
SFC	Strategic Forces Command
SOP	standard operating procedure
SPS	Strategic Program Staff
TD	technology demonstrator
UF6	Uranium Hexafluoride
VCDS	Vice Chief of Defence Staff

1 The oddities of Indian nuclear behavior

From the late 1970s until about 2004, India exhibited a pattern of lagging national security responses to unambiguous nuclear threats. Realist theory posits that states confronting protracted power rivalries and lacking the benefits of great nuclear power protection will acquire nuclear weapons.[1] India however bucked that trend until the late 1980s despite the increased threat from Pakistan's nuclearization and Sino-Pakistani nuclear collaboration. Even after India built nuclear weapons in the 1990s, it neglected to develop the institutional capacities necessary to wield them.

Organizational theorists who maintain that India's nuclear weapons program is the consequence of advocacy efforts by a "strategic enclave," the lobby of nuclear scientists and bureaucrats,[2] have never explained the 24-year gap between its first (1974) and second round (1998) of nuclear tests, or why the scientists and bureaucrats refrained from building a coalition with the Indian military, the surest route to a weapons program.

Similarly, explanations that cite prestige as the reason for not just why India has sought nuclear weapons but also for why it minimized their operational utility[3] prior to 1999 are unable to explain why four Indian governments during the 1990s kept the existence of the arsenal secret for a decade. Or why successive Indian governments in the last two decades, in a complete reversal of the logic of prestige, have committed themselves to developing an operational nuclear force even after India won the status of a *de facto* nuclear weapon power.

From the late 1970s on, Indian decision-makers had clear evidence of Pakistan's nuclear quest.[4] Indian national security elites understood that a Pakistani nuclear arsenal would be a game changer in South Asia. It would partly make irrelevant the conventional superiority India had historically enjoyed over Pakistan since their founding.[5] Of greater concern to them was the negative shift in the "balance of threat"[6] as evidenced by Pakistan's attempts at breaking up the Indian union, first by supporting secessionist insurgents in the sensitive Indian border states of Punjab[7] and later Kashmir.[8]

In the winter of 1986–1987 when India and Pakistan almost came to blows during a crisis triggered by India's Brasstacks military war games,[9] Pakistan communicated a nuclear threat through India's ambassador in Islamabad.[10]

2 The oddities of Indian nuclear behavior

India's response, beginning in the early 1980s, to these adverse shifts in the balance of power and threat was an experimental and disaggregated effort to develop advanced nuclear weapon designs and ballistic missiles.[11]

Sometime during the spring of 1988, top Indian policy planners and decision-makers received confirming evidence that China had passed on a nuclear weapon design tested in 1966 to Pakistan and that "Pakistan was in possession of at least three nuclear devices of 15–20 kiloton yield."[12] However, the Indian prime minister waited until the spring of 1989 before authorizing weaponization to formally commence and appointing a lead coordinator within government to oversee that effort.[13]

The late start of weaponization in 1989 had negative downstream effects for India during the decade of the 1990s. When the next Indo-Pakistani crisis blew up over Kashmir in the winter/spring of 1989–1990, India had no ready arsenal.[14] During this crisis, the Pakistani foreign minister delivered what Delhi thought was a veiled nuclear threat.[15] But the prototype weapon under development had until then not even been shown to the air force.[16] Nuclear command and control consisted of the prime minister, his principal secretary and the scientific advisor to the defense minister. Neither had the government done any nuclear contingency planning nor did there exist any institutional guidelines and procedures to help political authorities cobble up a nuclear response.[17]

Although many foreign powers assumed that India and Pakistan were nuclear capable in the early 1990s, it is highly unlikely that India achieved the technical capability to deliver nuclear weapons before 1994–1995.[18] But equally germane, the state did not develop the institutional capacity to manage its nuclear hardware in any instrumentally meaningful way in the decade of the 1990s. The term institutional capacity here means the civil–military chain of command, standard operating procedures, practice drills and ground rehearsals to coordinate action among and across the various agencies tasked with responding to a nuclear emergency. It also refers to operational planning in the military's tactical meaning of the term.[19]

This state of affairs briefly continued after India conducted nuclear tests in May 1998 and formally laid claims to nuclear power status, until the summer of 1999 when India suddenly found itself at war with Pakistan over the latter's unprovoked occupation of the Kargil heights in Kashmir. This was the historical moment when the Indian government initiated nuclear operational planning with the air force.[20]

Post-1998, India set out to create the ideational and institutional edifice for a "credible minimum deterrent."[21] Indian political decision-makers are now committed to taking nuclear capabilities beyond technological symbolism into realizable forces in the field. Between 1998 and 2005, the socialization of the Indian state into the operational practices of nuclear deterrence proceeded slowly leading to the observation that the distinguishing characteristic of the India's arsenal was operational passivity.[22] Thereafter, successive Indian governments have rapidly institutionalized the co-participation of the military in nuclear operational planning and established a semi-independent body led by a senior military officer to oversee the arsenal's long-term development. Following advice from the military, they also approved new and proactive procedures to enable the rapid mobilization of the arsenal during a crisis.

The effort to improve nuclear operations has now spawned the opposite and alarmist view that India, which was once the exemplar of nuclear restraint, is now an enfant terrible on nuclear steroids.[23] More remarkably, however, this newfound operational proclivity has disabused theories that have long attributed India's historical nuclear hesitancy to status seeking, symbolism, normative restraint, an absent strategic culture and civil–military distrust.

The research questions and this book's answer in brief

How did India, a regional power with a proven nuclear capability as early as 1974, end up in a scenario in the 1980s where it was forced to scramble to deal with a Pakistani nuclear threat? Similarly in the decade of the 1990s, despite the history of Pakistani nuclear threats, the high regional political and military volatility, and the threat of war with Pakistan ever present due to the latter's low-intensity operations in Kashmir, why did not India create institutional capacities to instrumentally manage its fledgling nuclear force? Odder still, how can one explain the variation between the initially slow and then accelerating pace of changes in the development of institutions governing India's nuclear arsenal during 1998–2010, a period characterized by stable regional rivalries with Pakistan and China?

These questions can be melded into a simpler and single one: Why were India's nuclear national security outcomes faltering between 1980 and 2004 and why have they become more normalized thereafter?

I answer the above question by analyzing three periods of Indian nuclear decision-making between 1980 and 2010. The year 1980 marks the approximate start date for India's decision to begin developing nuclear weapons. And the year 2010 marks a temporary end point in its rapidly maturing nuclear weapons-related institutional and technical developments.

Based on evidence from these three periods, I maintain that India's proliferation journey should not simply be read in terms of the commonly understood demand-side pull factors (national security) and supply-side constraints (economic, technological and normative). Beneath the hood of these structural factors, India's nuclear journey must also be understood as the outcome of a state's changing institutional learning capacities to forge competent policy choices under varying constraints of secrecy.

I argue that states respond to policy challenges by either adapting or learning. When adapting, states add new programs to old ones without synergizing the means-and-ends relationships. Change under adaptation is incremental as states settle for satisficing instead of optimizing. By contrast in learning, states think more holistically and seek to match the means-and-ends relationships. Change therefore becomes more substantial as states seek to optimize outcomes.

Through the combination of new data and insights from institutional, psychological and organization theories, I show that the Indian state's propensity prior to1998 was to adapt piecemeal to proliferation pressures. Post-1998, however, the Indian state has become more favorably disposed to institutional learning. India's faltering nuclear responses in the years 1980–2004 and its more normalized behavior thereafter are better explained through the lenses of institutional adaptation and learning.

This brings us to the related second-order question: How did India end up with adaptation in one historical period over learning in another? I maintain that adaptation and learning are contingent on a state's institutional capacity for developing mature information and knowledge banks, process data from those banks in a structured manner, and manage human capital robustly. States that acquire the capacity to perform these three functions successfully will tend to veer towards learning. Those that do not will end up adapting.

The challenge most covertly proliferating states confront is that they must of necessity undertake the development of nuclear weapons-related institutional capacities under the scrutiny of a hostile nonproliferation regime. States must perforce hide their nuclear activities due to the threat of sanctions and military attacks from hostile powers.[24] As a consequence, covert nuclear weapon programs generally tend to operate under a regime of exceptional and extreme secrecy.

At a basic level, the fundamental security challenge that states face in the international system is one of uncertainty. All states dealing with uncertainty confront three instrumental questions: What is to be accomplished? When must it be accomplished? And how should it be accomplished?

To deal with these questions, a state typically mobilizes the society's curators of knowledge, its epistemic actors. Epistemic actors are knowledge managers who enable decision-makers frame answers to the above questions. Through the process of issue framing and then filling those frames with content, they help educate decision-makers and by extension socialize the state into new learning practices.

Nonetheless, the strong institutionalization of epistemic actors alone is a necessary but insufficient condition for inducing learning within a state. For learning to occur, a second condition is necessary. The epistemic actors must operate in a decision-making environment that permits relatively open access to information and subjects policy planning to a "wisdom of the crowds" scrutinizing process.

The institutionalization of epistemic actors within the state and open-access policy planning constitute the base conditions for strong learning within the state. They reduce the scope for heuristics and cognitive biases in decision-making and pave the way for structured and relatively optimized policy outcomes.

Third and finally, decision-makers must develop the means, institutional and administrative, to effectively monitor their epistemic and bureaucratic agents to whom they delegate policy planning and program development. Otherwise, the agents who by default enjoy asymmetric advantages over information and knowledge can underperform on deliverables and manipulate decision-makers into accepting them.

However, a regime of extreme domestic secrecy retards the state's capacity to learn in three ways. First, it places limits on the state's willingness to mobilize a society's epistemic actors lest word of the programs leak out. Second, the secret programs tend to be compartmentalized into a number of isolated silos with few lateral interconnections between the actors and organizations involved in them.

These constraints on information and knowledge flows in turn prevent epistemic actors from developing programs holistically or successfully interrogating their progress at critical junctures. Information from the compartmented silos is often directly stove piped to decision-makers at the top without the intervening scrutiny of an inter-agency process. Finally, limits on shared information and knowledge help shield underperforming epistemic actors from the scrutiny of their decision-making overlords.

No doubt, secrecy is necessary to hide a covertly proliferating state's activities from the scrutiny of a hostile nonproliferation regime. Unfortunately for the proliferating state, secrecy also creates domestic challenges because of opacity and compartmented information. In effect, decision-makers become cocooned in a regime of information and knowledge scarcity. Until and unless, therefore, decision-makers consciously apply themselves to counteract the pernicious effects of this regime of scarcity, learning practices in the state will remain weak and performance lags will remain a recurring phenomenon.

The evidence I present in this book shows three interrelated causes for weak learning practices within the Indian state during the years 1980 and 2004. The first is Indian decision-makers' partial mobilization of national security-centric epistemic actors prior to 1998. This base condition was grafted on to a highly centralized, compartmented and monopolistic decision-making process that cumulatively attenuated the Indian state's capacity to craft nuclear policy. The secrecy and the compartmentalization of information also denied political decision-makers the means to effectively monitor the performance of their scientific and bureaucratic agents. Prior to 1998, therefore, India's nuclear policy outcomes were riddled with heuristic and cognitive biases alongside the weak actualization of instituted policies. Post-1998 as the state moved to reform these institutional practices, policy and program outcomes improved markedly.

Case selection and method

To develop my argument, I focus on three "within case" analyses of Indian nuclear decision-making between 1980 and 2010. Each case study is an analysis of decision-making episodes that approximately spans the length of a decade: the 1980s, the 1990s and the period from 1998 until about 2010. The first case concerns India's weaponization of nuclear devices, which were developed as part of its renewed weapons development program starting around 1980–1981.[25] The second analyzes India's lack of an operational nuclear capability during the 1990s in the aftermath of acquiring nuclear weapons. The third traces India's attempts to resolve institutional and organizational challenges related to the management of its nuclear force in the wake of its formal claims to nuclear status and international recognition of its arrival as a *de facto* nuclear weapons power.

Within-case studies are useful in domains such as proliferation where the N is small and the information concerning states' operational practices, especially among second-tier nuclear weapon powers, scarce. The within-case approach is especially relevant for sorting through the problem of "equifinality," a condition where outcomes have several explanations that allegedly produce the same outcome. The within-case method also helps in controlling for history, culture, and the effects of structural economic and security variables.[26] The contextualized and structured comparison keeps a leash on "conceptual stretching" and avoids the inclusion of cases that are not analytically equivalent. By undertaking to study this messy and compelling real-world problem, my goal is not to discover what Hempel described as general "covering laws."[27] Rather, my goal is to explain middle-range intervening processes that lie between the "start" and "finish" of phenomenon.[28]

The evidence I present combines historical "process tracing," and elite interviewing methods. The process-tracing method lends itself particularly well to detailed historical investigations and is useful to understand the interaction between leadership agency and systemic structure, leadership selection effects, sequential processes, path dependencies, and feedback loops.[29] I obtained substantial data for this book through elite interviews conducted in the field in India. Some of the data were obtained from the small number of senior civilian and defense officials who constituted India's informal nuclear network in the 1990s, prior to New Delhi's formal claiming of nuclear status. Other interview data come from senior advisors who formerly served in the prime minister's office (PMO), members of India's military elites and the newly formed Strategic Forces Command (SFC).

Some of the interviews were obtained on record. But most officials agreed to be interviewed on condition of anonymity. The data presented in this study are unique to the extent that no archival material in India pertaining to and related to the nuclear weapons program has been opened to scholars or the public. Further, much of what passed as institutional knowledge of India's nuclear weapons program in the pre-1998 era was not committed to paper for security reasons. It was orally transmitted among members of the nuclear network never numbering more than a dozen individuals. Thus the data used in this book represents one of the first attempts to study India's nuclear weaponization and operational planning processes through means of oral history.

Notes

1 T.V. Paul, *Power versus Prudence: Why Nations Forgo Nuclear Weapons* (Montreal: McGill-Queen's University Press, 2000).
2 Itty Abraham, *The Making of the Indian Atomic Bomb: Science, Secrecy and the Postcolonial State* (New York: Zed Books, 1998).
3 Karsten Frey, *India's Nuclear Bomb and National Security* (New York: Routledge, 2006).
4 *The Kargil Review Committee Report: From Surprise to Reckoning* (New Delhi: Sage Publications, 1999), p. 186.
5 For example, the late Chief of Army Staff General Sundarji published a series of papers on the effects of nuclear asymmetry on conventional war fighting in the early 1980s. "Effects of Nuclear Asymmetry on Conventional Deterrence," *Combat Paper No. 1* (Mhow: College of Combat, 1981); "Nuclear Weapons in a Third World Context," *Combat Paper No. 2* (Mhow: College of Combat, 1981).
6 I borrow this phrase from Stephen Walt who argues that states' balancing behavior is triggered not just by a shift in the balance of power but by their perceptions of threats inherent in that shift based on the opposing state's strength, geographical proximity, offensive capabilities and offensive intentions. Although Walt's argument concerns states' external balancing versus bandwagoning behavior, I extend his concept to "internal balancing." Stephen M. Walt, "Alliance Formation and the Balance of World Power," *International Security*, Vol. 9, No. 4 (1985), pp. 3–43.
7 "Joint Intelligence Committee (JIC) Paper No. 8/94 on Anti-India Activities of the ISI on the Indian Sub-Continent," cited in *The Kargil Review Committee Report*, p. 71.
8 Ibid., pp. 53–78.
9 P.R. Chari, Kanti P. Bajpai, Pervaiz Iqbal Cheema, Stephen P. Cohen and Sumit Ganguly, *Brasstacks and Beyond: Perception and Management of Crisis in South Asia* (New Delhi: Manohar, 1995), pp. 23–67.
10 *The Kargil Review Committee Report*, p. 191.
11 B.G. Deshmukh, "Keep the Faith," *Hindustan Times* (September 7, 2006), http://www.freerepublic.com/focus/f-news/1698250/posts (December 2010).
12 *The Kargil Review Committee Report*, pp. 188, 190.
13 Raj Chengappa, *Weapons of Peace: The Secret Story of India's Quest to Be a Nuclear Power* (New Delhi: HarperCollins Publishers India, 2000), pp. 332–333.
14 Ibid., p. 354.
15 *The Kargil Review Committee Report*, pp. 65, 204.
16 Shekhar Gupta, "Know What They Did That Summer," *Indian Express*, August 12, 2006, http://www.indianexpress.com/news/know-what-they-did-that-summer/10366/ (December 2010).
17 Chengappa, *Weapons of Peace*, p. 355.
18 According to Scientific Advisor to the Defense Minister A.P.J. Abdul Kalam's testimony before the Kargil Review Committee, weaponization was completed during 1992–1994. The records of this and other conversations pertaining to India's nuclear weapons program from the early 1980s until 1998 are contained in the annexure to the report, which has not been declassified. The author's interviews with several senior retired Indian Air Force officers at the highest levels suggest that India achieved an air deliverable capability sometime in 1995. See, *The Kargil Review Committee Report*, p. 205; interviews with senior Indian defense official (retd.) "Z", New Delhi, India, December 2009 and February 2010.
19 Interviews with senior Indian defense official (retd.) "X", New Delhi, India, October and November 2009.

20 Interviews with senior Indian defense official (retd.) "A", New Delhi, India, July and August 2010.
21 See section titled "Objectives" in National Security Advisory Board, *India's Draft Nuclear Doctrine* (New Delhi: Government of India, August 17, 1999).
22 Ashley J. Tellis, *India's Emerging Nuclear Posture: Between Recessed Deterrent and Ready Arsenal* (Santa Monica: Rand, 2001), p. 279.
23 Vipin Narang, "Five Myths about India's Nuclear Posture," *Washington Quarterly*, 36 (Summer 2013).
24 Vipin Narang, "Strategies of Nuclear Proliferation: How States Pursue the Bomb," *International Security*, Vol. 41, No. 3 (Winter 2016/2017), p. 115.
25 The term nuclear device refers to "…fission and fusion materials, together with their arming, fuzing, firing, chemical high explosive, and effects-measuring components, that have not yet reached the development status of an operational weapon…system designed to produce a nuclear explosion for purposes of testing the design, for verifying nuclear theory, or for gathering information on system performance." The end point of device development is not an actual test explosion in the field but technical completion in the laboratory. By contrast, weaponization refers to, "the conversion or modification of a nuclear test device into a combat-ready warhead," that "includes the design and production of a ballistic casing (and any required retardation and impact-absorption or shock-mitigation devices) as well as special fuses, power sources, and arming and safing systems or equipment." See, Chuck Hansen, *U.S. Nuclear Weapons: The Secret History* (New York: Orion Books, 1988), p. 13, 17.
26 James Mahoney, "Strategies of Causal Assessment," in James Mahoney and Dietrich Rueschemeyer eds., *Comparative Historical Analysis in the Social Sciences* (Cambridge: Cambridge University Press, 2003), pp. 360–367.
27 Alexander L. George and Andrew Bennett, *Case Studies and Theory Development in the Social Sciences* (Cambridge: MIT Press, 2005), p. 7.
28 For general arguments on the value of single-case and small-N studies see: Dietrich Rueschemeyer, "Can One or Few Cases Yield Theoretical Gains," in Mahoney and Rueschemeyer, *Comparative Historical Analysis in the Social Sciences*, pp. 305–336; Paul Pierson and Theda Skocpol, "Historical Institutionalism in Contemporary Political Science," in Ira Katznelson and Helen V. Milner eds., *Political Science: State of the Discipline* (New York: W.W. Norton & Company, 2002), pp. 713–718.
29 George and Bennett, *Case Studies and Theory Development in the Social Sciences*, pp. 205–232.

2 Secrecy and state learning

After sitting astride the nuclear fence for over two decades, India in 1998 finally elected to join the ranks of declared nuclear weapon powers, citing national security reasons.[1] In the decade following that decision, New Delhi doubled down on its attempts to acquire the technical and organizational accouterments of an operational arsenal. The arsenal is a work in progress and serious technical, institutional and organizational lacunae in India's operational capabilities remain. Nonetheless, the act of putting money where one's mouth is, has confirmed the logic of the Neorealist observation that states generally proliferate to manage the problem of nuclear uncertainty.

However, India's nuclear fence sitting, the longest in any nuclear weapon power's history, raises serious questions about the fidelity of Neorealist theory's fundamental observation that states respond to structural pressures through external and internal balancing. New Delhi's irresolution opened the door to a host of rival explanations. These latter explanations have variously linked India's nuclear behavior to peaceful norms, the absence of a strategic culture, prestige, the political economy of strategic restraint and so on.

Without doubt, each of these explanations holds some water. For example, Indian decision-makers insist on the impossibility of any nuclear use. But they are also simultaneously engaged in an ambitious nuclear buildup. Indian strategic elites often refer to India's "Hindu" culture to rationalize the lag in its operational nuclear posture. On the other hand, public opinion surveys consistently reflect the pride India's urban middle classes express in the country's nuclear arsenal. There is also considerable evidence that India's decisions to delay nuclear tests and prevaricate on an overt nuclear posture until 1998 were the consequence of perceived economic constraints on the part of prime ministerial incumbents.

Yet none of these explanations offers an argument that is internally coherent or entirely consistent with the historical evidence. The norms argument explains India's public hesitation in claiming nuclear status but cannot square with India's firm private commitment to a weaponization program from 1989 onwards. The strategic culture argument is also problematic. Cultures are sticky. They are resilient to change. If a cultural consensus on the symbolic nature of nuclear weapons had been widely prevalent within the

Indian state, four decision-makers in 1998 would have found it difficult to irretrievably turn the direction of the nuclear ship of state toward an operational course almost overnight. Similarly, the political economy of restraint is a reasonable explanation for India's hesitation to make overt and formal claims to nuclear power status. However, it is a weak explanation for the absence of intra- and inter-agency planning to give existing weapons operational punch in the years 1998–2004.

With more evidence now available on the covert nuclear weapons program in the two decades prior to the 1998 tests, the norms, strategic culture and prestige arguments increasingly appear less persuasive. Much of the evidence points to national security rationales, a point compellingly made in 1998 and thereafter. In that sense, Defensive Realism is the most persuasive residual explanation for Indian proliferation. And yet, although the broad contours of Indian nuclear outcomes conform to its logic, the details of Indian nuclear behavior are cause for puzzlement.

The three puzzles: India's delayed weaponization during the 1980s despite an unambiguous nuclear threat from Pakistan, the underdeveloped soft routines following weaponization during the 1990s, and more bafflingly still, the delays in infrastructure investments and the intra- and inter-agency coordination gaps in the five years immediately following the formal claims to nuclear status, cannot be reconciled with Defensive Realism's expectations. To be sure, the argument that operational gaps are inevitable when countries proliferate may have some validity. Yet the same is less true for when states proliferate overtly. In the latter case, states are less organizationally constrained from acting in their best interests. Visibility also has the effect of forcing proliferating states to act quickly to close any gaps between existing and proclaimed capabilities lest those capabilities be called to account in a crisis with a hostile adversary.

The problem with Defensive Realism is that it takes auxiliary mechanisms inside states for granted, which are the socialization and learning mechanisms that generate the outcomes the theory predicts occur in response to systemic pressures. Essentially, Defensive Realism has a very thin theory of socialization. It conflates states' adaptation to structural pressures with learning. But adaptation and learning are not the same. Learning entails a fundamental change in the values and belief systems of actors making the adjustment.[2] Adaptation to systemic pressures on the other hand may or may not stem from changes in values and belief systems. It may occur due to coercion or strategic calculation.[3]

Also problematic is the theory's assumption that state responses to structural pressures are nearly identical. In doing so, Defensive Realism subsumes rational choice, which imposes exogenous preference orderings on all decision-makers across the system without accounting for distortions. The heroic assumption behind this reasoning is that all states are socialized into isomorphic beliefs and practices, which emanate from the most successful states in the international system.[4]

Waltz, the leading proponent of Defensive Realism has argued that international selection and socialization are the mechanisms, which ensure that states mimic one another. Those states that do not keep up with their peers face punishment and decline in power for not doing so.[5] States also mimic the example of their most successful peers in the international system.

In the context of nuclear proliferation though, socialization pressures work in reverse. Although the competitive example of the most powerful states in the international system is nuclear proliferation, the socialization pressures generated through the nonproliferation regime penalize states for replicating those power institutions.[6] The standard channels of socialization that states usually rely on, foreign governments and international organizations, and transnational private actors, are for the most part blocked.

Structural theories are therefore at a loss to explain how the process of learning unfolds within proliferating states.

I

State learning

How then do proliferating states learn? In this chapter, I develop a theoretical framework to map the process of states' internal learning practices. My definition of learning concerns the modification of existing knowledge or the acquisition of new knowledge and its institutionalization into a state's habitual routines. Learning can be experiential, may occur due to a generational change in leadership or be induced through the success of epistemic actors in socializing decision-makers into new beliefs and practices.[7] The focus of my framework primarily concerns how states "learn to learn."[8]

What this means is the socialization process that occurs through: (a) interaction between epistemic actors and decision-makers, which is the appeal of arguments and persuasion[9]; and (b) institutional and organizational practices that enable states to adopt better analytic techniques, methodologies and processes to solve problems.[10] This framework of learning incorporates Philip Tetlock's "efficiency" criterion in which the measure of learning is the ability of state leaders to change their belief systems in a manner that reflects the world more accurately and make policy decisions that constitute a better fit between means and ends.[11] The phrase "state learning" is used in the abstract because all learning actually occurs at the level of individuals. It depends on the extent to which individuals are successful in transforming their beliefs into routine practices at the institutional and organizational levels in which they operate.[12]

Essentially, the process of learning across states is uneven because it is contingent on the growth of internal information and knowledge banks, the structured processing of information from those banks and the robust management of human capital. Learning in any state will only be as good as its institutional and organizational capacity to aggregate information and knowledge banks, integrate them with human capital and monitor the latter's performance.

However, learning in covertly proliferating states is problematic because it occurs under the fog of dense external and internal secrecy. The latter is necessary to hide the state's activities from the scrutiny of a hostile nonproliferation regime. Nonetheless, secrecy is also problematic because it spawns internal opacity and compartments information. These institutional conditions cocoon decision-makers in a regime of information scarcity. Unless decision-makers consciously apply themselves to counteract the pernicious effects of this regime of information and knowledge scarcity, learning and socialization practices in the state will be weak and performance lags will remain a recurring phenomenon.

States typically deal with challenges through the use of information and knowledge. The availability of information is generally not the problem. The world is awash in it. However, identifying relevant information is usually a challenge. Further, unprocessed information, like raw material, has limited value. Information must be processed into knowledge. There must be value addition to it before it becomes actionable.

Therefore, as a first step in managing uncertainty, states mobilize a society's curators of knowledge, its "epistemic community." Epistemic actors are central to identifying relevant information, interpreting that information, crafting a state's responses to problem sets, identifying alternatives and educating policy makers on actionable policies.

Second, states require structured information processing mechanisms to enable decision-makers to separate signals from noise. This is because research in cognitive psychology shows that individuals in isolated and informal decision-making contexts draw conclusions on the basis of heuristics and biases. The latter distort reality. However, decision-makers can reduce the problem of cognitive biases and errors by farming out problems to multiple epistemic agents and subjecting their output to independent peer review.

Third and finally, states are best able to deal with policy challenges when decision-makers have institutional mechanisms to monitor the activities of their epistemic and other bureaucratic agents. Successful monitoring depends on organizational transparency and an institutional permissiveness that allows various agents to monitor one another. It is also contingent on free-flowing information channels that allow information to percolate up the organizational decision-making chain.

This chapter is divided into two parts. The first part elaborates the theoretical substance of my arguments in three sections. Its first section draws on literatures from sociology and international relations that dwell on the learning and socialization roles epistemic actors and communities play in society. In international relations literature, epistemic communities are typically valorized for their role in diffusing ideas among states, socializing decision-makers into adopting specific policies and coordinating international action. But my specific theoretical framework elaborates how institutional practices related to epistemic actors are central to the formation of well-developed knowledge banks and corresponding state learning at the domestic level.

The second set of arguments tie learning in states to structured information processing and decentralized problem-solving. Using insights from cognitive psychology, I maintain that decision-makers operating in isolated organizational settings are vulnerable to heuristic fallacies. For a variety of reasons, which I specify, the compartmentalization of knowledge and isolated decision-making processes also slow the pace of policy innovation.

Part I's third and final section elaborates arguments regarding principal–agent problems of "information asymmetries" and "monitoring" in organizations. The principal–agent model is widely used in the study of markets, private firms, governments, and a myriad other institutions and organizations. Following this tradition, this chapter also uses theoretical frames from economics, agency theory, sociology, and ethics and applies them to the challenges of management and performance in proliferating states.

In Part II, I survey and critically appraise the more traditional explanations for India's nuclear proliferation behavior and outcomes.

The institutional role of epistemic actors

Epistemic actors and the broader "epistemic community" can be imagined as what Ernst Haas famously described as the "purveyors" of knowledge and expertise. In Haas's idealized characterization, the epistemic community is the vessel of a society's "consensual knowledge." Consensual knowledge is knowledge generally considered authoritative. It is derived through scientific and nonscientific means. Such knowledge does not transcend ideology or culture. Rather, consensual knowledge is a constructed mix of scientific knowledge and political choices. It differs from ideology to the extent that its internal validity is subject to verification challenges or "truth tests" from rival claimants of intellectual authority.[13]

Members of an epistemic community have a "substantive" or "technical" understanding of cause and effect insofar as it pertains to their domain expertise. They have internally agreed upon methods – formal and informal – for testing claims and reaching judgments. They favor analytic means and comprehensive solutions to problem sets. Above all, they are united by the belief that institutionalizing their knowledge through policy will provide effective solutions to the states' identified problems.[14] Epistemic actors and communities are by no means "hegemonic." Rather, they care about specific domains that correlate with their areas of expertise. And they try and shape policies in those areas.[15]

What epistemic communities bring to the table are shared views of the social and the physical worlds, particularly the ties that link causes to outcomes. For example, strategic nuclear theorists tend to see causal links between the acquisition of nuclear weapons by states and the denial of credible threats of nuclear use from their opponents. Arms controllers favor arms reductions and politically determined technological restraints as causal mechanisms for strategic stability. Experts who study global warming tie the rise in atmospheric temperature and climate change to an increase in the emission of greenhouse gases.

Members of an epistemic community are not restricted to any one particular profession. They populate most professions and are generally a diverse lot.[16] Epistemic communities are also different from bureaucracies and interest groups. Bureaucracies are organizations that often favor policy positions out of budgetary or organizational concerns. Similarly, interest groups are often coalitions of convenience.[17] In contrast, as sociologist Ben David has argued, the glue that binds epistemic actors is ethical. It is borne out of inner intellectual convictions.[18] In other words, epistemic communities hang together by normative and not professional codes.

There are different causal pathways for the formation of epistemic communities within states and the international system. Such communities can grow indigenously within states. For example, the arms control community that emerged in the United States in the 1950s and 1960s grew out of a network of scientists, scholars and policy practitioners from nuclear labs, universities and think tanks.[19] Members of this group wrote, published and played the role of public intellectuals. The critical dialogue among them was a form of "truth tests." It helped in the formation of "consensual knowledge," which they shared with US government officials and their Soviet counterparts during the Cold War and which ultimately became institutionalized through arms control agreements between the superpowers.[20]

Alternatively, groups of experts occupying critical positions in government within states can help forge a consensus on policy. Thus during World War II and its immediate aftermath, a group of liberal economists and policy planners in the United States and Britain helped shape the rules of a liberal world economic order that balanced elements of an open trading system with Keynesian government intervention, control and stability.[21] In another episode, a global epistemic community on food aid emerged out of international organizations and private sector initiatives between 1950 and 1990. Through international organizations, international conferences, publications and public criticism, this community reshaped the politics of food aid in the United States from one that in the 1950s lumped humanitarian with domestic agricultural and geopolitical objectives to one that acquired an overwhelmingly humanitarian focus by the 1990s.[22]

It is more likely that a nuclear weapons–centric epistemic community will grow indigenously within a proliferating state, although there may be exceptions to that rule. During the Cold War for example, the US arms control epistemic community helped one grow in the former Soviet Union. But because the majority of the states in the international system oppose nuclear proliferation, foreign governments and international organizations are less likely to play the role of socializers. Furthermore, the nonproliferation regime, despite its contradictions, has gained legitimacy over time.[23]

If anything, states and international organizations are more likely to diffuse norms and ideas to freeze and rollback nuclear proliferation. Within a proliferating state, therefore, an epistemic community will, in principle, emerge from the scientific community involved in developing and testing weapons. It will seek to build coalitions with epistemic actors from the strategic and international relations community in the government, the think tanks and universities grappling with the challenges, trade-offs and consequences of nuclear weapons acquisition. And ultimately, it will seek to incorporate representatives from the military on whom the doctrinal and operational challenges of the nuclear arsenal will ultimately devolve. It is also likely that some public intellectuals, bureaucrats and politicians could become part of the nuclear epistemic community. For the most part, however, the group's core membership will consist of experts from the fields of nuclear weapons design and testing, strategy and use.

In one sense, the nuclear epistemic community in clandestinely proliferating states will never be a true scientific community that transcends the state; of the type conceived in sociological and international relations literature.[24] This is because such a community cannot exist independently outside the state. Further, in light of the secrecy surrounding the nuclear weapons program, the relative paucity of information and political sensitivities surrounding public discussion of the program, a robust form of "consensual knowledge" will be hard to form.

Thus the nuclear epistemic community in a proliferating state can be reconceived as a "primitive" group"[25] consisting of professionals and policy specialists within and outside government who share a common normative understanding of nuclear deterrence. But exist it must in some institutional form within and outside the state. And transmit it must its expertise to key policy planners and decision-makers to give coherent direction to the proliferation effort.

The linkages between expertise, learning and policy outcomes are what make modern states modern. As Harvey Brooks puts it, "much of the history of social progress in the 20th century can be described as the transfer of wider and wider areas of public policies from politics to expertise." This does not of course mean that politics is absent from the process of policy making. All policy is ultimately political. However, episteme brings robustness to policy by defining its content, scope, and by providing alternatives to the status quo. The role of epistemic actors in this regard is to push the envelope of research and intellectual innovation, a process necessary to grow society's knowledge banks and provide decision-makers with optimized solutions to problems. In a sense therefore, the condition of a society's existing epistemic community is a broad measure of its intellectual frontiers in a specific domain at any given time.

The mere existence of an epistemic community in and by itself, however, is a necessary but insufficient condition for policy learning to occur within a state. For learning to happen, decision-makers must take the crucial step of mobilizing the society's epistemic actors. However, decision-makers will have incentives to undertake such a measure only when they commit the state to achieving a set of "expanded" and "interconnected" as against "limited" and "static" goals.[26] An expanded and interconnected set of goals in the context of nuclear proliferation, for example, would be the commitment to fissile material production, weapon development, testing, weaponization and operational planning as part of a program that is holistic and interlinked. The example of limited and static goals on the other hand would involve halting steps along each rung of the proliferation ladder over an extended time period. Leaders generally tend to rely on professional expertise when goals are complex, when they are expansive and tightly coupled. On the other hand, decision-makers are less likely to demand the sustained intellectual attention of an epistemic community when goals are limited, static or loosely coupled.[27]

Epistemic actors also tend to apply analytic methods to think through problem-and-solution sets. They carry the intellectual and emotional commitment to apply the cumulative knowledge of their domain expertise to a society's problems. They use holistic approaches to resolve the problem of misaligned means and ends. Instead of incremental advances they generally show a preference for strategic approaches that allow a fundamental rethinking of solutions to problems.[28]

In comparison to domain specialists, political leaders mostly lack expertise and tackle problems piecemeal. Not only that. They have short attention spans and even shorter time horizons. Epistemic communities carry within themselves policy innovators and executors. They play, in John Ruggie's characterization, the role of "switchboards." Although Ruggie and other international relations scholars have largely focused on the role epistemic communities play in interstate socialization and coordination functions in bodies such as the United Nations, such communities play an equally significant domestic role in educating decision-makers domestically.

The degree of policy innovation in a proliferating state will therefore depend on whether decision-makers decide in favor of an extensive versus a limited mobilization of a society's nuclear epistemic community. Mobilization apart, the strength of an epistemic community's institutionalization within a state will determine that state's speed of learning and policy innovations.

Institutionalization in the context of a state's administrative structure can be stated very simply as the "development of new organs, principles of action, and administrative practices…designed to improve the performance of the polity…"[29] Learning within the state will be most effective when epistemic actors are able to inject new consensual knowledge and institutionalize it into the state's habitual routines. In this regard, three measures are useful for assessing an epistemic community's institutional strength within a state.

The first is the community's longevity. This concerns the state of its continuous existence across successive governments and leaders. Expert communities that are institutionalized within the state are able to accumulate information and grow their expertise. Such gains in knowledge expand their institutional authority inside and outside the state over time. They become the sources of authoritative knowledge. In this capacity, they also serve as policy transmission belts and coordinating agents for decision-makers. Hence, entrenched epistemic actors with histories of long-term residency within the state's administrative and bureaucratic structure are in a strong position to educate decision-makers and the state by extension.

Second, epistemic actors should also have some access to sensitive information. The economist Douglas North illustrates this point by showing how rapid information turnover in the marketplace is crucial for firms' learning and survival.[30] In the policy-making world similarly, data availability facilitates the task that epistemic actors do best: judgment formation and idea contestation to prepare better policies for dealing with political challenges. Curtailed information flows on the other hand prevent epistemic actors from performing these tasks and from identifying policy flaws. Limited information sharing also prevents epistemic actors from coordinating action due to their inability to read from the same set of pages.

Information is a critical resource for another reason. Unlike well-functioning markets where alternative ideas and institutions often coexist, political markets embody a "winner takes all" approach.[31] This is especially true in the national security ideas markets where the relative scarcity of information and high costs make political decisions sticky. Initial decisions impose strong adaptive effects on other actors and in the process reinforce their own centrality. Hence, it is vital for epistemic communities to shape the status quo before it becomes self-reinforcing. Further, in the absence of information, epistemic actors will find it difficult to generate credible alternatives to the status quo due to the lack of supporting information.

For learning to occur, the epistemic actors must also possess some means to extract commitments for specific policy actions from decision-makers.[32] Decision-makers usually signal commitments to specific policies through political, institutional and budgetary means. These latter actions bind the agency of decision-makers for the long term because deviations from commitments are visible and likely to hurt their credibility and reputation.

In effect, commitments become a form of a "time lengthening" mechanism, which signals to epistemic actors that political actors are bound to a policy for the long term (Table 2.1).[33] Such mechanisms have the benefit of two functions. They provide epistemic actors the institutional means to monitor and evaluate the actions of decision-makers. They can do this by imposing reputation costs on shirking decision-makers. Equally significant, on a personal psychological level, the time-lengthening mechanisms serve as morale boosters for epistemic actors because their motivations are primarily professional and ethical. Credible political actions help them follow the strength of their intellectual and emotional commitments through.

18 *Secrecy and state learning*

Table 2.1 Epistemic actors and state learning

Condition	Impact
• Sustained institutional presence	• Sources of authoritative knowledge within government • Transmission belts for ideas • Coordinating agents for decision-makers
• High information turnover • Access to sensitive information	• Judgment formation • Idea contestation • Credible alternatives to status quo
• Ability to extract political, institutional, and budgetary commitments from decision-makers	• Bind agency of decision-makers • Monitor performance of decision-makers • Sustain intellectual and emotional commitments to policy

How monopolist decision making and psychological biases shape organizational learning

Structural theories also generally assume that nuclear decision-makers in emerging nuclear powers are rational choice agents. The belief is that nuclear aspirants in the international system seek to maximize strategic gains. These theories further assume that rational choices are possible because the nuclear decision-making process in proliferating states is secret, selective and isolated. The latter conditions prevent the rationality of decisions from being contaminated by the hurly-burly of domestic and organizational bureaucratic politics.[34] For the most part, the assumptions of secrecy and isolated decision-making are true. However, the related surmise that a highly select and relatively unitary or monopolistic decision-making process renders decisions optimal is problematic.

The weight of evidence from experiments in the fields of cybernetics and cognitive psychology as well as examples from the real world show that rational optimization is an abstract myth removed from reality. Decision-makers do not always have a well-defined set of utility functions. Nor do they systematically proceed down deductive decision trees making value and utility choices. More often, they lack the capacity to analyze in one sweep the entire range of choices before them. Nor do they fully anticipate the consequences of their choices. The decisions they make are often sequential, not comprehensive.[35] Issue frames and the order of choice critically shape decisions. Strong internally held biases compete with reason in the making of judgment calls. Decision-makers, to use Herbert Simon's famous characterization, are "boundedly rational."[36]

Insights from cybernetics and cognitive psychology offer more realistic approaches to understanding decision-making under monopolistic and secrecy conditions, which are the decision-making conditions one is likely to find in post-NPT proliferating states. In Streinbruner's cybernetic model, for example, decision-makers' primary motivation is uncertainty control and the retention of simplicity and consistency of their belief systems.[37] They achieve this by what Herbert Simon described as the "process decision of reality."[38] The latter is less like a constructed blueprint of reality and more like a recipe.

Decision-makers typically follow a set of instructions sequentially, produce an outcome without fully understanding its implications and then await environmental feedback to appraise the quality of their decision before making further adjustments.[39] Because environments are complex there is always tension between decision-makers' need for control and the demands of adaptation in a complex environment. Decision-makers usually have the choice of resolving this tension in two ways: First, they can maintain internal simplicity by screening out information and only accepting information through highly selective feedback loops. Second, they can decompose problem sets and assign fragmented bits to multiple individuals and organizations to resolve.[40]

If decision-makers choose to screen out information, chances are that optimization will be minimal. But even if they decide to parcel out problem sets to multiple individuals and organizations the issue of solution aggregation will remain a challenge. This is because in monopolist or highly centralized decision-making structures, problems can only be resolved sequentially in the manner in which they are raised. Hence, the challenge of aggregation will remain a critical roadblock to optimization. Decision-makers will tend to monitor feedback loops and discover the effects of their actions as they register feedback. If problems persist, then decision-makers can go down the path of "problemistic" search and scan the environment for solutions.[41]

But in a restricted and secret environment, such as the one encountered in proliferating states, they will generally turn to trusted sources and selective mechanisms already established. It is also likely that when dealing with the decomposed problems' components, decision-makers will choose to leave many of the optimization trade-offs unresolved. As a consequence, the system will evolve slowly evoking what Charles Lindblom characterized as the process of "muddling through."[42]

However, the cybernetic model has two limitations. First, it does not address decision-making under conditions of great complexity and uncertainty. And second, it does not deal with the role values play in judgment formation. Here, cognitive psychology helps us to understand how decision-making operates. Cognitive psychology's fundamental insight is that individuals simplify highly complex and ambiguous environments by imposing their internally held belief systems on those environments to give them structure and make them legible. The decision-making goal remains the same as before: economy, which amounts to bringing "simplicity" and "stability" to decision-making.[43]

Most individuals achieve this goal though what Herbert Simon termed as "satisficing" and not optimizing as rational choice theorists would have us believe.[44]

In other words, most individuals reach decisions once the thresholds of some internally held values and aspirations are satisfied. Research also shows that individuals tend not to make value trade-offs under conditions of uncertainty, as rational choice theorists would expect.[45] Rather, they do that only when compelled under the force of an external shock.

Research in the field of cognitive psychology also demonstrates that decision-makers tend to use analogies, wishful thinking, the notion of impossibility, social reinforcement and "groupthink" to manage uncertainty, which is essentially the gap between the environment as it actually is and their knowledge of it.[46] In the 1970s and 1980s, Kahneman and Tversky's "heuristics and biases" program and the experimental data it generated compellingly showed that individuals reach decisions through the use of heuristics or "simple rules of the thumb."[47]

Two heuristics in particular, the "representative"[48] and the "availability" heuristic,[49] explain decision-making more realistically than any rational-choice model. Both heuristics are anchoring phenomena, which operate on the principle of analogies. Experiments show that individuals reach conclusions about events and people not on the statistical probability of an event happening or the population size of their samples, but simply on the basis of how one event or a person is intuitively perceived as representative of another or on how vividly decision-makers can recall a similar situation or context from their memories. In Gilovich and Griffin's counterargument, the heuristics that most individuals use yield "serviceable solutions" to "compelling problems." But that which is serviceable is not necessarily optimal.[50]

To be sure, even when individuals do not deploy formal optimization models, their decisions can be intuitively rational. But this line of reasoning is more germane to specialists who acquire expertise over years of training and experiential knowledge. Chess grandmasters, for example, can often take in an entire game with a swift glance. But most political decision-makers are not experts in nuclear arcana. There is also a hidden problem with expertise itself. Most experts also zero in on problems through the use of heuristics.[51] In other words, the experts seek to problem-solve on the basis of what they already know, through what is strongly etched into their memory already and what they can easily recall. Unless specifically tasked, even experts typically do not optimize.

One of the methods that enable individual decision-makers to transcend individual cognitive limits is parallel processing, which is the parceling out of analysis and decision-making to specialized organizations. One of the central insights of the Carnegie School[52] was that organizations help solve problems of individual cognitive limits that constrain organizational optimization.[53] It was Weber who successfully argued that organizations embody rational choice. Simon and March subsequently made the point that unlike individuals who have limited attention spans and can only focus on one problem at a time, organizational parallel processing permits problem decomposition.[54] Although second-generation organizational theorists in the 1960s such as

Graham Allison popularized the view that organizations were the problem due to their standard operating procedures (SOP) and hidebound practices,[55] a less conventional view propounded by Landau and Wildavsky is that policy innovation occurs when organizations compete over policy choices.[56]

Parallel processing and the decomposition of problems across organizations enable optimization in four ways. First, decisions are based less on folk heuristics and more on scientific processes because professional organizations can chew through problem-and-solution sets. Second, the pooling of expertise creates room for the cross-fertilization of ideas. Third, just as good hardware engineering involves building redundancies into technological systems to guard against individual component and subsystem failures, redundancies in the decision-making process create an ecosystem for the coexistence of alternative logics that can compensate for the failure of any single dominant approach.[57] Finally, distributed decision-making serves as an institutional check against what Irving Janis identified as "groupthink," the tendency among closed groups of decision-makers to favor group harmony and consensus over critical evaluation of alternative points of view.[58] Thus monopolist decision-making concentrated in a few decision-makers retards the process of structured optimization (Table 2.2).

The "principal–agent" problem in proliferating states

Third and finally, positive learning and policy growth in a proliferating state will substantially depend on how well political principals manage their epistemic and other bureaucratic agents tasked with the execution of weapons development and its ancillary programs. In a proliferating state, the principals can be imagined as the key decision-makers in the political executive and their agents the scientists, the engineers, the bureaucrats, the strategic foreign policy analysts and the military. The challenge of principals effectively controlling their agents afflicts all organizations. However, regimes of information scarcity can exacerbate the dilemmas of effective organizational control and management.

In any principal–agent relationship, leaders in an organizational hierarchy (principals) assign and contract others down the chain (agents) to do tasks for them. Problems in this relationship arise due to two factors. First, the interests of the principals and their agents do not always overlap, a problem that can be summed up as goal divergence. And second, the agents are generally the experts in this interaction. Their expertise creates conditions of "information asymmetry" that often allow them, the agents, to effectively control their principals.

Goal divergence and information asymmetry are problematic in any principal–agent relationship because the act of risk taking and the responsibility for that risk are bifurcated. The agents take most of the risk but their principals bear most of the responsibility for that risk.[59] What this means for situations where the interests of the principals and their agents do not fully

Table 2.2 Rational optimization in closed and centralized versus open and decentralized decision-making systems

Goal	Process	Outcome
CYBERNETIC MODEL • Uncertainty control • Simplicity in decision-making	• Highly select and pre-established channels for problem-solving • Heavy pre-screening of information • Single environmental feedback loop for problem-solving	• Sequential resolution of problems • Solutions limited in scope and variety • "Muddling through" approach to policy challenges
COGNITIVE PSYCHOLOGY MODEL • Uncertainty control • Simplicity in decision-making	• Highly select and pre-established channels for problem-solving • Reliance on preconceived value judgments and the use of heuristics and analogies in problem-solving • Limited environmental feedback loop for problem-solving	• Serviceable but suboptimal policy solutions
OPEN & DECENTRALIZED MODEL • Uncertainty management • Complex decision-making	• Division of problems into parts • Parceling out of problem resolution to multiple actors and agencies • Use of scientific methods • Multiple and rival scrutiny of solutions by actors & agencies	• Cross-fertilization of ideas • Alternative policy solutions that guard against failure of a single dominant policy approach • Avoidance of "groupthink"

coincide is that the latter can take actions that have the potential for undermining the principals' interests.

A manifestation of this problem is "moral hazard." The concept of moral hazard refers to the idea that a party protected from the hazards of risk will act in a manner differently from one where it is not similarly shielded. For the most part, individuals and organizations protected from risk tend to make riskier decisions. In the principal–agent relationship, the agents are usually shielded from the responsibility of undertaking risky behavior. Conditions of information asymmetry often prevent principals from monitoring the activities of their agents effectively. Under such circumstances, it is not improbable to imagine that agents might take greater risks in policy than are warranted because the responsibility for those risks lies with their principals. The net effect of moral hazard is harm to the principals' interests.

The most popular application of the principal–agent model is the business firm where the interests of the shareholders and professional managers who run operations are often at odds with one another. Other successful applications of the model include small partnerships, nonprofits, charities, schools and governments.[60] When applied to business firms, the assumption is that property relations create natural incentives for agents to "shirk," unless the principals devise robust incentive-and-monitoring mechanisms to control them. Some sociologists and ethicists, however, contest the model's applicability to the public sector when it does not involve property relations and the maximization of profit.

Charles Perrow, for example, is skeptical of the principal–agent model because it goes against the grain of social cooperation.[61] Similarly "stakeholder" theorists such as Neil Shankman reject the unethical and depraved view of human nature and point to ethical commitments as the basis of cooperation.[62] They do not to deny that principal–agent problems do not exist in the public sector. Their argument is that the goal of agents in the public sector is the generation of public goods, not rent seeking. In one sense, the building of nuclear weapons is the ultimate public good as it enhances a polity's national security and prestige. Hence a safe assumption can be made that agents tasked with proliferation activities will possess a high professional and mission drive.

That said, a combination of "knights" and "knaves" will exist among agents even in the public sector. Further, individual agents themselves might combine qualities of both in some mix. Knights, according to Le Grand, are agents driven by professional and altruistic concerns and strive to promote the interests of their principals. The knaves on the other hand tend to be selfish and opportunistic.[63] What this means for a proliferating state is that the principals' agents who are knights will share a high nationalistic, professional and emotional commitment to proliferation. Their ethical norms will ease some of the tensions assumed in the more pessimistic business model. Nonetheless, the natural distribution of knaves in the population of agents will also be cause for some goal divergence with the principals.

The likeliest reason for goal divergence is that political principals represent a broad array of national interests. Even as they pursue proliferation goals, they will want to balance those goals with other competing domestic and foreign policy interests. In contrast, their agents who represent the nuclear labs, the military-industrial complex and the armed services, will exhibit a narrower set of professional and organizational goals. Many agents will share a propensity for pursuing narrower professional goals disproportionately. As a consequence, the principals will nearly always harbor some wariness toward their agents, because as decision-makers, they disproportionately shoulder all the residual risks of proliferation under a hostile nonproliferation regime.

The act of nuclear proliferation by any non-nuclear state is a dangerous enterprise because of the constant threat of punishment under the international nonproliferation regime. Hence, principals in a proliferating state will have incentives to maintain high external and internal secrecy to hide the program's existence. But external threats apart, principals will prefer secrecy for domestic political reasons too. The principals may fear that their agents could leak sensitive information to force their hand prematurely to commit to specific policy choices. The principals' fear of loss of agenda control will therefore constitute a secondary incentive to treat the weapon development effort as a black program.

The only way principals can avoid ceding agenda control to their agents is by compartmenting the proliferation program among and within the multiple agencies executing it. If parts of the program such as fissile material production, weapon design, carriage and operational planning are distributed across multiple agents and agencies, the principles will seek to retain agenda control through blocking or limiting inter-agent and inter-agency information exchange.

However, the twin processes of secrecy and compartmenting information also create a perverse problem for the principals in managing their agents. As the principal–agent theory informs us, agents enjoy the power of information and knowledge asymmetry. Principals usually find the costs of policing their agents to be very high due to cognitive problems of "bounded rationality" as well as their agents' domain expertise. Furthermore, the agents constitute the permanent state. They, the agents, are usually the masters of the bureaucratic process within their specific agency and the state in general. Given such circumstances, the best methods available to principals for monitoring their agents' actions are transparency and information availability. However, the latter conditions directly undercut the primary demand for secrecy.

In most organizations, there are three methods available to principals to reduce the cost of monitoring their agents. The first is transparency and easy information availability. This process renders the agents' actions easily visible to the principals. The second is competition among multiple agents. This process allows agents to monitor one another and also act as checks on each other. Further, mutual monitoring among agents is a relatively easy way for information to percolate up the organizational chain to the principals. Finally, decision-makers use institutionalized boards of independent experts (rival epistemic groups) to level information asymmetries between them and their agents in two ways. In the first, the boards vet actions at the initiation or project specification stage. In the second, they verify whether the outcomes are in line with the promises that agents made with the principals at the project initiation or specification stage.[64] If projects stall or fail, the boards then independently verify if the outcomes are the consequence of agents' shirking or due to random events outside their control.

However, the covert nature of most weapon programs makes transparency, information availability and multiple agent competition difficult. To be sure,

Table 2.3 Agent monitoring in closed versus open decision-making systems

Type	Process	Outcome
Closed decision-making systems	• Absence of transparency • Absence of inter-agent/agency competition	• Persistence of high information asymmetries • Minimal checks & balances • High degree of autonomy for agents
Open decision-making systems	• Transparency • Inter-agent/agency competition	• Reduction in information asymmetries • Robust system of checks & balances • Constrained autonomy for agents

even in imperfectly functioning information markets principals use screening devices[65] to ensure baseline quality. Just as education and schools serve as screening devices for employers to certify the credibility of potential employees amid uncertainty, the state's bureaucratic organizations, especially its scientific and technical organizations, have internal metrics to ensure quality control. Agents too can use signaling devices,[66] such as technical benchmarks and breakthroughs, thresholds and actual tests of weapon systems to help principals bridge the information gap.

However, the screening and signaling devices that work in the education and employment markets for example, do not work with analogous efficiency in the proliferation market. Nuclear proliferation falls in the category of large technological projects. Such projects are huge organizational efforts with vastly extended timelines. In such hugely complex projects, it is difficult for principals to distinguish if agent successes and failures are due to shirking or random effects.

Secrecy concerns also prevent covertly proliferating states from conducting full-scale audits such as weapon tests, thereby limiting the signaling capacity of agents. Further, unless institutionalized epistemic bodies can undertake independent peer reviews, the principals will find it hard to filter out signals from the background noise. In markets, product successes and failures are the ultimate benchmarks to verify the fidelity of agents' signaling. However, the likelihood that weapons of mass destruction will ever be used in war is exceptionally low, thus leaving the value of agents' signaling in the absence of a rigorous program of field tests or independent peer review, moot (Table 2.3).

II

The argument specific to India

More specifically in India's context, the theoretical argument of this chapter is that the nuclear policy lags observable during the years 1980–2004, were largely self-imposed. They emanated from the state's weak learning practices. I attribute the weak learning practices to a poorly functioning knowledge market inside the state, unstructured decision-making and skeletal institutional oversight.

Among the key reasons for this institutional state of affairs until about 2004–2005 was the extreme regime of internal secrecy surrounding India's nuclear weapons program. It should be noted in this regard that all proliferating states impose varying regimes of external and internal secrecy on their nuclear weapon programs. External secrecy has mainly to do with protecting the program from the prying eyes and interference of foreigners. Internal secrecy, on the other hand, protects the program from the critical scrutiny of domestic institutional actors and agencies. More germane, however, the logics that govern the regimes of external and domestic secrecy among overtly and covertly proliferating states differ.

Overt proliferators, especially legally recognized nuclear weapon states, even when they maintain external secrecy, feel less compelled to keep the nuclear weapons programs under wraps domestically. To be sure, large sections of the program will likely be walled off as is true for most sensitive national security programs. Yet, an overtly proliferating state will always have more latitude to build and institutionalize strong oversight and controls as it would for any other special program. Furthermore, overt proliferators enjoy the luxury of being able to more fully mobilize their epistemic communities in pursuit of their goals and reap the full benefits of parceling out the program's parts among the various bureaucratic agencies. This is largely because external pressures will be lower in the case of legally recognized nuclear weapon states or accounted for in cases of overt proliferators that operate outside the NPT.

Covert proliferators on the other hand must perforce operate under conditions of tight external and domestic secrecy. External knowledge of a nuclear weapons program invariably invites diplomatic pressure, sanctions and military counterforce actions with the goal of rollback. The corresponding regime of domestic secrecy for covert proliferators will also be tighter as any information leak within is likely to percolate to the external front. The tighter constraints for domestic secrecy mean that covertly proliferating states have less breathing room for the wide mobilization of epistemic actors, structured decision making, parallel processing and strong institutional oversight as would normally be the case with any of the state's other large technology projects.

India's nuclear weapons program from the early 1980s until 1998 was covert and operated under a regime of high external and internal secrecy. The country's regime of external secrecy was designed to minimize pressures for nuclear rollback from the United States as well as fend off threats of economic and technological sanctions. Indian leaders perhaps also found external secrecy a convenient cover to ritualistically comply with nuclear abstinence norms, which were a source of prestige and to which past prime ministers had committed the country to. And although India was privately no longer willing to comply with those commitments, a sharp break with existing norms was likely to prove embarrassing.

A corresponding regime of extreme internal secrecy was naturally extended to the weaponization program to prevent its details from prematurely leaking to foreign actors. Among other reasons, Indian leaders sought to control the tempo of the program to make it fit budgetary constraints as well as maintain control over the policy process against competing domestic political and bureaucratic actors. The regime of secrecy was also superimposed on India's nuclear and military research and development bureaucracies that in the decades since independence had already carved out protected institutional spaces within the state for themselves where they resisted external scrutiny and accountability. In addition, the secrecy extended to cover the country's problematic civil-military institutions that were characterized by an intermittent or what Anit Mukherjee has more accurately described as an "absent dialogue."

Left to their own devices and in the absence of access to the full-scale mobilization of the relevant epistemic actors, decision-makers chose to deal with the nuclear weapons program piecemeal, leaving gaps in several areas unaddressed. In the absence of well-institutionalized and structured nuclear weapons–specific information and knowledge evaluation processes, decision-makers selected policy options heuristically.

Policy in the two decades prior to 2004 devolved upon a fragile network of epistemic actors consisting of the topmost bureaucrats in the Prime Minister's Office (PMO) and the Ministry of Defense, a handful of nuclear and defense scientists from the Bhabha Atomic Research Center (BARC) and the Defense Research & Development Organization (DRDO), a former defense minister, a retired army chief, and the director of a defense ministry think tank outside government. As individuals these people were influential. The scientists were also institutionally rooted in some of India's most powerful nuclear and defense organizations. But when constituted as an informal group to advise the government on nuclear policy, they lacked the institutional power and authority to extract credible commitments from risk-averse decision-makers. Nor did they possess the means to impose a deductive and well-planned approach to the proliferation project on decision-makers.

Secrecy also denied the nuclear weapons program a "wisdom of the crowds" scrutiny from multiple actors and agencies within the state. The lack of an independent peer review process left several policy biases and lacunae in the programs unaddressed. Finally, the regime of dense secrecy not only succeeded in denying information about India's covert weaponization efforts to hostile outsiders but it also created knowledge asymmetries within the state, a condition that stymied efforts by political principals to successfully monitor their scientific and bureaucratic agents.

To be sure, these theoretical observations are more germane to the covert phase of India's nuclear policy developments (1980–1998). Yet, the negative path-dependency effects of past institutional practices persisted even after India emerged from its nuclear closet, until Indian governments beginning in 2004–2005 systematically sought to correct them.

Alternative explanations

In comparison to the above argument, the more traditional explanations for Indian proliferation outcomes fall into two categories. In the first are "nuclear demand" explanations, which dwell on the structural security imperatives that cause states to proliferate. These arguments are the most widely accepted explanations among the general public, academics and policy practitioners for India's nuclear state of affairs.

But because India's historical nuclear outcomes are arguably a weak fit with structural demand explanations, scholars have advanced "supply side" constraint arguments – normative, cultural and economic – to bridge the gap between the expected and actual outcomes.

The demand-side explanations draw from deductive general theories of international relations that function well at the systemic level. India like China, however, is often an exception to broad and generalizable trends in the international system. The supply-side explanations on the other hand are inductive and offer explanations that are specific to India. Together, the existing set of demand- and supply-side explanations help us map the key points in India's nuclear trajectory.

Nonetheless, the empirical data are more complex, and as the empirical chapters in this book will demonstrate, India's nuclear behavior eludes easy classifications.

Nuclear demand side arguments

Defensive realism

Structural Realism, especially its "Defensive" variant, is the most widely accepted theoretical explanation for India's nuclear behavior. The theory's fundamental tenets, which barely need repeating, are that the structural condition of anarchy in the international system forces states to rely on the institution of self-help. Nuclear weapons, because of their enormous destructive power, are game changers in the international system. States have the option of allying themselves with a nuclear weapons power and seeking the shelter of the latter's nuclear umbrella or developing nuclear weapons independently.[67]

In this framework, India faced a negative security relationship with its two regional neighbors: China and Pakistan. When confronted with independent nuclear threats from both countries, the impossibility of obtaining nuclear shelter from other nuclear weapon powers, as well as evidence of mounting nuclear collusion between China and Pakistan, New Delhi decided to build its own nuclear arsenal.[68]

The more nuanced Defensive Realist argument has been advanced by Paul who concedes that both Realism and Liberalism influence states' proliferation behavior.[69] He argues that unlike great powers, which are "greedy security maximizers," regional powers are "prudential realists." In their interactions with regional peers, they balance "interests, capabilities, and intentions" to avoid creating negative security dilemmas.[70] Paul typologizes the international system into regions of "high," "medium" and "low" conflict zones characterized by differences in the nature of state rivalries and conflicts.

Only states in regions of "protracted" and "enduring rivalries and conflict" are likely to follow the logic of "hard realism" and proliferate. States in regions of "medium" and "low" conflict will more likely be receptive to liberal norms and institutional incentives.[71] Unlike great powers, regional powers also do not proliferate easily. But those regional powers that harbor great power aspirations will have added incentives to acquire nuclear arms.[72] Thus in Paul's model and Structural Realism in general, India's decision to proliferate is self-explanatory.

The problem with Defensive Realism however is not the outcome but the outcome's delayed onset and its attenuated form until the middle of the last decade since the time India initiated a nuclear weapons program. The historical evidence that India delayed weaponization until the late 1980s, amid conditions of high political and military volatility, is puzzling. To be sure Indian scientists were working on "developing sophisticated nuclear weapons" through the 1980s, as B.G. Deshmukh who served as cabinet secretary and principal secretary to the prime minister subsequently disclosed. Yet, "… there was no major mission to integrate and manufacture deliverable systems."[73]

Although this may sound like a trivial distinction to the nontechnical observer, the developing of "technology" and the building of "technics" are distinct. Technology is "engineering know how, a practical knowledge of how natural principles can be put to work…" Technics on the other hand, are "actual tangible machines, apparatuses, and devices that are the product of labor and technology applied to natural resources."[74] The existence of the first is not interchangeable with the second. The Indian program illustrates this point well. Although 1989 was the start date for weaponization, the end date of its first phase was 1994. Further, it was not until 1995–1996 that India achieved the means to deliver nuclear weapons safely and reliably via aircraft. There was thus a six- to seven-year gap before technology could be transformed into technics.

More recent structural theories have a more refined explanation for states' extended responses to external nuclear threats. Vipin Narang's "Nuclear Acquisition Theory" for example divvies up the proliferation process into a series of steps that range from "technical," "insurance" and "hard edging" before states finally break into a "sprint" to acquire operational nuclear weapons.[75] According to Narang, China's emergence as a nuclear weapons power in 1964 caused the domestic consensus in India to shift from "technical" to a "hard edging" nuclear strategy. Thereafter, Pakistan's acquisition of nuclear weapons sometime in 1987–1988 forced India in 1989 into a "sprint" to develop an operational nuclear force.[76]

The best available historical accounts however attribute India's hesitancy in developing operational nuclear forces to Indian leaders' moral qualms and various supply-side material constraints (economic and technical). As a thought experiment, therefore, Narang might have asked, would Indian decision-makers have spent 25 years in "hard edging" absent these supply-side constraining factors? Likewise, Narang's theory is unable to explain the gap in India's institutional capacities to manage nuclear operations in the 1990s. Nuclear operations share several common characteristics with any complex emergency management task. The first institutional and organizational challenge is to establish a "common knowledge base" and "common operating base."[77] In India, however, the tight compartmenting of information regarding the weapons' existence comported against establishing any shared understanding among all the players.

Further, structural explanations have unpersuasive answers for why institutional anomalies in India's higher military command and inter-agency coordination practices, so crucial to address security dilemmas, remained unresolved for at least six years after the country publicly claimed nuclear power status and was accepted as much by the world's other great powers.

Essentially, Defensive Realism, like any good deductive theory, is concerned with parsimonious explanations and getting a few big things right. And the one big regularity it predicts is that states faced with structural conditions of anarchy will balance against them. By that measure, the theory is correct. India has balanced and acquired nuclear weapons. Arguably, the debate is over. And yet, the theory is short on details about the substantive nature of India's national security responses to structural pressures.

Nuclear "supply-side" constraint arguments

Indeed, India's quarter century of nuclear prevarication between 1974 and 1998 led most scholars to concur that the structural security demands for nuclear weaponry in India were overwhelmingly offset by a series of domestic factors that explained the reluctance of its decision-makers to break into a nuclear "sprint." These supply-side constraint arguments range from the normative, cultural to economic. Whereas the cultural and economic constraint arguments are fairly straightforward, the normative arguments encompass both positive and negative prestige values associated with nuclear weapons and cut in opposite directions. But in India's case, scholars argue that both factors in the past operated to restrain the hands of decision-makers.

This is somewhat ironic because in proliferation literature the positive prestige value of nuclear weapons is associated with a demand for them. In India's case, however, scholars argued that the positive prestige value when pitted against India's strategic culture and economic constraints meant that Indian leaders would likely settle for prestige emanating from nuclear tokenism and not a full-fledged operational capability. In that sense, positive prestige was less a demand factor and more a supply-side constraining factor.

Prestige

Prior to 1998 and immediately after, many scholars inferred from India's two decade – long nuclear fence sitting, the Hindu-nationalist nature of the government that ordered the 1998 nuclear tests and the rushed manner of the testing program itself, that India was invested in nuclear weapons overwhelmingly for prestige and not national security reasons.[78]

The Classical Realist argument went something like this: India cared for "prestige rather than power"[79] because prestige is the "everyday currency of international relations."[80] The sociological version of this argument stressed that some states cared for nuclear weapons as they might care for national flags and airlines. In these constructions, the value of nuclear weapons often has less to do with the weapons' functional logic, which is their strategic deterrent function. Rather, it has more to do with their buying into a shared system of beliefs where nuclear weapons constitute the greatest symbols of power in the international system.[81] To qualify as a great power, India had to have nuclear weapons. Karsten Frey summed up this view by saying that "in India's nuclear policy formulation, status seeking became a national interest in its own right…not by increasing the substance of state power…but by displaying it."[82]

The observations of the prestige theorists are not incorrect. But they also do not accurately capture the complexity and totality of India's nuclear politics. Without doubt, the post-independent Indian state and its elites have consistently deployed modern science and large technology projects (aviation, defense, heavy industry, hydroelectric and nuclear power, space) as scripts and props to infuse the country's post-colonial project of modernity with grandiosity, purpose and legitimacy.[83] In the minds of India's power elites, the actualization of these projects justifies the rejection of colonialism and closes the epistemic gap, albeit symbolically, between India and the more developed states in the international system, allowing India peer status regardless of large qualitative gaps in its material development metrics. Nonetheless, the secrecy surrounding India's nuclear weaponization project in the decade prior to its public reveal in 1998 alongside the program's current scale and complexity, testify to more complex national security rationales, something that prestige theorists do not adequately address.

The prestige theorists have generated a lot of prima facie evidence to support their claims. But they also ignore something fundamental, which is that prestige depends on public knowledge of the possession of a value or material object held in esteem because of its relative scarcity.[84] In cases involving India's large technology projects including atomic energy, defense and space

32 *Secrecy and state learning*

for example, publicity, performative displays and mythologizing are closely imbricated into the developmental fabric of those projects.

This is also true for the nuclear weapons project, but to a far lesser extent. Consider, for example, that from 1981–1982 when India began planning nuclear weaponization until the first phase of the project's completion in the late 1990s, Indian political leaders across three political coalitions (centrist, left and the right), chose not to disclose any aspect of the weaponization program in public. The prestige theorists therefore do not account for the fact that the pursuit of nuclear weapons in secret undercuts one of the basic operating principles of prestige, which is open public knowledge and publicity.

In India's case, scholars sometimes collapse the intrinsic and instrumental ends of prestige. At other times they parse them. In the intrinsic argument, nuclear weapons are associated with the post-colonial Indian state's foundational notions of legitimacy and modern identity. Consider for example Itty Abraham and Sankaran Krishna's casting of nuclear weapons as artifacts of modernity that dignify and satisfy the primordial nationalist urges of the subaltern post-colonial Indian state.[85] Their approach superbly unpacks the cultural meanings and symbolisms associated with the nuclear sector in the collective consciousness of Indian publics and elites. But it is impossible to tease out these symbolic associations from the more tangible national security drivers behind policies. Abraham and Krishna's arguments are also embedded in a "soft" epistemology, which even when insightful renders the task of measurement difficult.[86]

By comparison, instrumental prestige arguments, both domestic and external, are more measurable. In the early 2000s for example, Daniel Markey and Kanti Bajpai made the domestic version of this argument.[87] They claimed that India's decision to conduct nuclear tests and claim nuclear power status was causally linked to the rise of Hindu nationalism and the Hindu-nationalist Bharatiya Janata Party's (BJP) quest for electoral dividends. Nonetheless, both ignored the simple historical counterfactual that six prime ministers at the head of four centrist and left-of-the center coalitions supported the weaponization program for a decade prior to the 1998 tests. In fact, the tests would have been impossible without their support. Three prime ministers seriously considered nuclear tests in 1982–1983,[88] in 1995[89] and in 1996[90], before finally ordering them in 1998. To be sure, the tests proved enormously popular and the Hindu nationalists reaped some electoral dividends. However, the argument that the BJP ordered the tests solely to boost its electoral prospects is simplistic. More significant, in the post-1998 period as well, India's nuclear weaponization program has enjoyed strong support from all ruling coalitions that have governed the country.

On the external front, Karsten Frey advanced the claim that nuclear weapons are the petard with which India has sought entry into the exclusive club of nuclear great powers. To establish this claim, Frey uses the elite discourse analysis method. His evidence consists of a random sample of 705 nuclear-related editorials and opinions culled from four Indian newspapers between

1986 and 2005. This sample shows that the Indian elite discourse focused on security threats during the 1980s, shifted attention to the nonproliferation regime and identity-related status issues in the 1990s, reverted back to security issues in the wake of the 1998 tests and thereafter once again became fixated with status and identity issues.[91] In Frey's reckoning, for over 20 years, concerns of self, identity and prestige outpaced national security threats in the public discourse,[92] which can be treated as a proxy for the revealed preferences of its decision-makers.

Frey, however, did not consider that any political discourse takes its cues and has an interactive relationship with historical events. In India's case for example, as evidence of Pakistan's nuclear advances grew in the 1980s, national security primarily colored the nuclear debate. As the push to permanently ban nuclear testing and fissile material production as well as to permanently extend the NPT gained momentum in the 1990s, status and identity gained salience alongside national security issues in India. Post-1998, after India conducted nuclear tests, formally claimed the status of a nuclear weapons power, and reopened the debate about its nuclear future, national security once again leapt to the fore in editorials and commentaries. Subsequently thereafter, as the Indian government set out to negotiate its nuclear status with the United States and the other legally recognized nuclear weapon states, national security once again blended with identity and prestige discourses. What this tells us is that the mantle of public discourse rests on an inner fluid core of shifting events. The discourse invariably shapes itself to reflect on those events. But that shift in and by itself is not indicative of the predominance or the lack thereof of identity and prestige over national security.

Frey also proposed, without much supporting evidence, that because the Indian state lacked an institutionalized national security decision-making apparatus, the strategic elite outside the government was "able to monopolize the security discourse and thus hold an element of power which, in a Habermasian definition, comprising both 'communicative power' and 'administrative power' associated with the functions and institutions of the state."[93] This latter assumption vastly overestimates the elite's capacity to influence the state and underestimates the zealousness with which the Indian executive has historically guarded its prerogative over nuclear decision-making.

Hence in pronouncing India's nuclear quest as symbolic and prestige driven, the prestige theorists overstate their case on three counts. First, they ignore the reality that prestige associated with nuclear weapons has been a constant in Indian politics since the 1974 nuclear test. All prime ministers from 1982–1983 onward had the option to test and yet none chose to do so until 1998. Second, prestige depends on publicity. Yet, seven Indian governments between 1989 and 1998 elected against making India's nuclear capability public. Furthermore, nuclear issues have ceased to be an electoral issue in Indian politics. But for technical milestones such as platform acquisitions and missile tests that are visible to the general public eye, the more substantive organizational, institutional and doctrinal elements of nuclear force

34 *Secrecy and state learning*

development after 1998 receded into the background. Finally, the instrumentalists' surmise that India has sought nuclear weapons for display purposes is contradicted by the steady development of India's operational nuclear capabilities in the last decade even after being accepted as a "responsible state with advanced nuclear technology."[94]

Normative-ideological

The mirror image of the prestige through plumage display is that of abjuring it. In India's case, scholars and policy practitioners have pointed to this contradistinctive trend, which they believed made it highly unlikely that India would opt for an overt or operational nuclear posture. There was little doubt, they maintained, that India's power elites were obsessed with the power halo that nuclear weapons conferred on states in the international system. Nonetheless, the consensus in India on the positive power associated with nuclear weapons was fractured and influential members of the power elite also pronounced them as nihilistic and wasteful. The collision of these opposing cultural beliefs, many reasonably inferred, would produce a national compromise where India would develop key technologies and yet stop short of building an operational nuclear force.

The argument made in this context was that Indian leaders sought prestige by abjuring what would be considered the normal behavior of security-seeking states in the international system. Scholars maintained that Indian leaders sought to position India as a moral exemplar, a country that stands aloof and above the security maximizing states that populate the international system.[95] Indeed, Indian prime ministers until the late 1970s, Jawaharlal Nehru, Lal Bahadur Shastri and Morarji Desai, had a strong aversion to nuclear weapons and institutionalized their preferences through the state's public advocacy of global nuclear arms control and disarmament, as well as by rejecting domestic pressures for nuclear armament.[96] There is also evidence to show that the two key nuclear decision-makers in the 1980s, Prime Ministers Indira and Rajiv Gandhi, opposed weaponization on normative grounds.

However, the evidence is more muddied. Although senior policy planners who interacted with Rajiv Gandhi have described him a "reluctant believer" in the nuclear cause,[97] his mother and immediate predecessor's motives appear to be a mixed bag of economic realism and political risk-aversion.[98] That said, even Rajiv Gandhi followed a Janus-faced approach, which coupled moralism with an insurance strategy of allowing work on the weapon program to proceed.[99] In retrospect, it is evident that Rajiv Gandhi was the last of India's prime ministers who harbored doubts on the legitimacy of nuclear weapons in India's security matrix.[100]

More pertinently, prime ministers who succeeded the Gandhis after 1989 do not appear to have shared their normative predilections. India had a succession of six prime ministers in the period 1989–1998. At least three among them, V.P. Singh, Narasimha Rao and Deve Gowda, representing a broad swath of India's political spectrum to the left and center of the Hindu-right BJP, cited economic and not moral constraints for not conducting nuclear tests.[101] Further, all prime ministers from 1989 onward, including Rajiv Gandhi, privately supported the covert weaponization program, and allowed it to proceed even if they did not proactively commit to adding material and institutional means toward accelerating it.

The historical evidence, in fact, shows variation between the Indian prime ministers' public statements and private actions. Sociological Institutionalism informs us that actors generally follow two types of actions in public. The first is "obligatory" and the second "consequential." In performing "obligatory" actions, actors ritualistically comply with scripts that are deemed socially appropriate. In "consequential" actions on the other hand, actors consciously employ their agency to implement identified goals.[102]

Just because public actors formally abide by normative scripts does not mean that they actually believe in them or act on them in private. All this said, it must also be accepted that the force of obligatory norms likely played some role in India's formal advocacy of the Comprehensive Test Ban Treaty (CTBT) in the early and mid-1990s, a position increasingly at odds with the views of its own scientific, technical and military actors who manned the "deep state." Formal normative scripts in this period also likely reinforced the government's hesitancy to suddenly and forcefully end the policy of nuclear ambiguity and switch to nuclear power status.

Nonetheless, a deeper problem with the above normative argument is that it conflates the views held by prime ministerial incumbents with those of India's "deep state." This approach effectively black boxes the state. If we peer inside the black box of the state, we discover considerable support for the nuclear weapons program among scientist-bureaucrats and military leaders who viewed Pakistan's nuclear advances in the 1980s and 1990s with consternation and pushed for a hard Realist course of action.[103] Had India's "deep state" harbored a deep normative aversion to nuclear weapons, three decision-makers at the helm of a right-wing government in 1998 would have found it extraordinarily difficult to revolutionize the course of India's nuclear policy. That they did not, should serve as our canary in the coal mine of nuclear abstinence norms.

Related to normative nuclear abstinence norms is the argument concerning "strategic culture." Beginning in the late 1980s and early 1990s, as Indian decision-makers hesitated from formally claiming nuclear status even as evidence of India's basement arsenal grew, several scholars sought to explain away their hesitancy as stemming from the lack of a strategic culture.[104] The specific argument advanced in India's case was that the country's normatively freighted strategic culture imposed explicit and tacit restraints on military maximalism.[105]

This argument is generally popular with academics and policy makers. But considerable confusion abounds on whether the sources of cultural preferences that inform Indian strategic thinking are institutional or normative. It is also unclear if the strategic culture argument applies to "grand strategy," which is the "purposeful employment of all instruments of power available to a security community,"[106] or the narrower "military strategy," which pertains to the planning and execution by military organizations of strategic goals.[107]

In the absence of such specifications, the purchase of the strategic culture argument is unclear. Nuclear policy is referred to in a general way in many arguments. Some scholars have tied an entire stable of cultural preferences and beliefs (Nehru–Gandhi) to at least three evolving nuclear tableaus (option, recessed deterrence and overt posture) from the early 1980s to the last decade.[108] However, this attempt undermines the argument that cultural belief systems explain India's nuclear consistency and restraint in the face of system-level pressures.

The debate on cultural explanations for India's strategic behavior was triggered by Tanham's controversial claim in the early 1990s that India suffered from the "absence of strategic thinking." When making this claim, Tanham made no distinction between grand strategy and military strategy. He also based his claims on a mix of historical and cultural factors. At the historic plane, Tanham asserted that India lacked imperial unity for most of its history. Because India had not evolved into a modern state independently, it never developed a tradition of thinking about "national defense." However, Tanham tied the dominant reasons for India's lack of a strategic culture to Hindu religion: the Hindu "concept" or the "lack of a sense of time" and the treatment of life as vague and "mysterious." The latter, Tanham maintained, discouraged planning.[109]

The difficulty with Tanham's historical frame is that it ignores the two centuries of the British imperial interlude, the strategic planning that accompanied empire and the postcolonial Indian state's inheritance of both the imperial institutions as well as the imperial mindset. His cultural arguments also do not account for the materiality of the postcolonial Indian state and its primary post-independence project: centralized economic planning and development.[110]

Although Tanham never drew direct linkages between his claims on the "absence of strategic thinking" and Indian nuclear policy, leading Indian strategic thinkers such as K. Subrahmanyam and India's former foreign minister Jaswant Singh used it to frame what they described as the drift in India's nuclear policy. Nonetheless, a close study of Subrahmanyam's writings shows that both institutional and cultural reasons account for that drift and that these institutional reasons are the primary while culture is the secondary cause.[111]

Singh, on the other hand, accepted the validity of Tanham's reasons but argued that India's failings were specific to "grand" strategy and not "military" strategy.[112] Whereas Subrahmanyam's institutional critiques of Indian policy planning, borne out of his own experience in government, eclipse the cultural argument, Singh's criticisms have greater applicability to the grand strategic principles governing India's nuclear posture (covert versus overt) and the handling of nonproliferation pressures in general. They apply less to

Secrecy and state learning 37

the specifics of covert nuclear developments and related operational planning. More significant, Singh's arguments highlight the institutional path-dependency problems that arose from the personal and non-institutionalized system of foreign policy and strategic decision-making under Prime Minister Nehru's tutelage in the first two decades of Indian independence.[113]

To date, Rajesh Basrur has applied the strategic cultural argument most rigorously. He restricts his argument to a select historical period, narrows its scope to nuclear weapons excluding all other strategic questions, and develops a credible methodology of specific open-source content analysis and elite interviews to support his case.[114] Basrur identifies three elements in Indian strategic culture, which he argues are the basis for the continuing nuclear minimalism and restraint from the late 1970s until the early 2000s. These are: (a) a very limited acceptance of nuclear weapons as a source of national security; (b) political as against the technical/operational understanding of nuclear weapons; and (c) incremental responses to systemic-level structural pressures to expand nuclear capabilities.[115]

It is this restrained strategic culture, the "habits of mind, traditions, and preferred methods of operation," argues Basrur, which explains the slow institutional changes in India's nuclear responses: the options posture in the 1980s, the recessed posture during the 1990s and the overt posture post-1998.[116] Remarkably enough, Basrur characterizes the tectonic institutional shift between the recessed (pre-1998) and overt (post-1998) postures as non-radical, because of the general reluctance of the political class to develop an operational capability.[117] Thus cultural preferences in his view are the connective thread that tie three nuclear institutional postures and explain overall restraint.

Basrur's methodology, however, unearths something entirely at odds with his argument. It shows that the Indian elite's post-1998 nuclear beliefs and preferences are dichotomized along two lines: between the politicians who view nuclear weapons as political weapons and the strategic experts and the military who lean in the direction of espousing an operational framework for those same weapons.[118] In essence, Basrur's methodology reveals evidence of the existence of two competing subcultures within the Indian state, which uneasily cohabit a common political space. Although Basrur's data are restricted to the post-1998 years, his methodology when applied to earlier historical periods – the decades of the "option" and "recessed" posture – shows a similar cultural dichotomy between the political generalists and the professional military.[119]

In advancing the cultural argument, Basrur bucks the obvious institutional and organizational ones. In a regime of competing subcultures what conditions enable one set of cultural beliefs to prevail in the policy market place? Similarly, in a system characterized by cultural differences, why is there a systemic bias in favor of the status quo? Basrur indirectly answers these questions by showing that pre-1998 nuclear decision-making in India was the exclusive preserve of prime ministers to the exclusion of parliament, the civilian bureaucracy, the military and public opinion. By his own admission,

India's strategic culture is reduced to a set of cultural preferences held by prime ministerial incumbents,[120] a process that black boxes the state. Finally, and more significant perhaps, Basrur admits to the gradual shift toward an operational bias in Indian strategic culture[121] without accounting for the mechanisms behind new cultural learning in the system.

Economic

The final set of "supply side" constraint arguments concern the economics of nuclear restraint. This set has two variants. The first concerns India's economic constraints. The second argument is metaphorically akin to Putnam's "two-level game" model[122] where the outward/inward orientation of domestic political coalitions shapes the politics of nuclear restraint.

The strictly domestic-level argument is that India's weak resource conditions explain nuclear restraint in the years 1980–1998. In 1982–1983 for example, Prime Minister Indira Gandhi reportedly canceled earlier planned nuclear tests due to the implicit threat of US denial of World Bank and IMF funds.[123] Similarly in 1985, Prime Minister Rajiv Gandhi also shelved plans prepared by an interdisciplinary team consisting of scientists and the military for a proposed nuclear arsenal because he thought its budgetary price too high.[124] Similarly, Prime Minister Rao considered a program of nuclear tests in 1995–1996. But he decided against it lest the tests jeopardize the "structural adjustment" program then underway with the IMF's assistance.[125]

The economic constraints argument therefore credibly explains India's reluctance to conduct hot tests and embrace an overt nuclear posture until 1998. However, it does not address the puzzles raised in this book, which concern weaponization adjusted to the economic constraints of the time. Resource constraints, furthermore, should not impact operational planning, which is a software issue that concerns intra- and inter-agency coordination and planning.

More significant, in the decade following India's formal claim to nuclear status, economic constraints in the form of US sanctions ended with Washington's acceptance of New Delhi's *de facto* nuclear weapon power status. Likewise, the Indian economy's "tiger" performance in that period loosened the government's purse strings on military spending. However, even as these externalities changed, it took the Indian government until 2004–2005 to begin addressing the institutional and organizational lacunae in India's operational posture. The slowness of that response raises doubts about the economic constraints as the cause for India's nuclear restraint argument.

Etel Solingen has advanced a second economic argument. Solingen highlights the link between the orientation of domestic coalitions and grand strategy. Extending the analytic treatment that Jack Snyder and Mathew Evangelista applied to the domestic politics of great powers in the realms of war making and weapons procurement, she argues that nonproliferation outcomes are more likely to emanate from the economic practices of liberalizing domestic coalitions.[126]

In the context of nuclear proliferation Solingen makes two specific claims. First, domestic liberalizing coalitions care about access to international financial markets, trade, capital and investments. Such coalitions are aware that nonacceptance of full-scope nuclear safeguards can result in the denial of access to the global economy.[127] Second, nuclear weapon programs are usually bound up with domestic inward-looking "nationalist-confessional" coalitions. In contrast, liberalizers tend to deregulate the economy and disinvest in state-controlled strategic industrial sectors. The implications for nuclear weapon programs and the nuclear complex in general are that state liberalization of the economy and withdrawal from public sector industries will likely generate pressures that favor termination of nuclear weapon programs.[128]

Solingen caveats her argument by cautioning that her theory is more probabilistic than deterministic and that her models are more in the nature of Weber's "ideal types;" conceptual constructs and not "historical or true realities." Furthermore, leaders' ability to successfully implement liberalizing agendas will vary according to their strength vis-à-vis domestic competitors as well as whether neighboring regional states adopt similar liberalizing agendas. Equally significant, the temporal sequence surrounding nuclear weapons acquisition matter. Hence, the argument does not apply once critical nuclear thresholds are crossed. For example, leaders will find it harder to give up the weapons they may already possess than abandon steps in the direction of weapons acquisition already taken.[129]

But the empirical evidence to support Solingen's claims is problematic. Sasikumar and Way's hazard model shows for instance that trade liberalization is associated with higher risks of nuclear proliferation. Further, the expansion in gross domestic product (GDP) has a nonlinear relationship with states' nuclear quest. Per capita GDP expansion only above very high thresholds is likely to reduce the risk of nuclear proliferation. Higher levels of trade openness, to be sure, reduce the hazard. But participation in international regimes and organizations does not appear to inhibit proliferation.[130]

Solingen's test cases are restricted to states in the Far East and the Middle East. Her study excludes India and Pakistan. Nonetheless, India is an important test case because it meets all her theory's scope conditions: liberalizing coalition, effective domestic leadership, neighboring states with liberalizing agendas and a weaponization program in an inchoate phase. It also turns out to be the case, which refutes the liberalization as the means for de-nuclearization thesis. The weaponization phase of India's nuclear weapons program beginning in 1989 almost precisely overlapped with the launch of economic liberalization policies in the late 1980s. In the two decades following that decision, the weaponization program's scope has expanded even as the orientation of the Indian economy has taken an almost irreversible global turn.

To summarize the main points: the nuclear demand explanations focus on the role security competition plays in forming states' nuclear preferences. In India's case, however, they are unable to explain the lag in the actualization of those preferences. The nuclear "supply side" constraint arguments attempt to fill that gap by drawing on India-specific domestic explanations. Among them, prestige arguments underplay counterfactuals and read the evidence selectively. Normative accounts conflate the state's norms with those held by prime ministerial incumbents. Cultural arguments, on the other hand, are unable to decide whether the source of India's strategic culture is historical, normative or institutional. These arguments also ignore the institutional elephant in the room, which offers the obvious explanation for why amidst a host of competing subcultures, one subculture prevailed over the other. Finally, the economic constraint arguments are not germane to the issue of covert small-scale weaponization programs, institutional planning and organizational coordination.

Expectations of secrecy's rationality-bending effects model

In contrast to structural theories, which assume that states respond rationally and optimally to visceral national security threats, my argument suggests that secrecy generates distortionary effects, which stymies the process of rational decision-making. In my framework, the nonproliferation regime forces nuclear proliferation in post-NPT nuclear wannabe states underground. The process of covert proliferation hobbles nuclear learning because state leaders operate under a self-induced regime of information and knowledge scarcity. The secrecy regime's negative effects operate in three ways.

First, in every state, epistemic actors are central to the process of policy innovation and organizational learning. Epistemic actors play a critical role in forming consensual knowledge about problem-and-solution sets. They are also the key mechanism for transmitting that knowledge to policy makers, in helping them frame policy choices and in coordinating policy implementation across the state. Policy innovation occurs when states institutionalize new ideas generated by epistemic actors and communities into their habitual routines. However, one can expect that decision-makers in clandestinely proliferating states will only partially mobilize epistemic actors. Out of caution, they will more likely choose goals that are static and loosely coupled. Because such goals do not demand the sustained attention of an epistemic community, the latter will remain an underutilized resource within the state.

Since nuclear proliferation is an activity fraught with high risk, political decision-makers will also prefer autonomy and flexibility in the decision-making process. One can therefore reasonably expect that decision-makers will have incentives against strongly institutionalizing epistemic actors within the state. This is because strong institutions carry the risk of increasing decision makers' domestic audience costs and binding their agency. Weak institutions on the other hand protect their reputation and autonomy. Nonetheless, weak institutions also have the net effect of attenuating the state's policy capacity and reducing its scope for policy innovation. Further, because prevailing institutions create path dependencies, one can also expect the negative effects of secrecy to persist and create a drag on learning even after decision-makers openly commit themselves to proliferation policy goals.

Second, state learning is contingent on high information turnover, problem decomposition, distributed policy planning and independent peer review. Information abundance and structured processing of that information within states, or for that matter in any organization, reduce the scope for heuristics and biases in decision-making. However, one expects that decision-makers in proliferating states will favor low turnover of information and knowledge. They will prefer to hoard knowledge concerning the nuclear weapons program, curtail information flows within the state and centralize decision-making. One can reasonably surmise the net effect of such administrative behavior to be uncorrected cognitive biases among decision-makers and poorly optimized policy decisions.

Third and finally, political leaders need well-developed mechanisms within the state to monitor agents who they task with proliferation projects. However, the process of covert proliferation fragments knowledge inside the state and parcels it among various agents. Internal secrecy makes it extraordinarily hard for the decision-makers to accurately monitor and appraise the activities of their agents. Constraints on information and knowledge sharing also raise the transfer costs of knowledge among the agents themselves. One can therefore expect that political leaders, even in highly centralized settings, will lack effective means to monitor their agents and the nuclear program's progress precisely. It is also likely that lacunae in programs will go undetected.

Expectations of standard structural theories

In contrast, standard structural theories of international relations presume that proliferation decisions are primarily driven by raison d'état. As such their unfolding within the state will follow the path of supreme rationality. Due to the growing legal obstacles and moral norms against the acquisition of nuclear arms, the program will no doubt deviate from standard armament development projects. The project will likely grow within a walled-off secret enclave within the state. The epistemic actors mobilized to enact it will remain highly select. However, the actors will draw from a diverse set, which includes nuclear scientists and engineers, military specialists, bureaucrats and political decision-makers.

The epistemic actors will enjoy close proximity and access to decision-makers. The latter will tend to proceed with caution given the international opprobrium their actions if discovered are likely to provoke. Nonetheless, given the state's national security concerns and decision-makers' commitment to securing them, epistemic actors will enjoy considerable freedom of action, both in terms of access to information and material resources, to bring the nuclear weapons program to fruition. Epistemic actors will also likely find it relatively easy to secure decision-makers' commitments to a series of synergized program choices.

A related assumption is that the sequestered nature of decision-making within the walled off enclave will not affect its quality negatively. Structural theorists assume that cocooned decision-makers make more rational choices when removed from bureaucratic infighting and political compromises that afflict most programs. Within the state's sequestered enclave, segments of the state's scientific, engineering and military agencies will find the freedom to exchange information freely and cooperate to execute different but related elements of the project simultaneously. Thus fissile material production, bomb design and delivery systems will all be parts of a boutique but highly coordinated effort. Further, as with conventional weapons, the nuclear hardware once developed will naturally evolve to incorporate soft routines such as institutional oversight, strategic principles governing use, intra- and interagency coordination. No doubt, secrecy and sequestering will render the weapons special and remove them from the standard administrative processes of the state. The latter institutional conditions however should not immobilize those processes altogether.

Finally, structural theories do not expect that secrecy, reduced information inflows, or the relative absence of agent competition are detrimental to efficiency. The unstated assumption is that highly centralized and coordinated state settings will enable political principals to exercise control over their agents. High classification and internal opacity are not tantamount to the absence of oversight mechanisms in the state. Just that the state's normal administrative apparatus is unlikely to perform those functions. Given the significance of nuclear weapons and the power likely to accrue to leaders and the state from possessing them, political principals will seek to retain tight scrutiny over the program's direction and progress.

Overview of the book

In the remainder of the book I present empirical evidence to support the theoretical arguments developed in this chapter.

Chapter 3 revisits the puzzle of India's delayed weaponization in the 1980s. It highlights the challenges of imperfect information and uncertainty that confront most decision-makers and how weakly institutionalized epistemic actors and how constraints on information and knowledge sharing compound the challenges of accurately assessing national security threats. I show that India's sequential problem-solving approach and the decision-makers' underestimation of Pakistan's challenge are directly traceable to the unstructured information processing and national security decision-making system in the state. Further, Indian decision-makers' overestimation of the India's capacity to counter that threat bespeaks of the problems of effective agent monitoring in regimes of information and knowledge scarcity.

Chapter 4 dwells on India's problems of nuclear operational planning under domestic institutions of secrecy and international scrutiny in the decade of the 1990s. It presents evidence to show the linkages between poor knowledge aggregation within the state and the absence of deductive planning. In India's case, these directly contributed to many of the technical and organizational hurdles that hampered execution of the weaponization project during the 1990s. The evidence in this chapter also shows that decision-makers' cognitive biases prevented inter-agency planning and coordination on soft nuclear operational routines in this period. Information asymmetries and the decision-makers' lack of effective oversight over their agents were also the direct consequence of the state's internal regime of secrecy. The chapter concludes by demonstrating that contrary to foreign assumptions, India lacked an operational nuclear capability until the summer of 1999.

In Chapter 5, I examine the path-dependency effects of existing institutions even when decision-makers commit to new policy goals. I show how weakly instituted epistemic actors and compartmentalized planning adversely affected the actualization of nuclear operational practices in the six years following India's formal claims to nuclear power status, and how changes in institutional practices in 2004–2005 are gradually, but radically, altering outcomes. The chapter also shows that many of the technical and organizational bottlenecks that come in the way of smooth operational practices stem from classic principal–agent problems that arise in enclosed self-referential organizational systems.

Chapter 6, the concluding chapter, attempts a plausibility probe to expand the framework developed in this book to study three other cases of proliferation in the international system: France, Israel and Pakistan. It argues that compared to all three, India's case stands out as an exception. But the causality for Indian exceptionalism does not entirely run through either the nature of India's bureaucracy or its civil-military institutions. Rather the cause for the difference between India's nuclear performance and that of many other nuclear weapon powers stems from the variation in how self-referential systems are instituted domestically to manage their nuclear weapon programs.

In this regard, I draw distinctions between regimes of secrecy and hyper-secrecy. I argue that it is the latter, the regimes of hyper-secrecy, which are more prone to distorting rationality and producing suboptimal outcomes. The rationale for states selecting one over the other is variation in pressure: the threat of political and economic sanctions or military action from the United States, the principal enforcer of nuclear nonproliferation in the international system. There is a world time mechanism built into the enforcement principle. It has grown more rigorous since the passage of the NPT in 1969. Nonetheless, the historical evidence shows that US nonproliferation policy has varied in the treatment of friends and foes in the international system.

Notes

1 "Nuclear Anxiety: Indian's Letter to Clinton on the Nuclear Testing," *New York Times* (May 13, 1998), http://www.nytimes.com/1998/05/13/world/nuclear-anxiety-indian-s-letter-to-clinton-on-the-nuclear-testing.html (November 2012).

44 Secrecy and state learning

2   Jack Levy, "Learning and Foreign Policy: Sweeping a Conceptual Minefield," *International Organization*, Vol. 48, No. 2 (Spring 1994), p. 283.
3   For an overview on the practices of socialization see, Jeffrey T. Checkel, "Why Comply? Social Learning and European Identity Change," *International Organization*, Vol. 55, No. 3 (Summer 2001), pp. 556–564; "International Institutions and Socialization in Europe: Introduction and Framework," *International Organization*, Vol. 59, No. 4 (Autumn 2005), pp. 804–813.
4   Ibid.
5   Kenneth N. Waltz, "Reductionist and Systemic Theories," in Robert O. Keohane ed., *Neorealism and Its Critics* (New York: Columbia University Press, 1986), pp. 64–67.
6   For a theoretical framework that unpacks how international institutions socialize states', see Checkel, "International Institutions and Socialization in Europe: Introduction and Framework," pp. 804–813.
7   For a general overview of the literature on state learning see, Levy, "Learning and Foreign Policy."
8   Levy, "Learning and Foreign Policy," pp. 286–287.
9   Checkel, "Why Comply?" pp. 562–564.
10 Chris Argyris and Donald A. Schon, *Organizational Learning* (Reading: Addison-Wesley, 1980), pp. 26–28.
11 Philip E. Tetlock, "In Search of an Elusive Concept," in George W. Breslauer and Philip E. Tetlock eds., *Learning in US and Soviet Foreign Policy* (Boulder: Westview Press, 1991), p. 22.
12 Levy, "Learning and Foreign Policy," pp. 287–289.
13 Ernst B. Haas, *When Knowledge Is Power: Three Models of Change in International Organizations* (Berkeley: University of California Press, 1990), pp. 20–23; Haas, "Collective Learning: Some Theoretical Speculations," in Breslauer and Tetlock eds., *Learning in US and Soviet Foreign Policy*, pp. 65–66.
14 Haas, "Collective Learning: Some Theoretical Speculations," pp. 66–69.
15 Emanuel Adler and Peter M. Haas, "Conclusion: Epistemic Communities, World Order and the Creation of a Reflective Research Program," *International Organization*, Vol. 46, No. 1 (Winter 1992), p. 371.
16 Peter M. Haas, "Introduction: Epistemic Communities and International Policy Coordination," *International Organization*, Vol. 46, No. 1 (Winter 1992), p. 3.
17 Ibid., p. 19.
18 Ibid., p. 20.
19 Emanuel Adler, "The Emergence of Cooperation: National Epistemic Communities and the International Evolution of Nuclear Arms Control," *International Organization*, Vol. 46, No. 1 (Winter 1992), pp. 111–116.
20 Ibid., pp. 124–140.
21 G. John Ikenberry, "A World Economy Restored: Expert Consensus and the Anglo-American Post-War Settlement," *International Organization*, Vol. 46, No. 1 (Winter 1992), pp. 289–321.
22 Raymond F. Hopkins, "Reform in the International Food Aid Regime: The Role of Consensual Knowledge," *International Organization*, Vol. 46, No. 1 (Winter 1992), pp. 225–264.
23 See for example, Rublee, *Nonproliferation Norms: Why States Choose Nuclear Restraint*.
24 Haas, "Epistemic Communities and International Policy Coordination," pp. 16–20.
25 I borrow this characterization from John Ikenberry, See, Ikenberry, "A World Economy Restored: Expert Consensus and the Anglo-American Post-War Settlement," p. 293.
26 Haas, "Collective Learning: Some Theoretical Speculations," pp. 66–69.
27 Ibid.

28 Ibid., pp. 69–84.
29 Ibid., p. 89.
30 Douglas C. North, *Institutions, Institutional Change and Economic Performance* (Cambridge: Cambridge University Press, 1990), pp. 46–60.
31 Paul Pierson, "Increasing Returns, Path Dependency and the Study of Politics," *American Political Science Review*, Vol. 94, No. 2 (June 2000), pp. 257–262.
32 Paul Pierson, "The Limits of Change: Explaining Institutional Origin and Change," *Governance: An International Journal of Policy and Administration*, Vol. 13, No. 4 (October 2000), pp. 475–499.
33 Ibid.
34 Vipin Narang, *Posturing for Peace? The Sources and Deterrence Consequences of Regional Power Nuclear Postures*, PhD Dissertation (Cambridge: Harvard University, April 2010), pp. 143–144.
35 Charles Lindblom, "The Science of Muddling Through," *Public & Administration Review*, Vol. 19, No. 2 (Spring 1959), pp. 79–88; "Still Muddling, Not Yet Through," *Public Administration Review*, Vol. 39, No. 6 (November–December 1979), pp. 517–526.
36 Simon, "Alternative Visions of Rationality," pp. 19–23.
37 Steinbruner, *The Cybernetic Theory of Decision* (Princeton: Princeton University Press, 1974), p. 66.
38 Ibid., pp. 54–55.
39 Ibid.
40 Ibid., pp. 66–69.
41 Ibid., pp. 71–85.
42 Lindblom, "The Science of Muddling Through."
43 Steinbruner, *The Cybernetic Theory of Decision*, pp. 90, 109–112.
44 Simon, *Reason in Human Affairs*, p. 85.
45 Steinbruner, *The Cybernetic Theory of Decision*, pp. 112–121.
46 Ibid.
47 Daniel Kahneman, Paul Slovic and Amos Tversky, *Judgment under Uncertainty: Heuristics and Biases* (Cambridge: Cambridge University Press, 1982).
48 Daniel Kahneman and Shane Frederick, "Representativeness Revisited: Attribute Substitution in Intuitive Judgment," in Thomas Gilovich, Dale Griffin and Daniel Kahneman eds., *Heuristics and Biases: The Psychology of Intuitive Judgment* (Cambridge: Cambridge University Press, 2002), pp. 49–81.
49 Norbert Schwarz and Leigh Ann Vaughn, "The Availability Heuristic Revisited: Ease of Recall and Content of Recall as Distinct Sources of Information," in Gilovich, Griffin and Kahneman eds., *Heuristics and Biases*, pp. 103–119.
50 Gilovich and Griffin, "Introduction – Heuristics and Biases: Then and Now," in Gilovich, Griffin and Kahneman eds., *Heuristics and Biases*, p. 4.
51 Jonathan Bendor, *Bounded Rationality and Politics* (Berkeley: University of California Press, 2010), p. 42.
52 The Carnegie School is an interdisciplinary approach, which applies decision analysis, management science, and psychology to the organization and firm. It emerged during the 1950s and 1960s and is primarily associated with the works of Herbert Simon, James March and Richard Cyert.
53 Bendor, *Bounded Rationality and Politics*, pp. 164–165.
54 Ibid.
55 For a critique of Graham T. Allison's rational actor model see, Jonathan Bendor and Thomas H. Hammond, "Rethinking Allison's Models, *The American Political Science Review*, Vol. 86, No. 2 (June 1992), pp. 301–322.
56 Bendor, *Bounded Rationality and Politics*, p. 171.
57 Ibid., pp. 165–172; also see, Jonathan B. Bendor, *Parallel Systems: Redundancy in Government* (Berkeley: University of California Press, 1985), pp. 24–60.

58 Irving L. Janis, *Groupthink: Psychological Studies of Political Decisions and Fiascoes* (Boston: Wadsworth, 1982), pp. 174–175.
59 Oyvind Bohren, "The Agent's Ethics in the Principal-Agent Model," *Journal of Business Ethics*, Vol. 17, No. 7 (May 1998), pp. 746–748. For an overview of the application of the principal–agent theory to the discipline of political science in general see, Gary J. Miller, "The Political Evolution of Principal-Agent Models," *Annual Review of Political Science*, Vol. 8 (2005), pp. 203–225.
60 Eugene F. Fama and Michael C. Jensen, "Separation of Ownership and Control," *Journal of Law and Economics*, Vol. 26, No. 2 (June 1983), pp. 301–325. For an expanded version of the principal–agent model see, Richard W. Waterman and Kenneth J. Meier, "Principal-Agent Models: An Expansion?," *Journal of Public Administration Research and Theory: J-PART*, Vol. 8, No. 2 (April 1998), pp. 173–202.
61 Charles Perrow, "Agency Theory," *Complex Organizations: A Critical Essay* (New York: McGraw Hill, 1986), pp. 224–235.
62 Neil A. Shankman, "Reframing the Debate between Agency and Stakeholder Theories of the Firm," *Journal of Business Ethics*, Vol. 19 (1999), pp. 319–334.
63 Cited in Rosalind Levacic, "Teacher Incentive and Performance: An Application of Principal-Agent Theory," *Oxford Development Studies*, Vol. 37, No. 1 (March 2009), p. 35.
64 Fama and Jensen, "Separation of Ownership and Control," pp. 310–311.
65 Joseph E. Stiglitz, "The Theory of Screening: Education and the Distribution of Income," *The American Economic Review*, Vol. 65, No. 3 (June 1975), pp. 283–300.
66 For an overview of agents' use of signaling devices see, Michael Spence, "Job Market Signaling," *The Quarterly Journal of Economics*, Vol. 87, No. 3 (August 1973), pp. 355–374; also see, Paul Milogram and John Roberts, *Economics, Organization, and Management* (Englewood Cliffs: Prentice Hall, 1992), pp. 154–155.
67 Kenneth N. Waltz, "The Spread of Nuclear Weapons: More May Be Better," *Adelphi Paper 171* (London: IISS, 1981), pp. 7–8.
68 Tellis, *India's Emerging Nuclear Posture*, pp. 39–75; Sumit Ganguly, "India's Pathway to Pokhran II: The Prospects and Sources of New Delhi's Nuclear Weapons Program," *International Security*, Vol. 23, No. 4 (Spring 1999), pp. 148–177.
69 Paul, *Power versus Prudence: Why Nations Forgo Nuclear Weapons*, pp. 14–15.
70 Ibid., pp. 15–16.
71 Ibid., pp. 18–27.
72 Ibid., p. 18.
73 Deshmukh, "Keep the Faith."
74 Daniel Deudney, "Dividing Realism: Structural Realism versus Security on Nuclear Security and Proliferation, in Zachary S. Davis and Benjamin Frankel eds., *The Proliferation Puzzle: Why Nuclear Weapons Spread* (Frank Cass, 1993), p. 22.
75 Narang, "Strategies of Nuclear Proliferation: How States Purse the Bomb," pp. 110–150.
76 Ibid., pp. 136–146.
77 For an overview of some of the challenges of inter-organizational coordination during extreme events and emergencies see, Louise K. Comfort, "Crisis Management in Hindsight: Cognition, Communication, Coordination and Control," *Public Administration Review* (December 2007), pp. 189–197; Comfort, "Managing Intergovernmental Responses to Terrorism and Other Extreme Events," *Publius: The Journal of Federalism*, Vol. 32, No. 4 (Fall 2002), pp. 29–49.

78 Daniel S. Markey, *The Prestige Motive in International Relations*, PhD Dissertation (Princeton University, November 2000), pp. 19–31.
79 Hans J. Morgenthau, *Politics among Nations* (New York: Alfred A. Knopf, 1985), p. 95.
80 Robert Gilpin, *War and Change in World Politics* (Cambridge: Cambridge University Press, 1981), p. 31.
81 Sagan, "Why Do States Build Nuclear Weapons? Three Models in Search of a Bomb," pp. 73–76. In Sagan's version of the argument though, France is the exemplar of the prestige model. India's case is more representative of the organizational model where scientist bureaucrats seek to expand a large technology project for budgetary, organizational growth and prestige rationales.
82 Frey, *India's Nuclear Bomb and National Security*, p. 197.
83 Sunil Khilnani, *The Idea of India* (New York: Farrar, Straus & Giroux, 1997).
84 Barry O'Neil, "Nuclear Weapons and the Pursuit of Prestige," May 2002, http://www.sscnet.ucla.edu/polisci/faculty/boneill/prestap5.pdf (May 2011).
85 Abraham, *The Making of the Indian Atomic Bomb*, pp. 17–30; Sankaran Krishna, "The Social Life of a Bomb: India and the Ontology of an 'Overpopulated' Society," in Itty Abraham ed., *South Asian Cultures of the Bomb: Atomic Publics and the State in India and Pakistan* (Bloomington: Indiana University Press, 2009).
86 Landmark works include Abraham, *The Making of the Indian Atomic Bomb*; Abraham, ed., *South Asian Cultures of the Bomb*.
87 Bajpai, "The BJP and the Bomb," in Sagan ed., *Inside Nuclear South Asia*, pp. 49–57.
88 Perkovich, *India's Nuclear Bomb*, pp. 242–243.
89 Ibid., pp. 364–371.
90 Ibid., pp. 374–376.
91 Frey, *India's Nuclear Bomb and National Security*, pp. 28–46.
92 Ibid., pp. 44–46.
93 Frey, *India's Nuclear Bomb and National Security*, p. 30.
94 "Indo-US Joint Statement," July 18, 2005, http://www.hindu.com/thehindu/nic/indousjoint.htm (July 2005).
95 Perkovich, *India's Nuclear Bomb*, pp. 448–449.
96 Rajesh M. Basrur, *Minimum Deterrence and India's Nuclear Security* (Stanford: Stanford University Press, 2006), pp. 60–62; Perkovich, *India's Nuclear Bomb*, pp. 83–85, 199–204, 209–216.
97 Chengappa, *Weapons of Peace*, pp. 291–305.
98 Perkovich, *India's Nuclear Bomb*, pp. 242–244; Chengappa, *Weapons of Peace*, pp. 246–261.
99 Chengappa, *Weapons of Peace*, pp. 303–305.
100 Ibid.
101 Ibid., pp. 353–361, 367–371, 396–400; H.D. Deve Gowda, "Dear Prime Minister Sri Vajpayeeji," *Rediff on the Net*, May 22, 1998, http://www.rediff.com/news/1998/may/22deve.htm (June 2013).
102 Peter A. Hall and Rosemary C.R. Taylor, "Political Science and the Three New Institutionalisms," *Political Studies* XLIV (1996), pp. 946–950.
103 B.G. Deshmukh, *From Poona to the Prime Minister's Office: A Cabinet Secretary Looks Back* (New Delhi: Harper Collins Publishers India, 2004), pp. 163–166; Chengappa, *Weapons of Peace*, pp. 256–247, 257–261.
104 Examples include: George Tanham, *Securing India: Strategic Thought and Practice* (New Delhi: Manohar, 1996); Jaswant Singh, *Defending India* (Bangalore: Macmillan Press India, 1999); Michael R. Chambers ed., *South Asia in 2020: Future Strategic Balances and Alliances* (Carlisle: Strategic Studies Institute: U.S. Army War College, 2002); Basrur, *Minimum Deterrence and India's Nuclear Security*.

105 The most recent articulation of this argument is contained in, Stephen P. Cohen and Sunil Dasgupta, *Arming without Aiming: India's Military Modernization* (Washington, DC: The Brookings Institution, 2010).
106 Colin Gray, *War, Peace and International Relations – An Introduction to Strategic History* (Oxon: Routledge, 2007), p. 283.
107 Scott Sigmund Gartner, *Strategic Assessment in War* (New Haven: Yale University Press, 1999), p. 163.
108 Basrur, "Nuclear Weapons and Indian Strategic Culture," *Journal of Peace Research*, Vol. 38, No. 2 (March 2001), pp. 181–198.
109 Tanham, *Securing India: Strategic Thought and Practice*, pp. 72–75.
110 See for example, Sunil Khilnani, *The Idea of India* (New York: Farrar, Straus & Giroux, 1997), pp. 61–106.
111 For a snapshot see, K. Subrahmanyam with Arthur Monteiro, *Shedding Shibboleths: India's Evolving Strategic Outlook* (Delhi: Wordsmiths, 2005), pp. 1–28.
112 Jaswant Singh, *Defending India* (Bangalore: Macmillan India Limited, 1999), p. 14.
113 Ibid., pp. 22–58.
114 Basrur, *Minimum Deterrence and India's Nuclear Security*, pp. 57–59.
115 Ibid., p. 58.
116 Ibid., pp. 60–65.
117 Ibid., pp. 64–65.
118 Ibid., pp. 67–73.
119 For example see, General K. Sundarji, *Blind Men of Hindoostan* (New Delhi: UBS Publishers, 1993); Deshmukh, *From Poona to the Prime Minister's Office*, pp. 164–166.
120 Ibid., pp. 66–67.
121 Ibid., pp. 75–77.
122 Robert D. Putnam, "Diplomacy and Domestic Politics: The Logic of Two-Level Games," *International Organization*, Vol. 42, No. 3 (Summer 1988), pp. 427–460.
123 Perkovich, *India's Nuclear Bomb*, pp. 242–244.
124 Ibid., pp. 273–276; Chengappa, *Weapons of Peace*, pp. 297–305.
125 Perkovich, *India's Nuclear Bomb*, pp. 353–377.
126 Etel Solingen, "The Political Economy of Nuclear Restraint," *International Security*, Vol. 19, No. 2 (Autumn 1994), pp. 136–142.
127 Etel Solingen, *Nuclear Logics: Contrasting Paths in East Asia and the Middle East* (Princeton: Princeton University Press, 2007), pp. 40–41.
128 Ibid., pp. 41–42.
129 Solingen, *Nuclear Logics*, pp. 17–20, 44–45.
130 Sasikumar and Way, "Testing Theories of Proliferation in South Asia," in Scott D. Sagan ed., *Inside Nuclear South Asia* (Stanford: Stanford University Press, 2009), pp.79–81.

3 A disaggregated nuclear weapons option (1980–1989)

What happened between 1974 and 1989?

In May 1974 India exploded a nuclear device and dubbed it a peaceful nuclear explosion (PNE). But in its wake, India did not declare itself a nuclear weapon state. Nor did it seek such legal recognition internationally. Bucking the trend of other nuclear weapon powers until then, and somewhat paradoxically, India did not follow up this lone test with other field nuclear tests. Neither did it seek to incorporate nuclear explosives into its military planning.

Indian government representatives publicly insisted that the PNE was modeled after the US Ploughshares program,[1] which was an experimental attempt to leverage nuclear explosives in support of large engineering projects. These claims were plausible. However, they were never backed up by any Indian follow-up to use nuclear explosives for civil engineering programs. To policy practitioners schooled in realpolitik who thought the nomenclature of PNE a political cover for a weapons program,[2] there was also no accompanying evidence in the form of delivery systems, command control or organizational changes in the Indian military that would signify India's quest for an operational nuclear capability.[3]

India's lone nuclear test spawned the argument that it was not motivated by national security concerns.[4] However, the very likely answer to the riddle of India's lone 1974 test was the manageable risk of Chinese nuclear blackmail in the short term,[5] India's resource constraints, the lack of a diversified industrial infrastructure[6] and Western nonproliferation pressures.[7]

By the late 1970s, the balance of threat in the region began to change for the worse as clear indicators emerged of Pakistan's nuclear quest. In the case of Pakistan, the Himalayas did not present a geographic barrier as they did in the north vis-à-vis China. India's struggle against Pakistan was also ideological and existential. Pakistani revanchism became evident after India helped catalyze its break up in the Bangladesh War. Pakistan similarly hoped to reopen the disputed Kashmir conflict with India after it developed a nuclear capability.[8]

In a classic internal balancing act, India revived its nuclear weapons program after Indira Gandhi was reelected prime minister in 1980.[9] Gandhi's government also instituted a ballistic missile program in 1983. The Indian Air Force made purchases of dual-use combat aircraft capable of performing nuclear missions. These programs were ostensibly part of a balancing response against Pakistan's nuclear developments. India's "option" strategy as it became subsequently known, was interpreted from the outside as an attempt to assemble all the components of a working nuclear arsenal; a threshold capability that would give New Delhi the technical means to deploy an arsenal rapidly. The option strategy was also thought more economically manageable and far less likely to attract international "negative" balancing efforts in the form of sanctions.

The baseline assumption among most scholars was that India's response fit neatly into the standard rational-actor model.[10] But the trouble with this assumption as the subsequent evidence makes clear is that Indian decision-makers' notions of rationality were more imagined than real. The nuclear weapons development program was never clearly tied to the development of delivery systems. The weapons built in the nuclear lab did not fit onto dual-use combat aircraft. The ballistic missiles proved unsuitable for nuclear delivery.

Prime ministers and their top advisors underestimated the time it would take Pakistan to build nuclear weapons and were overly optimistic about India's capacity to counter the Pakistani nuclear threat. Pakistan acquired the ability to enrich uranium to weapons-grade in 1985; India did not obtain an uninterrupted supply of weapons-grade plutonium until 1988. Whereas Pakistan acquired two or three nuclear devices sometime in 1987, a comparable Indian capability emerged only in 1990.

How did India, a country with a proven nuclear weapons capability and a much larger nuclear estate and scientific-industrial infrastructure end up in a position of scrambling to counter a late proliferator like Pakistan, a country not only smaller but also far less materially endowed than its rival? This chapter provides answers to that question by showing that the organizational pathologies disrupted parallel coordination between India's nuclear estate, its defense agencies and its military. It also presents evidence to show that sequestered decision-making and the regime of information scarcity produced biases, which led Indian decision-makers into underestimating Pakistan's nuclear potential while overestimating India's own nuclear breakout capabilities. Finally, the evidence shows that the compartmentalization of information and the lack of institutional scrutiny undermined the task of managing the nuclear weaponization program successfully.

Compartmentalization and disaggregation

India revived its nuclear weapons program in 1980–1981. However, the program operated under a regime of severe internal opacity, which disrupted parallel coordination within the state. Between 1980 and 1989 less than a dozen individuals had specific knowledge of the program largely drawn from the Prime Minister's Office (PMO), BARC and DRDO.

Initiation of the nuclear weapons (1981) and missile development programs (1983) occurred in sequential order. The tasking requirements for the two programs proceeded on parallel tracks and were weakly coordinated. Strong internal firewalls also disrupted cooperation between the high-tech civilian space agency, the Indian Space Research Organization (ISRO), and the missile development agency, Defense Research & Development Laboratory (DRDL).

Within the armed services, the air force continued with routine capital acquisition and modernization programs without accounting for the challenges of potential nuclearization fully. Similarly, limited feedback loops between the agencies tasked with weapons development and the central executive coordinating arm of the government, the PMO, restricted the latter's independent scrutiny of the inputs it received from the former on the likelihood and potential effects of external sanctions, the state of Pakistan's nuclear progress and the speed at which India could resolve its own weaponization challenges.

India's top decision-makers believed that the discovery of the program would trigger technological and economic sanctions from the US and its western alliance partners. The resulting sanctions would cripple India's nuclear power sector and other high-tech sectors, and that economic sanctions would cause serious dislocations in the Indian economy. Such fears forced the program underground.

The extreme internal opacity and sequential planning had three effects. First, Indian leaders approached the nuclear weaponization program in increments. For the most part, they did not actively mobilize a nuclear epistemic community beyond the handful of nuclear scientists involved in the weapons development program. The latter condition constricted the process of learning among decision-makers. Second, even among actors with knowledge of the program, restrictions on the free cross exchange of information became an institutional roadblock for coordinating action among them. Third, the principals in the PMO sought to safeguard the secrecy of the program as well as their own autonomy by keeping the policy planning and decision-making process weakly institutionalized. As a result, the epistemic actors with stakes in the program never acquired the institutional means to extract policy commitments from their political masters. This last condition not only had negative effects on the morale of the agents but it also prevented the principals from monitoring the performance of their agents effectively.

This regime of internal opacity was substantially the child of fear born in the aftermath of India's 1974 nuclear test explosion. In its wake, the US led its alliance partners to deny sensitive nuclear fuel cycle technologies and equipment to states that did not accept full-scope International Atomic Energy Agency (IAEA) safeguards on their nuclear facilities. Nonproliferation pressures built up slowly: first through the Zangger Committee[11] and then the Nuclear Suppliers Group.[12] Further pressure came after the US Congress passed the Nuclear Nonproliferation Act (NNPA) in 1978. The NNPA changed US domestic law and forbade the supply of nuclear materials, equipment and technology to countries, which did not accept full-scope IAEA safeguards.[13] As international collaboration dried up, India's Department of Atomic Energy (DAE) was unable to meet the planned power generation target of 4,500 MW in the period 1970–1985. In 1985, a decade after the 1974 test, Indian nuclear reactors produced a mere 1,500 MW of power, one-third the original target. And the figure in 2000 was only 2,800 MW.[14]

Although the nuclear sector was the sole target of western technology-denial policies, yet the tightening of equipment, spares and nuclear material had a sobering effect on Prime Minister Indira Gandhi and her close policy advisors. Within India's space agency, for example, there was great concern that the fate of the nuclear sector would befall it as well. Vikram Sarabhai, the founder of the agency had opposed the nuclear explosives program on normative grounds. He had also argued against nuclear testing on grounds that building nuclear explosives was premature in the absence of supporting infrastructure that would enable India to field a nuclear force.[15] His successor Satish Dhawan, similarly opposed any militarization of the civilian space agency.[16] When Prime Minister Indira Gandhi authorized a secret medium-range ballistic missile program (Valiant) in 1972 using INR 60 million from the prime minister's "apex fund,"[17] Dhawan ensured that firewalls were erected between India's space and missile development agencies.

In the mid-1970s, engineers from the civilian space agency, ISRO and the Indian Institute of Science (Bangalore) conducted a peer review of the missile's liquid rocket engine.[18] However, Dhawan and his team avoided incorporating the engine developed for the Valiant rocket into the Polar Satellite Launch Vehicle (PSLV) program during the 1980s. For the latter, ISRO contracted to purchase the French Viking liquid fuel engine from Ariane, the French aerospace agency.[19] As Indira Gandhi's scientific advisor at the time saw it, the missile development agency, the DRDL became a victim of its own success. The prime minister, despite her wishes to the contrary, hesitated from forcing coordination and cooperation between the civilian ISRO and the military DRDL.[20]

In 1977, Indira Gandhi lost elections to Morarji Desai, a Gandhian who was morally opposed to the 1974 test and the nuclear weapons program in general. During his two-year tenure, the nuclear test team almost disintegrated due to his inattention and vocal opposition to the program. Despite the mounting threat from Pakistan, Desai moved the leader of the test team, Dr. Raja Ramanna out of BARC[21] to the position of scientific advisor to the defense minister.[22] In a public display of displeasure with the nuclear weapons establishment, the prime minister mocked the achievement of the Indian nuclear device team by publicly claiming that he was uncertain whether the 1974 test was caused by a nuclear device or by conventional explosives.[23] Nuclear scientists at BARC complained that they worked very hard during Desai's tenure to keep the 1974 nuclear device engineering and physics team intact.[24]

Between 1977 and 1979 evidence mounted of Pakistan's nuclear quest. In 1979, India's Joint Intelligence Committee (JIC) chaired by K. Subrahmanyam conducted its first thorough review of this development and concluded that Pakistan was pursuing a weapons program through the gas centrifuge uranium enrichment technique. US officials informed the Indian Foreign Minister A.B. Vajpayee during his visit to Washington that they believed that Pakistan could conduct a nuclear explosion within two or three years.[25] But Desai's government did not act on the JIC's report.[26] However, Indira Gandhi, who returned to power in 1980, did not share Desai's moral aversion to nuclear weapons. Confronted by nuclear developments in Pakistan and warnings from the nuclear establishment and India's intelligence agencies, she quietly revived the nuclear weapons program and reappointed Ramanna as director of BARC.[27] However, in doing so, she continued a pattern of secrecy and sequential decision-making. This method had a precedent in the 1974 test. But its urgency was felt greater in light of US nonproliferation pressures, the negative effects of technology denials on India's civilian nuclear power sector and the potential threat of economic sanctions.

In reviving the nuclear weapons program, Gandhi ensured that its goals were relatively static and loosely coupled. To avoid attracting international attention, the key elements of the program – fissile material production, device development, delivery system modification, force planning, command and control – were not pursued in a deductive manner. In the absence of a holistic approach to finding solutions to the challenge posed by the emerging Pakistani threat, the PMO deliberately mobilized only those epistemic actors that were absolutely essential during the program's early stages; these involved the nuclear physicists at BARC. The weapons development agency, the DRDO and a few of its labs were gradually brought into play. But high firewalls were left standing between them and BARC. The government also did not consider it prudent to coordinate action between the weapon development team, the team working on potential delivery systems and their actual users. All information was hived off in compartments with little lateral interflow between them. The net result of this approach was a regime of severe internal opacity, which rivaled the cloak of external invisibility.

Because of the weapon program's covert nature, its objectives were never debated purposefully in the cabinet, parliament, the committee of government secretaries (cabinet secretariat) or by the chiefs of staff. Little was committed to paper and all sensitive questions concerning the program were decided between the prime minister, the chairman of the Atomic Energy Commission (AEC) and the director of BARC. The chief of DRDO, who also doubled up as science advisor to the defense minister, was part of the technical circle of advisors because his agency was tasked with developing the non-fissile triggers for the devices under development. However, the DRDO chief's political overlord, the Defense Minister R. Venkataraman, had only occasional knowledge of nuclear developments such as an impending

54 *A disaggregated nuclear weapons option*

nuclear test.[28] Other decision-makers included members of the prime minister's inner circle including the cabinet secretary, her principal secretary, and occasionally her economic advisor.[29] The prime minister's principal secretary and the cabinet secretary also represented the PMO on the board of the AEC. However, given their non-technical status, the degree to which both were aware of the scope of the covert nuclear weapons program is debatable.[30] For the most part, the director of BARC and the chairman of the AEC were the two individuals privy to details of the program.[31]

In 1985, Prime Minister Indira Gandhi's son and successor, Rajiv Gandhi, experimented with a weakly institutionalized system of nuclear decision-making for a six-month period. Gandhi's informal "Policy Planning Group" consisted of two political leaders, the cabinet secretary, the Chairman Chiefs of Staff Committee (CCoSC), the chiefs of the AEC and intelligence agencies, the chief economic advisor and director of the defense ministry's think tank, the Institute of Defense Studies & Analyses (IDSA). However, Gandhi ended the experiment within six months and returned to the precedent of making decisions on the basis of consultations with his scientific and technical advisors.[32]

The available evidence suggests that the PMO did not make any deductive assessment of the type of weapons the Indian military might require in the Pakistan and China theaters. Such assessments could only have been possible through joint consultations between the PMO, the military and the scientists. However, the three cooperated only briefly to prepare a potential nuclear force sizing and cost estimate for the PMO in 1986.[33] Dr. A.N. Prasad who years later served as the director of BARC had this to say: "… the government set the Department of Atomic Energy no tasks, oversaw no military developments."[34] Nuclear scientists therefore proceeded with weapon designs without consulting the user services including the air force from which combat aircraft would most likely be drawn for nuclear missions or the DRDL that would supply rockets for delivering nuclear warheads.[35] Figures 3.1 shows an organizational schematic of optimal Indian nuclear decision-making and Figure 3.2 shows the actual Indian nuclear decision-making between 1970 and 1998.

The revived nuclear weapons program focused on reducing the size and weight of the 1974 fission device. It also very likely involved the design of a new device on the principle of fission boosting. Nuclear tests were planned in 1982–1983 and new shafts were sunk at Pokhran for the purpose.[36] However, the revived program was considered experimental and not one that would produce weaponized devices immediately. Thus there was no broad coordination among the nuclear and defense research and development agencies to make the weapons rugged and deliverable.

There was also no open debate on a viable long-term strategy for the nuclear weapons program. In fact, the AEC was divided on the overall direction of India's civilian nuclear power program and how that might parlay into the production of fissile material for a weapons program. Then AEC Chairman Sethna and BARC Director Ramanna led the dominant faction within the

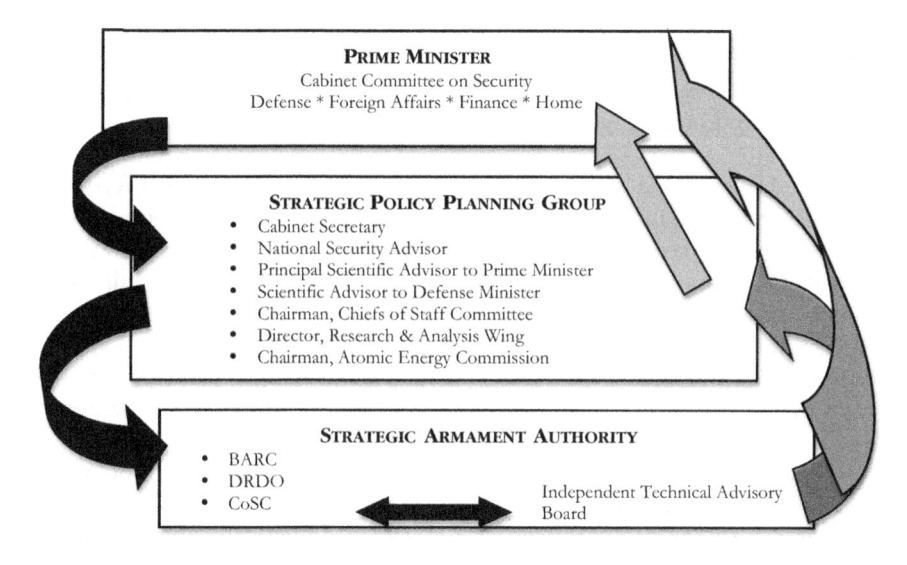

Figure 3.1 Imagined organizational schematic of optimal decision-making.

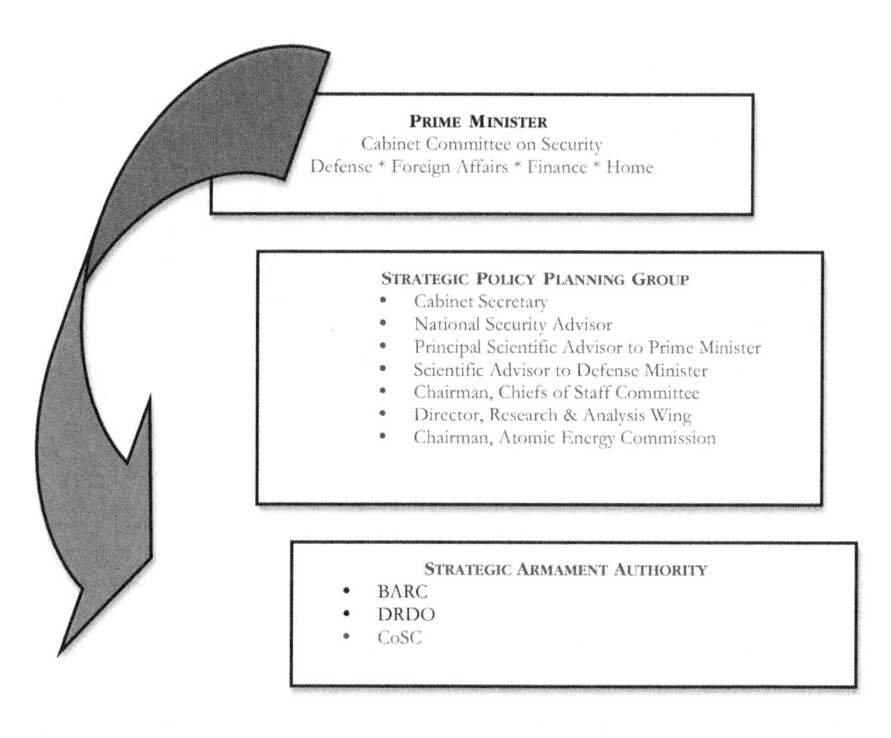

Figure 3.2 Organizational schematic of actual Indian decision-making (1970–1998).

AEC, which favored sticking with India's originally planned path of atomic energy development: the three-stage program with natural uranium heavy water reactors, fast breeder reactors and thorium reactors.[37] This approach would also produce weapons-grade plutonium for a weapons program in the long term.

However, a second school favored the light-water reactor (LWR) route using low-enriched uranium (LEU). The Soviet Union offered to build LWRs for India on the condition that such reactors be placed under international safeguards. Moscow was also prepared to relax the condition of full-scope safeguards to build such reactors in India. The latter route was favored by the M.R. Srinivasan (subsequent chairman of India's AEC) faction and viewed as the means for reviving the nuclear power program, which had stalled in the wake of the 1974 test explosion.[38] However, it implied bifurcating the power and fissile material production programs. But there was no debate outside the AEC and Prime Minister Indira Gandhi did not come down in favor of either. Her successor Rajiv Gandhi favored the LWR plan as a means of reviving the nuclear power program. However, the new prime minister's inclination caused serious fissures in the AEC's leadership, including between Ramanna and the prime minister,[39] further dampening the drive toward information cooperation between the agencies.

Even as India revived an experimental nuclear weapons program in 1980–1981, critical decisions on potential delivery systems for those weapons were pushed further down the road. In 1983, the Indian government launched the Integrated Guided Missile Program (IGMDP)[40] under DRDO's direction. This was a continuation of the ballistic missile programs from the1970s. However, the IGMDP envisaged the development of a diverse array of missile systems: anti-tank, air defense and two ballistic missile programs. The ballistic missile programs, the short-range Prithvi[41] and the medium-range Agni[42] had strategic implications as potential carriers of nuclear munitions. However, in the absence of strategic direction from the government, DRDO sought to sell the short-range Prithvi to the services as a version of long-range artillery.[43] On the other hand, the Agni, with its longer range, actually held greater promise as a potential nuclear delivery system. But it was conceived as a "technology demonstrator," a proving ground for technologies and subsystems (Table 3.1).[44]

Table 3.1 Indian ballistic missile programs (1970–1990)

Year	Name	Type	Range
1973	Valiant	Liquid fuel	Medium-range
1983	Prithvi	Liquid fuel	Short-range
1983	Agni Technology Demonstrator	Liquid fuel/solid fuel	Medium-range

The compartmentalization between the missile and nuclear agencies, the DRDO and BARC, is evident indirectly from the weight and size of India's fission warhead design in the 1980s. DRDO's missiles were designed to carry a generic one-ton payload, the presumed weight of a first-generation nuclear warhead. However, warheads designed for missiles place greater demands on design and shape requirements compared to aircraft.[45] Such warheads must of necessity fit into the narrow cone of the missile's warhead casing. They must be sufficiently rugged to withstand the shock of vibrations and the heat of reentry during flight.

According to a senior air force officer with some knowledge of the program, the weight of the first nuclear bomb was between 1,000 and 1,500 kg.[46] Had missile carriage been the intent, BARC would have designed a lighter warhead. Further, the DRDO's missile development and BARC's warhead design schedules proceeded independently of each other. For example, India commenced weaponization in the spring of 1989. However, the Prithvi's testing and certification schedule continued until 1994–1995. It was not until the late 1990s, most likely around 1996–1997 that nuclear warhead trials commenced for the Prithvi.[47] On the other hand, the testing of the Agni technology demonstrator began in 1989 and ended in 1994 after which the government authorized DRDO to begin development of a follow-on all-solid rocket motor ballistic missile for operational deployment.[48]

The first fission weapon was designed with the air force's Jaguar in mind. However, high internal firewalls and information compartmentalization precluded information sharing between BARC and the air force. The weapon that emerged out of BARC had a diameter that was too large for carriage beneath the aircraft as it left very little ground clearance. Of the early trials in the 1980s that DRDO conducted to test the potential of the Jaguar to serve as a potential delivery system, a test pilot on the team had this to say:

> we were groping in the dark. We had no interaction with the scientists who were actually making the bombs. They had never flown an aircraft and we were not involved in the bomb's development...we argued that unless we knew what the left hand is doing how can the right hand bring it together.[49]

Between 1987 and 1990, DRDO borrowed a Mirage 2000 from the air force to test its feasibility for nuclear missions.[50] However, DRDO circumscribed the test pilot and squadron base commander's communications with Air Headquarters in New Delhi.[51] Outside India it was presumed was that India's Jaguar and Mirage 2000 aircraft purchased from Britain and France were nuclear-capable, providing India with a rapid nuclear breakout capability. According to senior air force officers closely associated with negotiating the Jaguar and Mirage deals in the 1970s and the early 1980s, there was only a generic query from the government about nuclear feasibility. The air force was not tasked to perform detailed feasibility studies on conversion of the aircraft for nuclear missions.[52]

The disaggregation within India's strategic technical estate was not an exception. India's nuclear policy knowledge resources were equally fragmented. For example, the Indian military's inputs on the security implications of the impending Pakistani nuclear revolution did not receive a full hearing within government until the latter half of the 1980s. Despite remaining on the policy sidelines, the army instituted an "Experts Committee" in 1975 to plan for modernization in the 21st century. One section of the report that came out of that process dealt with India's nuclear response to regional threats.[53] Although the army submitted its report to the defense ministry in 1976, the latter did not pass on the plan to the PMO for consideration. It was not until 1982 that then army chief Krishna Rao who was also chairman, CoSC, brought the army's recommendations to Prime Minister Indira Gandhi's attention and briefed her on its sensitive nuclear section.[54]

Beginning in the early 1980s the Indian army began experimenting with a mobile defense and offense-in-depth conventional war strategy based on mechanization that was supposed to be conducive for conducting conventional operations under nuclear, biological and chemical warfare conditions against Pakistan. In the Army's College of Combat at Mhow, Lt. General Sundarji kicked off a series of seminars on conventional operations under conditions of nuclear asymmetry, which became the basis of the famous *Mhow (Combat) Papers* and the core of his subsequent nuclear advocacy and strategy for India.[55]

Sundarji's main argument was that India's conventional superiority would cease to matter under conditions of nuclear asymmetry, as the army would be unable to concentrate in mass for fear of nuclear annihilation. Scattering forces to reduce the army's vulnerability to a potential nuclear attack would allow the enemy (Pakistan) to chew up Indian forces piecemeal.[56] Sundarji's effort, however, was driven by his own academic interest in nuclear weapons and warfare. Due to the lack of any strategic direction from the government there was no institutional attempt to provide military officers with training on the subject at staff colleges.[57] Sundarji's arguments only received full attention after he became army chief in 1986 and came to enjoy the backing of the Minister of State for Defense Arun Singh who ran the ministry on behalf of the prime minister who at the time also held the cabinet post for defense.[58] However, the military chiefs had no formal means of bringing their concerns before the cabinet. Nor did the PMO solicit their views.

The disaggregation of the state's nuclear epistemic actors apart, those elements of it that were mobilized were weakly institutionalized within the state. They had no legal or institutional means to extract political commitments from the political leadership. Commitments, as I argue in Chapter 2, are "time lengthening" mechanisms, which signal the strength of the decision-makers' commitment to resolving problems. Epistemic actors, the knowledge brokers and specialists, are the ones most committed to holistic solutions and suffer loss of morale when they find such commitments lacking. This is evident from the Indian case as well.

Two episodes highlight these dynamics during the 1980s. In late 1982 for example, Prime Minister Indira Gandhi approved a program of nuclear tests. However, she retracted her decision within a day of making it. The DRDO chief, V.S. Arunachalam who was privy to that episode recalls the emotional impact of that decision on him and other members of the nuclear epistemic community. In his words:

> Once we were to ready to test for the first time...myself, Dr. Ramanna... in 1982. Ramanna who pressurized it insisted that I follow it up with Mrs. Gandhi, why we should test it...it is important and so forth...reduction in size, increased efficiency etc. etc. I don't want to mention who all else were sitting in that meeting. Mrs. Gandhi said yes and Ramanna rushed to Bombay to get things organized. And I went to another location to organize a few other things.

> In the evening my Defense Minister Venkataraman called me. He called me and said: It's off. I asked: what is off sir? He said the testing is off. I said that the PM gave her yes during the meeting. He said but now she has changed her mind.

> So I rang Dr. Ramanna. He just was so furious. He said: No! Go seek an immediate appointment with the prime minister and talk to her. He was in Bombay and trying to come by the next flight.

> So I went to my minister and said: is it alright sir if...can I meet the prime minister? He said: the prime minister doesn't want to see you...very clearly.

> And I told Ramanna: I couldn't get an appointment...it is up to you. The next morning he [Ramanna] comes to my house and after breakfast says: this is not right...I am going to see (the prime minister). I have asked for an appointment...I think it was...the prime minister's secretary was there. But the appointment never came. It was over. I saw the prime minister many times after that. I decided that I will not ask her. If she doesn't want to see me on this...I have my own pride and I am not going to ask her why did she said no.[59]

The former head of the JIC, K. Subrahmanyam, who participated in Rajiv Gandhi's "Policy Planning Group" for a short six-month period in 1985, similarly recalled the emotionally enervating effect of weak institutions on epistemic actors. In Subrahmanyam's recounting of those meetings:

> ...the person who was opposed to it [India going nuclear] was the economic advisor...Jalan. Most of the people kept silent. Ramanna [Chairman, AEC] didn't say anything. But everyone knew Ramanna's views that he was in favor of development. I know Arun Singh [Minister of State for Defense]

60 *A disaggregated nuclear weapons option*

was in favor of development...but I don't remember his saying anything in public. The Cabinet Secretary was against it and the intelligence chief didn't say anything openly. But I know that he, Gary Saxena, was for it. And I think the Intelligence Bureau chief also should have been for it.

The main problem is that in a meeting like this with the prime minister presiding over the meeting, you don't find many people talking very freely. Of course I was the exception. Most people weren't sure what the prime minister's opinion was. And I have a feeling...guess...they didn't want to...if they hadn't already taken a stand like Ramanna and myself...they didn't want to take a stand in contradiction of the prime minister's opinion. They wanted to play safe...[60]

The downside of sequestered decision-making and inferences drawn on the basis of value judgments

The fundamental challenge before Indian decision-makers during the 1980s was one of uncertainty. The uncertainty stemmed from imperfect information concerning: (a) how the United States would respond to an Indian nuclear weapons program; and (b) the progress and state of Pakistan's nuclear program. Cybernetic decision-making models suggest that decision-makers in isolated settings routinely attempt uncertainty control by simplifying the ambiguity that surrounds them. They do this by using highly selective channels to screen incoming information in order to ensure consistency of their belief systems. Cognitive psychology also informs us that in conditions of ambiguity, decision-makers resort to heuristics and substitute knowledge gaps with value-based judgments.

In India, the deliberately induced scarcity of information limited the extent to which decision-makers could seek feedback from within and outside the state. Further, given the dilemmas of incomplete information, the decision-makers essentially substituted factual assessments with value judgments based on "anchoring" and "availability" heuristics. The latter were based on memories anchored in India's 1974 nuclear test and the very real threat of US technological sanctions, proven by the ruin of India's civilian nuclear power sector. Equally significant, the decision-makers' beliefs were also anchored in India's vast nuclear and rocket technological estate, which could have produced nuclear weapons and rockets to deliver them with relative ease, and the relatively thin Pakistani nuclear and missile infrastructure by comparison.

This brute material reality had three bias effects. First, it produced over-caution in the minds of Indian decision-makers about what might or might not the United States do.[61] Second, it led them to overestimate India's indigenous nuclear breakout capability. And third, it produced a bias train, which led them to underestimate Pakistan's capacity to produce nuclear weapons. The net result of this approach was that despite India's vast technological and resource advantages over Pakistan, found itself in a position of rough equivalence and even slight disadvantage when confronted with Pakistani nuclearization in 1987.[62]

From the late-1970s, the threat of US sanctions was very real. For example, international collaborators, who prior to the 1974 nuclear test had eagerly participated to help India build up the complete nuclear fuel cycle, train its scientists and engineers and set up a vast ancillary infrastructure, withdrew their cooperation as India became the exemplar of the dangers of the dual-use "Atoms for Peace" program. Although Indian nuclear scientists and political leadership had aspired to make the nuclear program self-sufficient, they were almost entirely dependent on foreign, particularly western assistance.

India's first swimming pool-type reactor was built almost entirely with British assistance.[63] Canada built the 40 MW CIRUS research reactor at Trombay, which later provided the plutonium for India's 1974 test.[64] General Electric from the United States built the first power generation reactors at Tarapur on a "turnkey" basis.[65] All the reactor's components including the supporting equipment and machinery were imported. Similarly, the first unit of the heavy water reactor in Rajasthan was a Canadian import. Indian engineers worked under Canadian supervision. But India did not gain design competencies or outfit the plant with any indigenous machinery or equipment.[66]

This heavy dependence on foreign suppliers, design, and engineering expertise caused the entire program to falter once external assistance ceased. There was also another reason that compounded the nuclear power sector's weak performance. Indian nuclear scientists starting with the first head of the DAE, Homi Bhabha, had oversold the benefits of cheap nuclear power to their political overlords in the 1950s and 1960s.[67] In their eagerness to prove nuclear energy's viability against alternative sources, they embraced relatively untried and untested technologies.

According to Ashok Parthasarathi who advised the PMO on scientific issues, there was no "operational feedback" on the reactor India bought from the Canadians. Thus serious engineering problems cropped up in the wake of operating this "premature Canadian technology."[68] Examples of problems included the cracking of the reactor's end shield and the poor performance of the "zero leak" pumps and valves used to circulate the reactor's heavy water.[69] Leaky valves and the discharge of highly radioactive waste caused serious operational problems in the Tarapur reactors as well.[70] Resolution of these design and operational problems took over a decade of trial and error. Further, it took India's DAE 12 years to build a heavy water reactor indigenously after Canada withdrew assistance in 1976[71]. Similarly, India's heavy water plants and the plutonium reprocessing facility at Trombay also performed below par.[72]

However, western technology denials in the wake of the 1974 test were a mixed bag. Western collaborators did not immediately end civil nuclear cooperation with India. Although Canada ended cooperation on the second phase of the Rajasthan atomic power project, the United States continued supplying low enriched uranium (LEU) for the Tarapur reactors. In the early 1980s as the supply of LEU became increasingly contested in the United States due to congressional pressure, the Reagan administration allowed India to negotiate a substitute nuclear supply agreement with France. Further, the technology export control regime the United States instituted to deny the sale of sensitive technologies was not watertight. For example, a CIA report from the early 1980s concluded that India was relatively immune to US supplier disruptions due to the existence of an international "grey market." As the report put it:

> Largely through the use of the international 'grey market,' India has been able to maintain a nuclear weapons capability…India's purchasing activities challenges US efforts to work with other nuclear supplier states for tighter export controls and demonstrate that the Nuclear Suppliers Guidelines have serious weaknesses.
>
> India has evaded Western supplier-state export and nonproliferation controls by avoiding government-to-government agreements and not importing complete nuclear facilities. Instead, India has established direct relations with foreign vendor firms, used intermediaries to disguise the end use of its purchases, and bought many components piecemeal. [73]

The report further stated:

> …we expect the European exporting countries and Japan to continue to resist US efforts to curb their nuclear exports by arguing that they will be replaced by the Soviets in the Indian market if they are curtailed.[74]

In a "grey market" an acquirer state violates the spirit if not the letter of the supplier state's export control laws. Equipment is purchased from private vendors piece-by-piece, subsystem-by-subsystem or component-by-component. Export controls that would normally apply to the sale of a complete nuclear reactor or reprocessing plant do not apply to individual components such as pressure valves, vessels, control instruments that could be incorporated into a larger facility.[75] Indeed, starting in 1976, Pakistan systematically imported an entire gas centrifuge uranium enrichment plant piece-by-piece from Western Europe based on vendor lists pilfered by A.Q. Khan out of the Netherlands.[76]

Equally significant, India's missile agency learnt lessons from the case of sanctions applied to the nuclear sector. Anticipating technology denials for India's ballistic missile program in the 1980s, the DRDO set up a "Special Purchase Team," which stocked up on gyros, accelerometers, hydraulic actuators, computers, motion simulators and three-axis measuring machines from Sweden, France, United States and West Germany.[77] For the critical carbon–carbon heat shield then under development for the medium-range Agni missile's reentry vehicle, the team purchased a special six-axis filament-winding machine with computer controllers in the United States. In order to escape scrutiny from US export control authorities, the machine was routed through an Indian textile manufacturer.[78]

Indian nuclear and missile entities were aware of the complexities of the international technology market and the manner in which export controls could be circumvented. The scientists had far greater confidence that India could proceed with a nuclear weapons program and overcome the retarding effects of technology sanctions.[79] However, the debilitating effects of technology denials anchored the PMO's view that scientists had oversold the nuclear power program. Despite promises that they could resolve technological problems, they had proved unsuccessful.

The PMO's nuclear hesitancy was anchored in the threat of the potential denial of World Bank loans and the IMF's restructuring package by the United States. These, the PMO believed could cause serious damage to the Indian economy.[80] Reflecting these fears, the prime minister remarked rhetorically to Ramanna during a private meeting where they discussed the possibility of nuclear testing: "Do you want our skulls cracked?"[81] In this clash between the PMO and the scientists, the PMO's view prevailed. In order to maintain the nature of India's nuclear response covert, the prime minister and her top advisors did not consult widely within the government about the potential disruptive effects of sanctions. Likewise, the scientists had few institutional means to force decisions on the prime minister and her inner council.

As India tentatively began planning for a nuclear test in 1982–1983, US spy satellites discovered renewed activity at the Pokhran test site. In May 1982, Lawrence Eagleburger, the US undersecretary of state for political affairs confronted India's foreign secretary Rasgotra about the impending tests during the latter's trip to Washington.[82] The cat was thus out of the bag. And yet, top Indian leaders continued to believe the program's existence could be denied by keeping weapons development compartmentalized, a condition that stymied coordination across the state's various agencies. Equally significant, the progress of Pakistan's clandestine procurement efforts was visible to Indian intelligence agencies and the political leadership. So was the US handling of Pakistan with kid gloves.[83] To be sure, Pakistan was a special case during the 1980s because it rented strategic space to the United States and became a frontline state in the struggle against the Soviet Union in Afghanistan. In the hierarchy of US foreign policy and national security interests, this struggle superseded the struggle against nuclear proliferation.[84]

During the 1980s the US also discovered a program of substantial Chinese material assistance to Pakistan's nuclear weapons effort. This included the supply of an actual weapon design based on China's fourth nuclear test among other things.[85] However, the Reagan administration proved unwilling or helpless to stem this tide of cooperation. Undoubtedly, US treatment of India was different, especially in light of New Delhi's close ties with the Soviet Union and its thinly veiled anti-US positions. And yet, the US handling of

Pakistani proliferation provides a rough indicator of potential US flexibility in handling proliferation challenges. However, Indian prime ministers in the 1980s took the view that the US would apply blanket economic and technological sanctions on India, which could in principle cripple India's economy and high-tech sectors. Despite initiating a nuclear explosives and ballistic missile program known to the United States, they kept the programs isolated, their assumption being that opacity would facilitate deniability.

In any situation of uncertainty, there are what the former US Secretary of Defense Donald Rumsfeld identified as the know knowns, the known unknowns and the unknown unknowns. In assessing the Pakistani nuclear threat, Indian prime ministers' decisions were substantially driven by the known knowns. Among the latter was the very real disparity between the nuclear estates of the two countries. India was the competitor with the larger resources and the greater technical manpower advantage. Its nuclear sector had deep roots and was relatively self-sufficient in the plutonium fuel cycle. India's nuclear estate included uranium mining, milling and fuel rod fabrication facilities, heavy water plants, research and power reactors and plutonium reprocessing.[86]

By this scale of comparison, Pakistan's nuclear estate was miniscule. It possessed only lab-scale spent-fuel reprocessing capabilities to extract weapons-grade plutonium[87] Above all, India had a proven nuclear device, which it had already exploded. Further, with the revival of the nuclear weapons research and development program in 1980s, India was working on advanced boosted-fission designs and miniaturized versions of the fission design tested in 1974.[88] This extant materiality anchored Indian prime ministers' belief of India's superiority in any nuclear competition vis-à-vis Pakistan. V.S. Arunachalam, the chief of DRDO and scientific advisor to India's defense minister, who became the informal point person for the nuclear project between 1983 and 1992, summed up the decision-makers point of view to the author:

> …there was no reason to panic…the panic will come if we didn't know what is a nuclear weapon, if we didn't know how to make it, if we didn't know how to deploy it…what can the panicking do…there is no reason to panic…[89]

The key challenge in producing a nuclear device is mastering the nuclear fuel cycle to obtain fissile material. Within the nuclear physics and engineering community, the design of a first-generation nuclear device is generally regarded a relatively simpler task. By this measure, India possessed the fissile material. Pakistan did not. Pakistan's original attempt at obtaining plutonium through plans to build natural uranium reactors and import a French plutonium reprocessing plant was blocked by the United States in 1976–1977.[90]

In response, Pakistan switched to the uranium enrichment route. Under A.Q. Khan, Pakistan elected for gas centrifuge technology, an extremely

A disaggregated nuclear weapons option 65

difficult process to master. Centrifuges spin at extraordinarily high speeds. They require special materials, precision design and exquisite engineering. Their successful operation is also dependent on well-trained scientific and engineering teams with the formal and tacit knowledge to operate them.[91]

Indian beliefs about the state of Pakistan's advances were anchored in their own experience with centrifuge enrichment technology. India began building its own centrifuge enrichment facilities in the early 1970s. However, it only succeeded in enriching uranium on a pilot scale at BARC by 1985. Construction of a larger plant to enrich uranium started in the mid-1980s at Rattehalli in Karnataka and the plant came online in 1990. The Indian enrichment program had significant operational problems due to "...corrosion and failure of parts" and was beset by delays.[92] The difficulties of getting this complex technology to work became a cause of skepticism in the minds of top scientists within India's nuclear establishment about the ability of their Pakistani counterparts to get the technology to work.

Top Indian civil bureaucrats and their scientific counterparts in the AEC were contemptuous of Pakistan's nuclear capabilities. For example, in response to Pakistani Prime Minister Zulfikar Ali Bhutto's famous statement after India's 1974 test that Pakistan would acquire a matching capability even if Pakistanis had to eat grass, P.N. Haksar who was formerly Indira Gandhi's principal secretary remarked sarcastically:

> If by eating grass one can produce atom bombs, then by now cows and horses would have produced them. But, of course, the people of Pakistan under the great and charismatic leadership to which they are now exposed might produce a bomb on a diet of grass.[93]

Top Indian nuclear scientists similarly expressed contempt toward their Pakistani counterparts. They harbored the biased belief that Pakistan was blustering. A former AEC chairman in the mid-1980s claimed: "We did not take A.Q. Khan seriously. He was a metallurgist. They would not be capable of doing these things."[94] Similarly, Arunachalam, then scientific advisor to India's defense minister, volunteered to the author that he would not have hired A.Q. Khan for any of his labs.[95] Likewise, former AEC Chairman P.K. Iyengar, a central figure in India's 1974 test and the thermonuclear weapon design, informed the author: "I didn't believe it...they could [Pakistan] probably...perhaps build one or more bomb at most...but not more."[96] Dr. M.R. Srinivasan, who served as the chairman of India's AEC between 1987 and 1990 while admitting to Pakistani advances in uranium enrichment, summed up the Indian atomic establishment's view of Pakistan's nuclear capacity in the following words:

> Although there are certainly competent scientists and technologists in Pakistan, its nuclear technological base is rather limited, so its scientists have apparently gathered parts from various international sources...

although Pakistan claims parity with India in nuclear capabilities, there is an order of magnitude difference in the overall capabilities, not the least in terms of trained personnel and industrial capability.[97]

The Indian nuclear establishment in making assessments of Pakistan's advances lacked perfect information about its actual state of progress. The known knowns in this case were that Pakistan had succeeded in acquiring blueprints for a centrifuge-based uranium enrichment plant from Urenco in the Netherlands; that A. Q. Khan had succeeded in procuring an entire uranium hexafluoride gas plant from West Germany; that Pakistani agents in Europe had purchased special steel known as maraging steel to manufacture centrifuge cylinders; and that Pakistan had also obtained high-frequency power units to drive the centrifuges from Western Europe.[98]

Nonetheless, the known unknowns were whether Pakistani nuclear scientists and engineers had the explicit and "tacit" skills to get the complex technology up and running.[99] In scientific-industrial processes, tacit hurdles are some of the hardest to transcend. There are limits to the degree to which foreign consultants, suppliers, and technology transfers can bridge the gap between the formal and tacit means of doing things.[100] In the absence of precise knowledge of the state of Pakistan's tacit skills and knowledge, the Indian nuclear establishment relied on its own operating experience with centrifuge enrichment to make inferences about Pakistan.

In addition, Indian nuclear scientists at the highest levels retained connections with their Pakistani counterparts such as the former chairman of the Pakistan Atomic Energy Commission (PAEC), Dr. Munir Ahmed Khan. The latter had a bitter falling out with A.Q. Khan whose Engineering Research Labs (ERL) sidelined the PAEC's pursuit of fissile material through the plutonium route.[101] The likes of Munir Ahmed Khan spoke "disparagingly" of A.Q. Khan to their Indian counterparts whom they routinely met on the sidelines of annual International Atomic Energy Agency (IAEA) meetings in Vienna.[102] In the process, the PAEC inadvertently undermined A.Q. Khan's reputation and underscored the Indian nuclear establishment's skepticism of Pakistani claims.

In comparison, Indian intelligence agencies dutifully reported the advances in the Pakistani nuclear weapons program to the PMO. In early 1981 for example, Indian intelligence informed the PMO that Pakistan would have sufficient weapons-grade uranium by July–November that year; and that Islamabad had initiated preparations for an underground test explosion in the Rashkoh Mountains in Baluchistan.[103] In 1982, Indian intelligence agencies estimated that Pakistan very likely possessed weapons-grade fissile material for a bomb "core or two."[104] Indian intelligence reports duly reported Pakistan's purchase of krytron switches used to deliver pulsed electric charges in a nuclear device. They also tracked Pakistan's purchase of X-ray machines used for high-speed flash photography. The latter is used for testing the non-nuclear trigger assembly of a nuclear device. They noted Pakistan's purchase of software for simulated implosion test analysis on computers.[105]

By the mid-1980s, all signals suggested that Pakistan was developing a nuclear device. Based on these inputs, Indian external intelligence agency in the mid-1980s recommended a counter Indian weaponization program to Prime Minister Rajiv Gandhi.[106] However, Gandhi was "skeptical," according to K. Subrahmanyam, who sat in on the "Policy Planning Group" in 1985. The prime minister "...asked a lot of questions."[107] Similarly, former AEC chairman P.K. Iyengar affirmed Gandhi's skepticism with the raw intelligence. Gandhi, according to Iyengar, was more confident about what the nuclear establishment told him. "He asked me how I could or could not be confident that the Pakistanis were enriching uranium...I explained him how. And he then believed me."[108]

Like their intelligence counterparts, India's top military leaders also urged the prime minister's nuclear haste. In the early 1980s, the army chief General Rao led that charge circumventing the defense ministry's normal channels of communications with the PMO.[109] His successor, General Sundarji, lobbied for nuclear weapons even more vociferously, both in his official capacity as army chief and through his close personal relationship with Arun Singh, who was Rajiv Gandhi's confidante and managed the defense ministry for the prime minister as minister of state.[110] The Indian air force did not lobby for nuclear weapons directly; however, after Israel's destruction of Iraq's Osiraq reactor in 1981, its operations staff prepared an internal study on similar options against Pakistan's Kahuta uranium enrichment plant.[111] The latter was allegedly discussed and rejected by the PMO.[112]

Concerns also grew within India's military that Pakistan had begun supporting insurgents in India's Punjab, confident in the belief that its emerging nuclear arsenal had immunized it against a potential Indian conventional counter response. In 1986, the Indian army conducted *Operation Brasstacks*, its largest war games in history to test Sundarji's technical and organizational reforms for mechanized maneuver warfare in the Pakistan theater.[113] The exercise almost spun out of control and triggered war as nervous Pakistani leaders counter-mobilized and threatened undefended Indian territory in Punjab.[114]

The bulk of the evidence suggests that preemptive war was not India's intent. However, the exercise was certainly regarded as a show of force, a means to coerce Pakistan into terminating support for the insurgency in the Punjab.[115] At the height of the crisis, when Rajiv Gandhi considered the idea of initiating war against Pakistan, General Sundarji counseled the prime minister to do just that as it was India's last probable realistic chance to destroy Pakistan's nuclear weapons program in the cradle.[116]

The above evidence shows that there was a diversity of opinions within the Indian government during the1980s about the state of Pakistan's nuclear progress and what India ought to do about it. Decision-makers in the PMO were aware of nuclear developments across the border but uncertain of the precise nature of the Pakistani threat. They were over-cautious in determining an Indian counter response because of their biased view of the extreme reaction it might induce from the United States. The PMO's extreme caution was also reinforced by its almost exclusive reliance on the atomic energy establishment for assessments of Pakistan's nuclear progress. Although leading Indian nuclear scientists favored faster progress on nuclear weapons development, they also harbored deep skepticism about Pakistan's claims to achieving nuclear weapons capability.

Their skepticism was not based on incontrovertible data. It drew on the wellsprings of biases fed by India's own difficulties with mastering the gas centrifuge uranium enrichment process. In contrast, Indian intelligence and military chiefs held more alarmist views of Pakistan's nuclear quest and its consequences for India. Once again, their views did not rest on certainty. However, as James Surowiecki explains in the *Wisdom of Crowds*, crowds have a lower tendency for judgment errors in the face of uncertainty because their independent errors cancel each other out, a phenomenon less likely in decisions by individuals and closed groups. The key to better prediction amidst imperfect information is independence, diversity of opinion and a way of aggregating diverse opinions.[117] In India, however, the sequestered process of decision-making cut off the oxygen of crowd sourcing within the government, which amplified the biases of the decision-makers.

The big unknown before India in the 1980s was whether Pakistani nuclear scientists had acquired the tacit knowledge to work the Kahuta uranium enrichment plant and build nuclear weapons. Unbeknownst to the Indian nuclear weapons establishment and its intelligence agencies were the extent and depth of the secret nuclear cooperation between Pakistan and China. For example, Indian prime ministers were briefed on reports in the early and mid-1980s that China had likely shared a nuclear weapon design with Pakistan. However, Indian intelligence agencies were able to confirm that only in 1988.[118]

New evidence from US intelligence sources and US nuclear scientists with extensive contacts within the Chinese nuclear weapons complex suggests that China cooperated with Pakistan extensively during the 1980s. The nature of that cooperation included: training Pakistani scientists in nuclear weapons design starting in 1982–1983, the transfer of the CHIC-4 implosion type enriched uranium warhead, assistance in the design of explosive lenses for an implosion device, the transfer of a neutron initiator for the device, and ultimately the conducting of an actual nuclear test (Event 35) for Pakistan at China's Lop Nur test site on May 26, 1990.[119]

Throughout the 1980s, US intelligence sources tracked the presence of Chinese nuclear scientists and engineers at the Kahuta uranium enrichment plant as well as the Wah Cantonment complex near Islamabad. Similarly, Pakistani nuclear scientists and technicians were constant fixtures at sensitive nuclear weapons–related facilities in China.[120] For example, Thomas Reed and Danny Stillman, former veterans of the Lawrence Livermore and Los

Alamos nuclear labs[121] claim that the 1990 Event 35 at the Lop Nur test site in China was:

> ...a fairly crude but reliable enriched uranium design, unboosted but using a Chinese neutron initiator scheme, all in a configuration that had been successfully cold tested within Pakistan during the 1980s.[122]

Historians of Pakistan's nuclear weapons program including Feroz Khan have downplayed the scope of Chinese cooperation.[123] However, unlike the US nuclear labs and intelligence agencies, Khan provides no evidence to back this claim. However, even Khan admits that China transferred enriched uranium sufficient for two nuclear bombs to Pakistan in 1981.[124]

Clearly, Pakistan was much further ahead on the nuclear learning curve than the Indian nuclear establishment and PMO knew or had imagined.[125]

Weak inter-agent competition and principal-agent problems

Biases in sequestered institutional settings, as the evidence above shows, expand the scope for decision-making errors. The other negative consequence of sequestration and low information turnover is the very real constraint on political leaders' ability to police the activity of their subordinates (agents) within the state.

In proliferating states, external opacity is not only useful to protect the state's autonomy for action from pressure by adversarial states. Equally significant, domestic opacity also serves to protect decision-makers' autonomy of action within the state, lest they be pushed to take up their agents' agendas, which might not be in their own best interests. Leaders do this by compartmentalizing programs and information concerning them and limiting cooperation between agencies and their agents. However, in any organization, transparency, high-information exchange and inter-agent competition are the keys to leaders' obtaining credible information about programmatic choice. The downside of a regime of information scarcity is difficulty in agent management and leaders' commitment to public-policy choices without fully understanding the risks involved in making them.

In the remainder of this chapter I demonstrate the logic of this argument by comparing principal–agent problems in India's nuclear power sector in the late 1960s under conditions of information monopoly and their subsequent mitigation through inter-agent competition. I compare the course correction in India's nuclear power program with the 1974 nuclear test in which there was a serious dispute within BARC about the yield of the exploded device. In the latter case, however, information about the dispute did not percolate up to the PMO due to the lack of inter-agent/agency competition.

I next show that during the 1980s internal opacity and the lack of alternative sources of information led successive prime ministers to harbor unduly optimistic assessments of India's capacity for a nuclear breakout, both in the

70 *A disaggregated nuclear weapons option*

context of a steady supply of fissile material as well as the potential for transforming prototype-stage nuclear devices into deliverable weapon. Further, information asymmetries between political leaders and their technical advisors produced suboptimal choices in India's ballistic missile program. The net consequence of these asymmetries was that the missiles ended up representing the missile development agency's organizational interests and not those of the users for potential deployment and use. Finally, the absence of agent monitoring between the nuclear and air force teams had highly negative consequences for resolving the challenges of air delivery.

The history of India's civilian nuclear power sector provides an example of how low information turnover and the lack of inter-agent competition produces adverse programmatic choices. It also serves as an example of how the introduction of internal policing through agent competition induces palliative effects.

The institutional legacy of India's nuclear sector is one of secrecy for reasons that have a lot to do with its defense implications, the desire to place atomic energy outside the calcified purview of India's bureaucracy, and the close personal friendship between Prime Minister Nehru and the founding chairman of the DAE, Dr. Homi Bhabha.[126] The AEC board exercised oversight over the entire atomic energy sector and made all the critical program choices. On the board sat two "technical" members, both representatives of the DAE. They alone had the competence to appraise the technical quality of programmatic choices. Other members on the board included the prime minister's principal secretary, the cabinet secretary and the finance member. These non-DAE members had no technical competence and they concerned themselves with procedural, financial and organizational matters, and generally approved decisions that were subsequently rubber-stamped by the PMO and approved by the cabinet.[127]

Critical examples of program choices included the decision to purchase different reactor types from the United States and Canada when commercial reactor operations were largely unproven. Other prominent and controversial examples include the famous Sarabhai Profile (1970), which urged the quintupling India's nuclear power-generation capacity from 600 MW in the early 1970s to 2800 MW by 1980. The Sarabhai Profile also outlined ambitious plans to double the capacity of power reactors from 200–230 MW to 500 MW without accounting for India's industrial capacity for reactor construction, natural uranium mining, fuel fabrication, heavy water production or the ability of the electrical grid to uptake the power generated.[128]

The DAE also artificially lowered the cost of nuclear power generation to make it competitive with alternative sources of energy. It achieved this through accounting sleights of hand, by deliberately not factoring for the cost of heavy water, waste disposal or the price of dismantling the reactors at the end of their life cycle. More alarmingly, the DAE hid the problems of reactor operations such as heavy water leaks, radioactive contamination, reactor damage and fuel rod damage. The DAE also did not appraise the PMO about other problems afflicting the nuclear sector including the poor performance of the sensitive plutonium reprocessing plant.[129]

By the early 1970s, as Prime Minister Indira Gandhi consolidated power, the PMO expanded its institutional reach and hired agents to monitor the DAE. Ashok Parthasarathi who served as scientific advisor in the PMO narrates the saga of agent competition between him and the AEC chairman Vikram Sarabhai. As a consequence of the independent inputs from Parthasarathi, the PMO rejected the Sarabhai Profile after initially approving it, split the DAE and space department into two separate agencies, gave Sarabhai charge of the latter, and removed him as head of the atomic energy department. Plans for generating nuclear power were subsequently revised downward. The plan for building 500 MW reactors was also dropped. Due to Parthasarathi's independent monitoring, the PMO was also made cognizant that the costing estimates for nuclear power were rigged.[130] However, the prime minister's principal secretary at the time, P.N. Haksar, decided to ignore these rigged estimates, because he felt "…there were larger objectives to our [India's] nuclear program than nuclear power and those objectives cannot be compromised at any cost."[131]

In the case of the 1974 nuclear test, however, there was no inter-agent competition. There were only three points of contact between the PMO and the nuclear team at BARC: Homi Sethna, Raja Ramanna and P.K. Iyengar. During Mrs. Gandhi's visit to Trombay in 1972 when the decision to build the device was approved, the four agreed not to commit anything to paper, especially from the PMO.[132] After the test, AEC Chairman Homi Sethna publicly announced the yield of the device between 10 and 15 kt.

Initial analyses of the device's yield were based on seismic measurements and not on post-shot analysis of the yield debris from the explosion crater. Indian nuclear scientists Raja Ramanna and P. Chidambaram subsequently presented a scientific paper at the IAEA in Vienna, in which they claimed the implosion device had a yield at 12 kt. However, their estimate too was calculated on the basis of seismic verification, not on post-shot analysis of the crater's debris. BARC subsequently undertook a post-shot analysis[133] and the internal findings of its radiochemistry division placed the yield far lower at 5 kt.[134]

A senior official who served in BARC's radiochemistry division at the time and participated in that analysis revealed to the author in 2010:

> Now Chidambaram was there at Pokhran…I established mass spectrometry as a method of measurement and analysis. And I did all the isotopic measurements. And I did isotopic measurements on the Pokhran debris. And my yield was…much lower…and they threw the book at me…and classified my report… so I questioned that. I became unacceptable after that. They started looking at me with suspicion. I didn't say anything. I didn't tell anybody. I didn't go to the newspaper. I gave an internal report saying that your calculated values are not correct. It is higher than what I am getting.[135]

72 *A disaggregated nuclear weapons option*

However, former AEC Chairman P. K. Iyengar discounted the radiochemistry division's report on grounds that the method of sampling the debris had a 40%–50% chance of error. Iyengar reported to Ramanna that the yield was in the ballpark of 10–12 kt.[136] Subsequently, Iyengar lowered his estimate of the yield to 8–10 kt.[137] However, Ramanna, who served as chairman of the AEC during 1983–1986 continued to insist even as late as 1991, when he published his autobiography, that the yield of the Pokhran I device was between 12 and 15 kt.[138]

The scientific controversy on the Pokhran I yield remained buried inside BARC. It resurfaced after 1998 when rumors arose that the thermonuclear device and its boosted fission primary, which BARC claimed was the highlight of the second round of tests in 1998, had underperformed. Indirect evidence of the Pokhran I device's failure is available in a recently declassified State Department cable drafted by Steve Ghitelman in January 1996. Written in the context of impending Indian nuclear tests, the cable states:

> Technicians want to test…the activity brings the site [Pokhran test site] to a heightened state of readiness in the event Rao [Prime Minister Narasimha Rao] makes a decision to test, but it says nothing about his decision to do so. Rao's scientists may be pushing for one or more tests of India's unproven nuclear designs, which need significant reworking after the near-failure of the 1974 test.[139]

In 1996, former AEC Chairman Sethna admitted to George Perkovich that the radiochemical analysis, the gold standard for assessing yield in the nuclear test business, had shown a yield lower than the one publicly announced. When Perkovich questioned a subsequent AEC Chairman P.K. Iyengar why the results of the radiochemical analysis had never been published, the latter responded: "what does it matter if it was 8 or 12 kt?"[140]

The significance of this controversy is not just about the sociology of settling scientific controversies and method. It also has real-world implications for the political and military leadership. In the absence of any oversight authority, institutionalized inter-agent competition, and one-way channels of information on sensitive nuclear weapons–related secrets, the prime ministers were in the dark about the controversy surrounding the Pokhran I device. Assumptions about its performance became the basis for subsequent presumptions about India's nuclear breakout capabilities.

Through the 1980s and 1990s, succeeding AEC chairmen and BARC directors had a monopoly on nuclear weapons–related inputs to the PMO, with literally no outside scrutiny. Former AEC Chairman M.R. Srinivasan admitted as much to the author in an interview with the caveat that prime ministers on occasion also consulted some of their close bureaucratic advisors and senior cabinet colleagues on political decisions surrounding nuclearization.[141] Another AEC Chairman, P.K. Iyengar downplayed concerns about the lack of agent competition in questions of science and technical expertise and argued that

> ...we should stop looking at the issue from an American point of view. During the Manhattan project, the government [US] trusted the scientists. In one instance, General Groves attempting oversight by pointing out a mathematical error during a meeting with scientists. However, the scientists told Groves that they were concerned with the physics of the issue and not necessarily strict mathematical accuracy. In the case of Manhattan project, the US governments had no proof that the Hiroshima device would work...but the president trusted the scientists.
>
> Most political systems at inception of great scientific and technical projects rely on trust. Institutions follow at later stages when projects mature. In the Apollo program...Kennedy had no credible means for assessing if the mission to place man on the moon was indeed possible. However, he and his aides proceeded on the basis of trust.
>
> In India's case as well there is a great tradition of trust between prime ministers and senior scientists....embodied in the rapport shared by Nehru and Bhabha and thereafter by leaders of the DAE. American notions of institutions, laws, and regulations are misplaced largely because such mechanisms are a weak substitute for trust and actually indicate the absence of trust in society.
>
> It was trust which operated between Indira Gandhi and the top BARC hierarchy during the 1974 test...and also throughout the decades of the 1980s and 1990s when nuclear weapons development at BARC was kept secret from the prying eyes of foreign powers.[142]

Indeed, based on private assurances from the scientists, Prime Minister Rajiv Gandhi claimed publicly in 1985 that if India were to decide on becoming a nuclear weapons power it would only take a few weeks or a few months to do so. Or as the scientists put it to the prime minister, "...if the government should ever want this capability you shall have it."[143] These assurances were based on the work on the weapon program in the lab and not the real world of production, deployment and use.

For example, until 1985 India had no consistent source of weapons-grade plutonium. In the past, India had used the Canadian supplied CIRUS reactor for generating spent fuel, which was then reprocessed to extract weapons-grade plutonium. Prior to the 1974 test, the reactor used US-supplied heavy water, which is one reason why India dubbed the 1974 test a PNE. India could not have legally conducted nuclear weapon explosions using plutonium fuel from CIRUS because of the peaceful assurances it had made to the US and Canada.[144]

What India needed was an indigenous research reactor dedicated to the production of weapons-grade plutonium. The construction of a scaled-up indigenous version of the CIRUS reactor was made a top priority starting 1981. This reactor, the 100 MW R-5 or Dhruva, went critical in 1985.[145] However, the reactor shut down as soon as it started. A fuel leak caused radioactive contamination in the coolant system. The problem was ultimately traced to vibrations generated from the coolant system, which resonated with the frequency of the core, causing the fuel rod damage and leaks. The reactor was restarted in December 1986 and operated at one-fourth of its rated capacity until 1988 when it achieved full power.[146] What this means is that compared to Pakistan, which achieved the capacity to enrich uranium to weapons grade in 1985,[147] India's capacity for a sustained weaponization program was severely constrained until 1988.

Further, in the absence of multiple agent inputs, particularly from the military, Gandhi was unaware of the challenges of fitting the lab weapon into a pod for air delivery. Attempts to sling the first-generation weapon under the air force's Jaguar had already failed because of problems emanating from the weapon's large diameter and low ground clearance of the aircraft.[148] The Jaguar, according to senior air force officers involved with the aircraft, could in theory have served as an ideal delivery platform. In the case of the Jaguar, the air force had succeeded in rewriting the software code for the aircraft's electronic warfare and navigational attack systems. That process took about "500 flights to clear...and five to six years," according to a senior air force officer involved in the program.[149] This was not the case with Dassault's Mirage 2000, which the Indian Air Force acquired from France in the mid-1980s. However, due to the lack of inter-agency sharing, the weapon that came out of the lab was unfit for delivery by the Jaguar.

The design of a subsequent delivery casing for the Mirage proceeded in secrecy at the Terminal Ballistics Research Laboratory and Armament Research & Development Establishment without any timelines. As one of the members in the design team put it: "...our bosses seemed satisfied with whatever pace we set," until the weaponization decision in 1989 when the tenor changed to: "...the house is on fire. All this should have been ready yesterday. Now rush, rush!"[150]

Another senior air force officer complained about the DRDO's "amateurish" way of designing the weapon without interaction with the user service. As he put it, "DRDO underestimates the intellectual, technological, and managerial challenges of building complex systems, or deliberately underplays the challenge of the tasks to game the system...knowing full well that the weapon system would never be delivered on time...but that the system could be gamed indefinitely."[151] Recalling his interaction with DRDO's chief Arunachalam, he went on: "...Arunachalam had the habit of proposing accelerated time lines for weapon development that was divorced from reality."

In the case of air-delivered nuclear bombs, "the design of reliable height burst fuses is extraordinarily difficult and such fuses are critical for accurate airburst." Recalling the DRDO's failures in the design of conventional runway denial and cluster bombs, the air force officer disclosed that he ordered DRDO to "halt tests and stop wasting the air force's money."[152] In the absence of institutional representation from the air force, decision-makers in the PMO were unaware of the potential of such technical and organizational minutiae to delay the program.

The final exhibit of the negative consequences of weak inter-agent/agency competition comes from the case of India's ballistic missile program in the 1980s. The short-range Prithvi missile that emerged out of it, and which alone at the time could conceivably have served as a nuclear delivery vehicle, was explicitly designed around the DRDO's organizational legacy, which was an attempt to reverse engineer the Soviet SA-2 surface-to-air missile's liquid fuel engine.[153] Classified as the "Devil" program in the 1970s, no operational weapon system had emerged out of it, leaving the agency demoralized. The DRDO therefore tried to rebuild its missile lab's morale by resuscitating the Devil program in the avatar of the short-range Prithvi. The political leadership signed off on the program without understanding its operational viability.[154] The missile that emerged out of the program flew successfully. However, its toxic fuel, corrosion problems associated with fuel-storage, long fueling routine before launch, short-range and large logistics train made it unsuitable as a nuclear weapon carrier of choice.[155]

Conclusion

This chapter focuses on how political leaders in India managed nuclear weapons–related national security risks during the decade of the 1980s. Defensive Realism assumes that decision-makers automatically respond to threats with efficiency and optimality. The evidence presented here shows that structural pressures in themselves are insufficient conditions for generating efficient and rationally optimized responses to threats. Rather, efficiency and optimization are contingent on the quality of states' domestic institutions and decision-making processes. Critical to efficient and optimized decision-making is a sophisticated awareness of a state's internal and external realities.

Decision-makers need access to well developed and functioning knowledge markets seeded by epistemic actors and sophisticated institutional processes that vet raw information through the scrutiny of multiple eyes. The latter are essential for cancelling out biases and errors as well as for producing more accurate forecasts in environments characterized by uncertainty and imperfect information. Secrecy and stove piping of information through one-way channels also constitute a poor means for political principals to manage their bureaucratic agents. The data on Indian nuclear decision-making from the decade of the 1980s shows a number of erroneous assumptions and miscalculated responses. It also demonstrates that Defensive Realism's assumptions of automaticity, efficiency and optimality are simplistic.

Evidence presented in this chapter also supports the claim that India's nuclear restraint during the 1980s in the face of a looming Pakistani threat

76 *A disaggregated nuclear weapons option*

was not the consequence of the normative beliefs of decision-makers steeped in Gandhian-Nehruvian moralism. To the contrary, Indian decision-makers pursued a Janus-faced strategy that combined a serious military option with political restraint. The political restraint, however, was rooted in their subjective comprehension of risk. That subjective comprehension exaggerated the negative political and economic consequences of a more aggressive proliferation strategy on the one end and underestimated the technical and military complexity of the challenge India faced in developing an operational capability on the other.

It is also evident that the sclerotic pace of India's nuclear arsenal development in this decade was not the consequence of decision-makers' belief that that the symbolic aspects of nuclear weaponry were sufficient to achieve deterrence. Rather, the sclerotic pace stemmed from the sequential and hence incremental pace of technology development and integration. More significant, the weak institutional processes attenuated Indian leaders' capacity to actualize instituted options into a more fast-paced and robust strategy.

Nor was the lack of formal institutional participation of the military in nuclear planning a sign of civil-military distrust. The "absent dialogue" between India's civilian and military leaders, as Anit Mukherjee characterizes the issue, is an institutional anomaly even in normal times.[156] But the state's exaggerated emphasis on internal opacity exacerbated this anomaly. Decision-makers justified the military's formal exclusion on grounds that the weapon program was in its infancy. They rationalized that the military would become part of the planning process once the program matured.

For India, the outcome of a weakly seeded knowledge market and even lesser developed decision-making and agent management processes was a strategy of muddling through the challenges of covert nuclear proliferation. But most observers within and outside trying to make sense of India's nuclear direction behind its thick fog of secrecy tended to interpret this muddling through approach as a rational strategy of economic caution, moral hesitancy or some combination of the two. Neither, it turns out, was correct.

Notes

1 Project Ploughshares was an experimental program launched by the United States in the 1960s to leverage the use of nuclear explosives in large civil engineering programs. The US Atomic Energy Commission also explored the idea of conducting PNEs in India to quell its quest for prestige and use nuclear excavation to resolve "some of its basic river problems." However, the program was unsuccessful in the United States because of the negative environmental fallout and public opposition. It was finally terminated in 1977. For an overview of the program, see Scott Kaufman, *Project Ploughshare: The Peaceful Use of Nuclear Explosives in Cold War America* (Ithaca: Cornell University Press, 2013); also see, Perkovich, *India's Nuclear Bomb*, p. 91.

2 In the wake of the 1974 test, Indian Prime Minister Indira Gandhi wrote her Pakistani counterpart Zulfikar Ali Bhutto: "we [India] remain fully committed to our traditional policy of developing nuclear energy for peaceful purposes."

A disaggregated nuclear weapons option 77

To which Bhutto replied that there was no technical distinction between a nuclear explosion for peaceful or military purposes. See, A. Appadorai and M.S. Rajan, "Developments since 1972," *India's Foreign Policy and Relations* (New Delhi: South Asian Publishers, 1985), pp. 578–579.
3 Perkovich, "India Explodes a 'Peaceful' Nuclear Device," *India's Nuclear Bomb*, pp. 170–189; Yogesh Joshi, "The Imagined Arsenal," *Nuclear Proliferation History Project*, June 2015, http://www.wilsoncenter.org/publication/the-imagined-arsenal (July 2015).
4 Ibid.
5 L.K. Jha, "Nuclear Policy," *Prime Minister's Secretariat* (New Delhi: P.N. Haksar Files, Sub. F. – 111, Nehru Memorial Library, May 3, 1967).
6 Perkovich, *India's Nuclear Bomb*, pp. 121, 173–174.
7 Ibid., pp. 173–174.
8 *Kargil Review Committee Report*, pp. 185–187.
9 Ibid., pp. 199–206.
10 Narang, "Strategies of Nuclear Proliferation," pp. 135–146.
11 The Zangger Committee was formed between 1970 and 1974 by a group of advanced industrial countries to regulate the supply of fissile material and equipment that could be used to process fissile material to any non-nuclear state unless the equipment or fissile material was subject to international safeguards. See, "Communication Received from Members Regarding the Export of Nuclear Material and of Certain Categories of Equipment and Other Material," *International Atomic Energy Agency Information Circular*, INFCIRC/209, September 3, 1974, http://www.fas.org/nuke/control/zangger/text/inf209.htm (May 2013).
12 The Nuclear Suppliers Group was formed in 1975 by a group of advanced industrial countries to coordinate their export control policies on the supply of nuclear material and sensitive nuclear fuel-related technologies and equipment to non-nuclear states. See, "The Nuclear Suppliers Group at a Glance," *Arms Control Association*, October 2012, http://www.armscontrol.org/factsheets/NSG (May 2013).
13 See full text of the 1978 NNPA in, "Nuclear Regulatory Legislation," *United States Nuclear Regulatory Commission*, NUREG-0980, Vol. 3, No. 10, http://www.nrc.gov/reading-rm/doc-collections/nuregs/staff/sr0980/v3/sr0980v3.pdf (May 2013).
14 Parthasarathi, *Technology at the Core*, p. 106.
15 See Vikram Sarabhai's press statements cited in, Perkovich, *India's Nuclear Bomb*, p. 121.
16 Parthasarathi, *Technology at the Core*, pp. 172–173.
17 Ibid., pp. 170–171; Chengappa, *Weapons of Peace*, pp. 131–145.
18 Chengappa, *Weapons of Peace*, pp. 169–174.
19 It also needs noting that the French Viking engine represented off-the-shelf technology that could easily be incorporated into the PSLV whereas the Valiant was still in the research and development phase.
20 Parthasarathi, *Technology at the Core*, pp. 171–180.
21 BARC is the nerve center of India's nuclear weapons design and development program.
22 Bharath Karnad, *Nuclear Weapons and Indian Security: The Realist Foundations of Strategy* (New Delhi: Macmillan, 2002), pp. 338–344; Chengappa, *Weapons of Peace*, pp. 218–219.
23 The spokesman for India's Department of Atomic Energy responded to Desai's statement by saying: "the funniest thing I have heard so far." See, "Desai Claims He Has Some Doubts about India's Nuclear Test in '74," *New York Times*, June 3, 1981 http://www.nytimes.com/1981/06/03/world/desai-says-he-has-some-doubts-about-indian-nuclear-tests-in-74.html (May 2013).
24 Chengappa, *Weapons of Peace*, p. 219.

78 *A disaggregated nuclear weapons option*

25 *Kargil Review Committee Report*, p. 186.
26 Ibid.
27 Ibid., pp. 199–200; Chengappa, *Weapons of Peace*, pp. 246–247; Perkovich, *India's Nuclear Bomb*, pp. 227–232.
28 R. Venkataraman, *My Presidential Years* (New Delhi: HarperCollins Publishers India, 1994), p. 323.
29 Perkovich, *India's Nuclear Bomb*, pp. 242-244.
30 Interview with Dr. P.K. Iyengar, Chairman, Atomic Energy Commission/Secretary, Department of Atomic Energy (1990–1993), Mumbai, India, June 20, 2010.
31 Interview with Dr. M.R. Srinivasan, Chairman Atomic Energy Commission/Secretary, Department of Atomic Energy, Government of India (1987–1990), Bangalore, India, July 8, 2010.
32 Chengappa, *Weapons of Peace*, pp. 294–305; Perkovich, *India's Nuclear Bomb*, pp. 273–276.
33 Ibid.
34 Bharath Karnad, *India's Nuclear Policy* (New Delhi: Pentagon Press, 2008), p. 80.
35 Ibid., p. 82. The lowering of internal firewalls between BARC and India's missile agency occurred around 2002–2003. According to Indian missile scientists and engineers, the phenomenon of high firewalls prevented optimization of nuclear missile designs until then.
36 Perkovich, *India's Nuclear Bomb*, pp. 242–244.
37 Raja Ramanna, *My Years of Pilgrimage* (New Delhi: Viking, 1991), pp. 109, 115.
38 M.R. Srinivasan, *From Fission to Fusion: The Story of India's Atomic Energy Program* (New Delhi: Viking, 2002), pp. 182–192.
39 Ramanna, *My Years of Pilgrimage*, p. 115; Srinivasan, *From Fission to Fusion*, p. 184.
40 Indranil Banerjee, "The Integrated Guided Missile Development Program," *Indian Defense Review*, July 1990, pp. 99–109.
41 *The Integrated Guided Missile Development Program* (Delhi: Defense Research & Development Organization, 2008), pp. 63–109.
42 Ibid., pp. 110–116.
43 Ibid., 63–109.
44 Among all three missiles, the Agni Technology Demonstrator held the greatest promise for an operational ballistic missile system because of its light weight, solid fuel first stage motor and medium range. Yet, the Agni was not accorded priority until the late 1990s when the missile's hybrid configuration of a solid fuel motor first stage and liquid fuel engine second stage were resolved in favor of solid motors.
45 Verghese Koithara, *Managing India's Nuclear Forces* (Washington, D.C.: Brookings Institution Press, 2012), p. 126.
46 Interview with Air Marshal (retd.) "N," New Delhi, India, January 2010.
47 Chengappa, *Weapons of Peace*, p. 406.
48 Ibid., p. 387.
49 Ibid., p. 327.
50 Interview with Air Marshal (retd.) "N."
51 Ibid.
52 Ibid.
53 Chengappa, *Weapons of Peace*, pp. 253–255.
54 As General Krishna Rao summed it: "The chiefs of staff had taken up the case with the prime minister that we must go nuclear. Before this, the military had never made a suggestion like this. I must add that was also a part of the Expert Committee's recommendations." See, "China Was the Real Concern: In Conversation with Gen. K.V. Rao," *Force* (December 2004), p. 31; Chengappa, *Weapons of Peace*, p. 255.

55 Sundarji, "Effects of Nuclear Asymmetry on Conventional Deterrence."
56 Sundarji, *Blind Men of Hindoostan*, pp. 21–48.
57 Interviews with K. Subrahmanyam, Noida, India, October 2009.
58 Deshmukh, *A Cabinet Secretary Looks Back*, pp. 163–166.
59 Interview with Dr. V.S. Arunachalam, Scientific Advisor to Defense Minister/Secretary, Defense Research & Development Organization (1983–1992), Bangalore, India, May 19, 2009.
60 Interviews with Subrahmanyam.
61 Scholars such as Sumit Ganguly believe that Indian decision-makers' assessments of the threat of US sanctions were correct.
62 The doyen of Indian strategic analysts K. Subrahmanyam subsequently claimed that "in the period between 1987 and 1990 India was totally vulnerable to a Pakistani nuclear threat." See, K. Subrahmanyam, "Indian Nuclear Policy – 1964–1998 (A personal recollection)," in Jasjit Singh ed., *Nuclear India* (New Delhi: Knowledge World, 1998), p. 44.
63 Abraham, *The Making of the Indian Atomic Bomb*, pp. 82–86.
64 Ibid., pp. 86–91, 120–124.
65 Perkovich, *India's Nuclear Bomb*, pp. 49–59.
66 Parthasarathi, *Technology at the Core*, pp. 115–117.
67 Abraham, *The Making of the Indian Atomic Bomb*, pp. 91–98; Parthasarathi, *Technology at the Core*, pp. 18–19, 118–125.
68 Parthasarathi, *Technology at the Core*, pp. 115–116.
69 Ibid.
70 Ibid., pp. 110–112.
71 Parthasarathi, *Technology at the Core*, pp. 117–118; Perkovich, *India's Nuclear Bomb*, pp. 197–199.
72 Parthasarathi, *Technology at the Core*, pp. 17–18; Perkovich, *India's Nuclear Bomb*, p. 201.
73 "India's Nuclear Procurement Strategy: Implications for the United States," *Directorate of Intelligence*, CIA-RDPS00854R00020012000-0 (Approved for Release: July 1, 2011), p. iii.
74 Ibid., p. 12.
75 Ibid., p. 6.
76 For details of Pakistan's clandestine procurement efforts see, Leonard S. Spector, *Going Nuclear* (Cambridge: Ballinger Publishing Company, 1987), pp. 113–117; Sreedhar, *Pakistan's Bomb: A Documentary Study* (New Delhi: ABC Publishing House, 1986).
77 Chengappa, *Weapons of Peace*, pp. 314–315.
78 Ibid., pp. 346–347.
79 Srinivasan, *From Fission to Fusion*, p. 271.
80 Perkovich, *India's Nuclear Bomb*, pp. 243–244.
81 Chengappa, *Weapons of Peace*, p. 260.
82 Ibid., pp. 255–257.
83 *Kargil Review Committee Report*, pp. 184–190.
84 Between 1979 and 1985, the US Congress granted special exemptions to Pakistan from the NNPA. In 1985 it passed a special amendment, the Pressler Amendment, to allow for continued economic and military aid to Pakistan, so long as the US president could certify to Congress that Pakistan was not in possession of a nuclear device. See, Spector, "Pakistan," *Going Nuclear*, p. 104; "Context of August 1985: Pressler Amendment Passed, Requiring Yearly Certification That Pakistan Does Not Have Nuclear Weapons," *History Commons*, http://www.historycommons.org/context.jsp?item=a0885pressleramendment (May 2013).
85 Thomas C. Reed and Danny B. Stillman, *The Nuclear Express: A Political History of the Bomb and Its Proliferation* (Zenith Press, 2009), pp. 252–253.

80 *A disaggregated nuclear weapons option*

 86 Spector, *The New Nuclear Nations*, pp. 106–109.
 87 "Analysis of Six Issues about Nuclear Capabilities of India, Iraq, Libya and Pakistan," Report Prepared for The Committee on Foreign Relations, United States Senate, *Congressional Research Service* (January 1982), pp. 1–6, 13–18; Spector, *Going Nuclear*, pp. 126–127.
 88 Perkovich, *India's Nuclear Bomb*, pp. 242–243.
 89 Interview with Arunachalam.
 90 Spector, *Going Nuclear*, p. 102.
 91 For details of Pakistan's uranium enrichment effort see, Feroz Hassan Khan, *Eating Grass: The Making of the Pakistani Bomb* (Stanford: Stanford University Press, 2012), pp. 139–161.
 92 M.V. Ramana, "India's Uranium Enrichment Program," *INESAP Information Bulletin*, No. 24, December 2004, http://www.cised.org/uraniumenrichment_INESAP.pdf (May 2013).
 93 Jacques E.C. Hymans, *The Psychology of Nuclear Proliferation: Identity, Emotions and Foreign Policy* (New York: Cambridge University Press, 2006), p. 186.
 94 Quoted in Perkovich, *India's Nuclear Bomb*, p. 275; also see, Ramana, "India's Uranium Enrichment Program."
 95 Interview with Arunachalam.
 96 Interview with Iyengar.
 97 Srinivasan, *From Fission to Fusion*, pp. 278–280.
 98 Ibid., p. 279.
 99 For the classic text on the subject of "tacit" knowledge, see, Michael Polanyi, *The Tacit Dimension* (Chicago: University of Chicago Press, 1966).
100 See, Jacques E.C. Hymans, *Achieving Nuclear Ambitions: Scientists, Politicians and Proliferation* (New York: Cambridge University Press, 2012), pp. 205–220.
101 Khan, *Eating Grass*, pp. 147–150.
102 Srinivasan, *From Fission to Fusion*, pp. 279–280.
103 *Kargil Review Committee Report*, pp. 187–188.
104 Ibid.
105 *Kargil Review Committee Report*, pp. 189–190.
106 Interview with Subrahmanyam.
107 Ibid.
108 Interview with Iyengar.
109 Chengappa, *Weapons of Peace*, pp. 255, 260.
110 Deshmukh, *A Cabinet Secretary Looks Back*, pp. 163–166; K. Subrahmanyam, "Introduction," in K. Sundarji ed., *Vision 2100: A Strategy for the Twenty-First Century* (New Delhi: Konark Publishers Ltd., 2003), pp. xvii–xxxii.
111 According to the Indian Air Force's director of air operations at the time: "In the wake of the Israeli attack on Osiraq, the IAF's Offense Operations Directorate drew up plans…I was its director at the time. But this was contingency planning…just a four-page plan. I do not know if it went up to the Air Chief of Staff. I don't know whether Air Headquarters and the political leadership considered attacks on Kahuta in 1984. They may have, but I do not know about it. And I did not ask the concerned individuals about it. It would not have been difficult to destroy Kahuta, the surface structures. Destruction of underground structures would have required bunker penetrating bombs…for which we could have turned to the Israelis." Interview with Air Commodore (retd.) Jasjit Singh, former Director, Center for Airpower Studies, New Delhi, India, May 6, 2009.
112 Scott D. Sagan, "Indian and Pakistani Nuclear Weapons: For Better or Worse?" in Scott D. Sagan and Kenneth Waltz eds., *The Spread of Nuclear Weapons: A Debate Renewed* (New York: W.W. Norton Company, 2003), p. 93.

113 Bajpai, Chari, Cheema, Cohen and Ganguly, *Brasstacks and Beyond*, pp. 27–33.
114 Ibid., pp. 49–60.
115 Perkovich, *India's Nuclear Bomb*, p. 278.
116 Ibid., p. 280.
117 James Surowiecki, *The Wisdom of Crowds* (New York: Doubleday, 2004), pp. 1–142.
118 *Kargil Review Committee Report*, p. 188.
119 Reed and Stillman, *The Nuclear Express*, pp. 252–253.
120 Jeffrey T. Richelson, *Spying on the Bomb: American Nuclear Intelligence from Nazi Germany to Iran and North Korea* (New York: W.W. Norton Company, 2006), p. 343.
121 William J. Broad, "The Hidden Travels of the Bomb," *New York Times*, December 8, 2008, http://www.nytimes.com/2008/12/09/science/09bomb.html?pagewanted=all (April, 2013).
122 Reed and Stillman, *The Nuclear Express*, p. 253.
123 Khan, *Eating Grass*, p. 175.
124 Ibid., pp. 188, 190.
125 Ibid.
126 Abraham, *The Making of the Indian Atomic Bomb*, pp. 34–68.
127 Parthasarathi, *Technology at the Core*, p. 20.
128 Ibid., pp. 99–109.
129 Ibid., pp. 17–18, 114–115, 116–117, 118.
130 Ibid., pp. 118–124.
131 Ibid., p. 124.
132 Interview with Iyengar.
133 Perkovich, *India's Nuclear Bomb*, pp. 181–183.
134 Interview with Iyengar.
135 Interview with senior BARC official (retd.), Bangalore, India, July 7, 2010.
136 Interview with Iyengar.
137 Ibid.
138 Ramanna, *Years of Pilgrimage*, p. 91.
139 US Department of State Case No. M-2009-00895, Doc No. C17601478, August 15, 2012.
140 Perkovich, *India's Nuclear Bomb*, p. 182.
141 Interview with Srinivasan.
142 Interview with Iyengar.
143 Perkovich, *India's Nuclear Bomb*, p. 268.
144 "India's Nuclear Program – Energy and Weapons: An Intelligence Assessment," *Directorate of Intelligence: Central Intelligence Agency*, July 1982, SW 8210056C/SC 00406/82 (approved for release, July 19, 2010), p. iv.
145 Former AEC Chairman Raja Ramanna claimed in 1991 that the *Dhruva* went critical in 1983 and functioned "…without any trouble…at its maximum capacity." His successor M.R. Srinivasan pushed the date to 1985 and admitted to vibrations-induced fuel damage. Former Indian Cabinet Secretary Deshmukh has also admitted that a consistent supply of plutonium became available to the Indian government in 1988 after *Dhruva* went critical. See, Ramanna, *My Years of Pilgrimage*, p. 111; Srinivasan, *From Fission to Fusion*, p. 272; Chengappa, *Weapons of Peace*, p. 332.
146 David Albright, "India's Military Plutonium Inventory, End 2004," *ISIS*, May 7, 2005, http://isis-online.org/uploads/isis-reports/documents/india_military_plutonium.pdf.
147 Reed and Stillman, *The Nuclear Express*, p. 251.
148 Chengappa, *Weapons of Peace*, p. 285.

149 Interview with Deputy Air Chief of Staff (retd.) "G," Gurgaon, India, February 9, 2010.
150 Chengappa, *Weapons of Peace*, p. 336.
151 Interview with senior Air Marshal (retd.) "N."
152 Ibid.
153 Chengappa, *Weapons of Peace*, pp. 164–174.
154 Ibid., pp. 276–279; A.P.J. Abdul Kalam with Arun Tiwari, *Wings of Fire* (Hyderabad: Universities Press, 1999), pp. 114–117.
155 Zian Mian, A.H. Nayyar and M.V. Ramana, "Bringing the Prithvi Down to Earth: The Capabilities and Potential Effectiveness of India's Prithvi Missile," *Science & Global Security*, 7, no. 3 (1998), pp. 333–360.
156 Anit Mukherjee, "The Absent Dialogue," *Seminar*, No. 509 (July 2009), http://www.india-seminar.com/2009/599/599_anit_mukherjee.htm (July 2015).

4 Behind the veil of nuclear opacity (1989–1998)[1]

In the spring of 1989, Indian Prime Minister Rajiv Gandhi finally decided to follow Pakistan's lead and authorized the building of air deliverable nuclear weapons. Although this decision was a highly classified secret, by the early 1990s it was generally assumed outside that India and Pakistan were *de facto* nuclear weapon powers. The *de facto* was taken to mean that both countries had the technical capability to assemble and deploy nuclear weapons as well as the organizational capacity to use them instrumentally.

In his history of the Indian nuclear weapons program, for example, George Perkovich cited evidence that during 1988–1990, India readied "at least two dozen nuclear weapons for quick assembly and dispersal to airbases for delivery by aircraft in anticipation of retaliatory attacks against Pakistan."[2] Writing in 1992, George Quester downplayed the challenges of "weaponization" and declared the issue of nuclear delivery a minor one.[3] Both Perkovich and Quester claimed that whatever nuclear weapons India possessed at the time were readily deliverable via its fleet of Mirage, Jaguar and MiG combat aircraft.[4]

Carnegie's Leonard Spector similarly echoed these claims independently.[5] Summing up the prevailing view of the state of Indian nuclear capabilities at the time, Steve Coll of the *Washington Post* reported in 1991 that, "while the exact status of the military nuclear programs in India and Pakistan is being kept secret, US officials believe both countries have acquired the ability to produce and deploy quickly a small number of nuclear weapons…both countries possess sophisticated fighter aircraft that could conceivably penetrate air defenses while carrying one or more nuclear bombs."[6]

These prevailing views were reinforced by US government officials who never tired in public of pointing to the immediacy and severity of the proliferation threat in South Asia. During the 1989–1990 Indo-Pakistani crisis over Kashmir,[7] a senior US defense official suggested that "If readiness is measured on a scale of one to ten and the Indians are normally at six, they have now moved to nine."[8] US intelligence sources estimated that India was capable of building nuclear weapons within a matter of days and that weapons could be delivered by combat aircraft, a point reinforced by Lynn Davis, the US Undersecretary of State for International Security Affairs.[9]

In a February 1993 hearing on proliferation threats before the US Senate Committee on Governmental Affairs, then CIA Director R. James Woolsey stated: "The arms race between India and Pakistan poses perhaps the most probable prospect for the future use of weapons mass destruction, including nuclear weapons. Both nations have nuclear weapons development programs and could, on short notice, assemble nuclear weapons...advanced aircraft are often the delivery system of choice for weapons of mass destruction, and they are now commonplace among proliferating countries...the aircraft available to these countries are fully capable of delivering nuclear weapons..."[10]

However, there was a broad consensus both among US officials and nongovernmental experts that neither India nor Pakistan maintained assembled weapons that were immediately employable. Between 1988 and 1998, the two common conceptual frames used to describe Indian and Pakistani nuclear postures were "non-weaponized" and "recessed" deterrence. Although these frames of reference were often used interchangeably, they convey different meanings. This is why it is important to distinguish between them. George Perkovich popularized the term "non-weaponized deterrence" in 1993 and advanced it as a policy alternative that India and Pakistan could conceivably use as a bridge between the two extremes of fully deployed nuclear arsenals and nuclear rollback. In what he described as the "third" way, Perkovich drew the line at building nuclear weapons and deploying ballistic missiles.[11] Under it, deterrence would stem from the mere existence of nuclear capability and the ability of either country to build nuclear weapons quickly. It would allow both countries to reap the security benefits of nuclear weapons without running afoul of the international nonproliferation regime.[12]

Perkovich acknowledged, however, that "only a small minority of tight knit elites" in both countries had knowledge of the actual nuclear state of affairs and their views on "non-weaponized deterrence" were "difficult to ascertain."[13] Furthermore, Perkovich's non-weaponized deterrence proposal was exploratory and largely aspirational. But by 1996–1997, scholars including Rosalind Reynolds baldly asserted with little evidence that emerging nuclear weapon powers were tacit adherents to the regime of non-weaponized deterrence.[14] India, Reynolds claimed, abided by the regime out of normative concerns in order to safeguard its reputation as a disarmament advocate and remain a good international citizen. Reynolds also expanded Perkovich's non-weaponized schema to include the absence of strategic planning involving nuclear weapons and their integration into the military. She viewed the lack of operational planning as evidence that emerging nuclear powers such as India and Pakistan treated nuclear weapons as diplomatic and not military assets.

In contrast, Jasjit Singh's notion of "recessed deterrence" assumed that India possessed all the elements of a working nuclear arsenal: warheads, delivery systems and operational routines. However, all the working elements of the arsenal were deliberately withheld from operational readiness.

Hence, the characterization "recessed." More important, in Singh's conceptual frame, this lack of operational readiness was not the consequence of India's normative commitment to nonproliferation. Rather, it stemmed from Indian decision-makers' concerns for strategic stability. That apart, the condition of the arsenal, from its normally unconstituted state to an operationally deployed form, was contingent upon threat assessments. In Singh's assessment, the arsenal's operational readiness would parallel the changes in threat levels.[15] Hence, the crucial difference between "recessed" and "non-weaponized" deterrence frameworks was their presumed causal driver. In non-weaponized deterrence the causal driver was deference to nonproliferation norms. In recessed deterrence the causal driver was strategic stability.[16] Nonetheless, the "recessed" state diplomatically dovetailed with the choice of a "non-weaponized" arsenal whether or not the decision-makers deliberated or intended it that way.

In this chapter, I present evidence to show that most assumptions about the state of India's nuclear capabilities in the decade prior to the 1998 nuclear tests were wrong. India did not possess deliverable nuclear weapons until at least 1994–1995.[17] Although India elected to build weaponized nuclear devices in 1989, the process of integrating them with aircraft stretched out for nearly seven years, until 1994–1995.[18] Similarly, warhead integration on the short-range Prithvi ballistic missiles did not reach fruition until 1996–1997.[19] In other words, for the greater part of the decade, the default non-weaponized state of the Indian arsenal stemmed from technical and managerial bottlenecks and not from any normative choice to abide by nonproliferation principles.

After weapons became available in the mid-1990s, Indian leaders consciously decided to maintain them in a disassembled form out of concerns for safety and strategic stability. However, they elected against developing the soft institutional and organizational routines to manage those weapons operationally. My evidence shows that cognitive biases stemming from heuristic decision-making, not arms-control norms or cultural understandings of nuclear weapons as political weapons shaped the latter choice. Likewise, assumptions of an extant recessed operational capability turned out to be a vast overestimation. The earliest Indian operational routines, by which is meant the civil-military chain of command, standard operating procedures, practice drills and ground rehearsals to coordinate action within and across various agencies tasked with responding to a nuclear emergency, were devised during the Kargil War[20] in the summer of 1999,[21] a year after India conducted nuclear tests and formally claimed nuclear power status.

With the help of new evidence based on interviews with senior Indian civilian and military officials involved in the weaponization program during 1988–1999, I highlight some of the challenges India faced in developing operational nuclear forces under the scrutiny of a hostile nonproliferation regime. I show that in covertly proliferating states, political leaders fear pressures for nuclear rollback from nonproliferation watchdogs in the international system.

These pressures force the proliferation process underground, deep into the bowels of the state. To prevent information leaks, sensitive nuclear weapons–related information is usually tightly compartmented and hived off within small and informal social networks. Decision-makers only partially mobilize epistemic actors and approach programmatic decisions sequentially. Secrecy concerns also create disincentives against decomposing problems and parceling them out for resolution to multiple bureaucratic actors.

Institutional secrecy thus creates management roadblocks in the path of hardware development and operational planning. It also generates demands for highly centralized and monopolist decision-making, a condition that accentuates cognitive biases among policy planners and prevents operational optimization. Finally, secrecy short-circuits the state's normal institutional oversight and control mechanisms. This last condition creates huge information asymmetries between decision-makers and their agents and compounds the challenges of management. The low information turnover and absence of the "wisdom of the crowds" scrutiny by multiple individuals and agencies leave many problems unidentified and unaddressed. Under these circumstances, most learning that occurs in the political system follows external shocks and crises. Overall, the regime of internal opacity and the unstructured nature of decision-making militate against policy optimization.

"Seat-of-the-pants" nuclear learning

By 1987–1988, there were multiple signs that Pakistan had acquired nuclear weapons or was on the verge of acquiring the capability to build them. There was some uncertainty within India's nuclear establishment and its external intelligence agency, the Research & Analysis Wing, about the precise state of Pakistani nuclear advances.[22] However, Indian leaders had few doubts about Pakistan's direction. Triangulating through Indian intelligence sources, US government leaks and open source publications, they concluded that Pakistan was rapidly proceeding down the path of nuclear weaponization.[23] By late 1988 it also became evident that there were no takers for Prime Minister Rajiv Gandhi's global nuclear disarmament plan. Domestically, pressure mounted on the prime minister from the defense and nuclear scientific agency heads, DRDO and BARC, as well as his principal secretary to act. Ultimately in March 1989, Rajiv Gandhi authorized a program to commence weaponization.[24]

However, the weaponization program had a narrow technical focus. Between 1989 and 1994, it exclusively concerned the production of a small number of miniaturized and ruggedized fission weapons that could be safely and reliably delivered by means of combat aircraft. The weaponization process essentially concerned taking the device beyond its basic "physics package." This involved a reduction in the size and weight of the weapon, the use of metallurgically stabilized nuclear material, nondegradable high-explosive lenses, and anticorrosive materials within the weapon to ensure easier storage, maintenance and longer shelf life. It also involved the development of reliable electronic subsystems such as high-voltage capacitors, electronic safety and arming systems, and barometric fuses to ensure accurate height burst for the weapon.[25]

For successful air carriage on the designated Mirage 2000, weaponization involved reduction in the size, weight and casing of the weapon to avoid upsetting the aerodynamics and center of gravity of the aircraft.[26] It entailed redesign of the Mirage's wiring system to enable the bomb's electrical connectivity. Other tasks concerned the reconfiguring of the aircraft's electronic interface to enable the sighting, arming and safe release of the weapon; the rewiring of the aircraft's electronic interface to feed the bomb's ballistics into computers; electromagnetic pulse (EMP) protection; and the strengthening of the suspension points for the weapon on the aircraft along with the "airframe along certain high stress zones and joints."[27] The last component of the weaponization program was the training of pilots in the arming, fusing and delivery of nuclear bombs.

The focus on the technical aspects of weaponization did not mean that India's national security managers had no appreciation for the accompanying institutional and organizational routines to embed those weapons within the air force operationally. In the late-1980s for example, Prime Minister Gandhi directed DRDO chief Arunachalam to undertake precautionary routines to reduce some of the worst vulnerabilities of the fledgling Indian nuclear weapons program to a surprise attack.[28] Subsequently, with the weaponization decision behind him, Gandhi also felt an imperative need to expand the circle of officials with knowledge of the program.[29] V.P. Singh, who succeeded Gandhi as prime minister, shared this concern and complained to his principal secretary about the lack of shared institutional knowledge and planning.[30] Nonetheless, neither prime minister undertook serious institutional measures to resolve their concerns.

Hence the weaponization program remained isolated from the institutional and organizational demands of operational use. Even as knowledge of the weaponization program expanded vertically within the scientific and engineering enclave tasked with its various subprojects, horizontal networks within the state privy to knowledge of the program shrank.

To oversee the effort, Gandhi appointed Defense Secretary Naresh Chandra as coordinator.[31] However, because the program was treated as technical, relatively static and sequential, there was no corresponding attempt to expand the planning and decision-making circle to include cabinet members, a larger group of civil servants in the foreign ministry or the military. B.G. Deshmukh, who served as both cabinet and principal secretary to Prime Ministers Gandhi and Singh later disclosed that although he closely participated in the weaponization decision in 1988–1989, his involvement in monitoring the program's progress declined thereafter.[32] The prime ministers henceforth dealt directly with Naresh Chandra and the heads of DRDO and BARC. Arunachalam himself complained in an interview with the author about the "loneliness" and the "burden" of being one of the sole institutional repositories of India's nuclear secrets in this period, without the luxury of being able to share them with anyone.[33]

Central to this lack of institutionalization and the horizontal expansion in the decision-making circle were concerns about potential breaches in secrecy. As Chandra put it to the author, "…because of the fundamental inefficiency and sloppy approach of the bureaucracy…the latter could not be relied upon to keep matters secret. Hence the smaller the numbers [in the know] the better."[34] He recalled an episode from the mid-1980s when foreign spies penetrated the office of P.C. Alexander, who served as principal secretary to Prime Ministers Indira and Rajiv Gandhi.[35]

Secrecy, Chandra insisted, also enabled deniability to domestic constitutional authorities such as parliament and the office of the Comptroller and Auditor General.[36] However, the cause of Indian decision-makers' acute desire for secrecy did not lie in domestic factors alone. It stemmed from their perceptions of India's economic vulnerability to US nonproliferation pressures. Three contingent factors in the early 1990s compounded their sense of vulnerability: the collapse of the Soviet Union which had been India's long-standing superpower ally, an acute balance of payments crisis, and the resort to an IMF bailout package.[37] As a result, decision-makers shielded the weaponization program even more than might have been warranted.

Ironically, in 1985–1986, Prime Minister Rajiv Gandhi made a feeble attempt at institutionalizing national security planning and nuclear decision-making through a national security council. That attempt ended dismally within six months.[38] Next, he invited the service chiefs and the heads of the nuclear and defense research agencies to provide the government with preliminary numbers and cost estimates for a small nuclear force.[39] However, he allegedly "pigeonholed" that report.[40] During these years, service chiefs such as Generals Rao and Sundarji also took advantage of their excellent personal ties with Prime Ministers Indira and Rajiv Gandhi to lobby them personally in favor of nuclear weapons.[41] For a short while, Rajiv Gandhi also was in charge of the defense portfolio in the cabinet. This gave then army chief General Sundarji, who was also by then the military's foremost expert on nuclear matters, unprecedented direct access to the prime minister.[42] Sundarji lobbied the prime minister in favor of the bomb with such alacrity that it aroused the ire of then Cabinet Secretary B.G. Deshmukh.[43]

However, once weaponization got underway, the program was cordoned off almost entirely. All information sharing was restricted to the heads of the AEC and DRDO, the incumbent prime minister, and the president. Cabinet ministers, the group of department secretaries and the military chiefs were kept in the dark. According to Arunachalam, it was easy to exclude the army and navy chiefs because their services were not involved in the delivery program.[44] The "air force chiefs," Chandra maintained, "only found out about it [the weaponization program] because the air force was tasked with nuclear delivery."[45]

To avoid unnecessary attention from foreign intelligence agencies, government officials and offices, which were normally the sites for specific programmatic decisions, were also excluded. In contrast, the small group of officials with critical knowledge of the program remained involved in it regardless of their formal positions within government. Furthermore, these officials retained their involvement without the knowledge of their political or bureaucratic overlords.[46] This small and informal network of individuals did not emerge by design. As Chandra put it, "it emerged from necessity...almost to the extent that it became self-constituted...a minimal response by relevant individuals within the state who responded to a critical national security challenge."[47]

This fractional mobilization of India's nuclear epistemic actors effectively decoupled scientific-technical developments from the military's operational planning. The net effect of such excessive compartmentalization was that when a crisis in Kashmir with nuclear overtones suddenly erupted in 1990, the air force was in the dark about the parameters of the weapon then under development.[48] Because India had no suitable nuclear delivery system at the time, there is some evidence to suggest that the air force autonomously and internally debated kamikaze missions as a possible nuclear delivery method in the late 1980s and early 1990s.[49] During the decade of the 1990s, its interaction with DRDO was primarily technical, restricted to modification of the Mirage 2000 for nuclear missions and the training of a handful of pilots to deliver nuclear weapons using dummy bombs. Until 1996 when Prime Minister Narasimha Rao privately confided to Air Chief Marshal Sareen that India possessed nuclear weapons, no air chief had official knowledge of the program.[50] The air force's role, in the memorable words of another air chief who served in the 1990s, was simply that of a "delivery boy."[51]

Thus in the pre-1998 era, the institutional link between the scientific agencies that designed and built nuclear weapons and the services was severely restricted.[52] The data on nuclear weapons effects, meteorology and demographics, that General Sundarji used for preliminary estimates of nuclear weapon effects in land warfare for example, were derived from open-source literature such as foreign military training manuals or from military training courses that individual service members had attended abroad.[53] A select few air force test pilots were trained in the mechanics of air delivery.[54] However, procedural plans for operational deployment and use were not developed with the air force. Nor did the government task the services with developing an epistemic community in the realm of nuclear strategic thought and warfare. To the contrary, senior cabinet ministers such as Narasimha Rao rejected suggestions from the defense ministry's quasi government think tank, the IDSA, to educate the military on nuclear issues due to concerns that it would suggest to the outside world that "we are developing nuclear weapons."[55] India's schools where staff officers trained for higher command duties therefore offered no training or courses on nuclear subjects.[56]

Beginning in the early 1990s, a small number of civilian officials working with the scientific agencies drew up "paper plans" for an assured retaliation posture. But they did not give teeth to this posture by developing operational plans with Air Headquarters to move weapons from the "stockpile-to-target."[57] A secret committee, the Arun Singh Committee, sat in the summer of 1990, in the aftermath of the Kashmir crisis with Pakistan, the subcontinent's first serious nuclear crisis, to plan India's nuclear emergency response measures.[58] The committee's "only specific recommendation," recalled the late K. Subrahmanyam who participated in its deliberations, was "...to create separate storage for missiles and warheads...what should be the drill for them being brought together...and then...the communications from command and control."[59]

As George Perkovich reports in his history of the Indian nuclear weapons program, "...the group called for designating air force units to receive nuclear devices and deliver them according to previously prepared orders that base commanders would possess under seal."[60] The piecemeal nature of decision-making can be inferred from the fact that the committee's key recommendation was not implemented until certification of the air delivery platform in 1994–1995. Only subsequently in 1995 did Prime Minister Rao approve the enactment of dispersal and concealment routines planned for safeguarding fissile cores and non-fissile trigger assemblies from a preemptive attack.[61] Meanwhile, wartime operations planning to coordinate action between the air force and scientific agencies to enable the air force plan nuclear missions were delayed still further.[62]

The partial mobilization apart, the nuclear epistemic community's weak state of institutionalization further minimized its capacity for policy learning; especially insofar it concerned integration and coordination issues. No doubt, many of the scientists and technologists in BARC and DRDO had long careers that spanned successive governments, sometimes as long as three decades. For example, nuclear scientists including Ramanna, Iyengar, Chidambaram, Kakodkar, Sikka and their DRDO counterparts such as Nagchaudhuri, Arunachalam, Santhanam and Kalam enjoyed long stints in government. Ramanna, the leader of the 1974 explosion team for example, went on to become the chief scientific advisor to the defense minister, the head of AEC, member of parliament and minister of state for defense. Arunachalam continued for a decade as the scientific advisor to the defense minister and the lead advisor on the weaponization program to five prime ministers. K. Santhanam who became involved in the weaponization program in the mid-1980s, served as the coordinator between DRDO and BARC in his position as chief technology advisor to the defense minister's scientific advisor at the time of the 1998 tests.[63]

Their individually powerful positions notwithstanding, as a group the scientists were not institutionalized within any agency such as a national security council or a secretariat that could provide them with a structured platform to advance their views. As members of an epistemic community, the scientists and technologists existed as an informal social network. There were no established legal or even quasi-legal administrative rules of business to guide their interaction. Nor did they have independent access to other government agencies such as the military or power centers such as the cabinet or parliament. In the absence of legal and administrative authority, entrée and continued participation in the network depended on either a personal relationship with prime ministerial incumbents or with their coordinating agents.

These institutional weaknesses left the scientific-technological epistemic community in a weak position to extract "credible commitments" from political principals. From 1974 until 1998, the nuclear scientists were mostly unable to get successive prime ministers to authorize any further testing. Even after Rajiv Gandhi approved weaponization in the spring of 1989, the program was reduced to "bar charts" detailing "when the (bomb) trigger would be ready, what type of platform would carry the bomb, how the bomb was to be mated to a delivery vehicle, the type of electronic checks..." with the prime minister retaining veto over the crossing of every technical threshold.[64] The armed services were never part of the network except at its very fringes.

A retired air chief who served in this period brutally summed up the institutional constraints of his office when he stated "...no air chief wants to approach the prime minister about nuclear issues only to be told to go mind his own business!"[65] Indeed as the air force's nuclear air delivery system came online by the end of 1995, some bureaucrats within DRDO such as Santhanam supported operational planning with the air force. However, this was not the consensus view among the senior scientists and civilian bureaucrats responsible for policy planning. Senior air force officials who interacted with them concluded that the scientists were only cogs in the wheel. They lacked the political clout to force operational planning on the political leadership.[66]

As India's longtime weaponization manager Arunachalam put it,

> Our task was to see...can we have an efficient and successful system? That is what I was involved in...I was not involved in saying...what would be... how many squadrons will be involved in this...what will be the pattern of the squadrons...and who will...and that particular part of it...we were not involved in those kind of discussions...force synthesis...the integration of technical, organizational, and ideational elements is a political decision, which must be coordinated from the top. Scientific bureaucracies working on the technical parts of a weapon system cannot on their own undertake such decisions. [67]

Compartmentalization, cognitive biases, and constrained optimizing

The organizational dysfunction associated with the regime of internal opacity had the cumulative effect of stymieing India's operational nuclear capabilities during the entire decade of the 1990s. The compartmenting of information meant that policy planners and their decision-making counterparts approached problems sequentially. Secrecy concerns similarly prevented problem decomposition and parallel planning by multiple agencies within government. Many technical bottlenecks therefore remained unidentified by planners until pressed by the force of circumstances. Such extreme compartmenting of information also led to weak intra-and interagency coordination and planning, especially insofar as command, control and operational planning went. Above all, institutional secrecy and the absence of multiple actors and agency reviews contributed to policies based on erroneous analogies and biases.

When thinking of nuclear operationalization, it is generally useful to draw distinctions between a "device" and a "weapon." A device can, according to Chuck Hansen, commonly be understood as "…fission and fusion materials, together with their arming, fusing, firing, chemical high explosive, and effects-measuring components, that have not yet reached the development status of an operational weapon…system designed to produce a nuclear explosion for purposes of testing the design, for verifying nuclear theory, or for gathering information on system performance."[68] But a weapon system is considerably different. It involves "the conversion or modification of a nuclear test device into a combat-ready warhead," which "includes the design and production of a ballistic casing (and any required retardation and impact-absorption or shock-mitigation devices) as well as special fuses, power sources, and arming and safing systems or equipment."[69]

If we use the above definitions as the base for measurement, then India did not possess a nuclear weapon until at least 1990. To be sure, Indian nuclear scientists were working on advanced boosted-fission and perhaps even thermonuclear weapon designs by the late 1980s. As early as 1982–1983, they likely planned to test a lighter and more sophisticated version of the 1974 device. But the sequential nature of planning ensured that it was not until 1985–1986 that Rajiv Gandhi's government put in motion a plan to develop a weapon system of reduced weight and size that was safe, reliable and deliverable. India neither possessed such a weapon system in 1986–1987 when the Brasstacks Crisis erupted with Pakistan nor did it possess such a weapon at the time of the Kashmir Crisis in 1989–1990. Indeed, the doyen of Indian strategists and nuclear consultant to nearly all prime ministers since the late 1970s, K. Subrahmanyam subsequently disclosed that "in the period between 1987–1990 India was totally vulnerable to a Pakistani nuclear threat."[70]

Further, until the prime minister reached a decision in 1989 to commence weaponization, the scientific agencies did not seriously engage the air force to resolve the technics of nuclear delivery. Many observers in the 1990s assumed that India's Jaguar and Mirage combat aircraft were capable of performing nuclear missions. However, the grounds for such claims are suppositions not facts. In India's case, Prime Minister V.P. Singh recalls DRDO chief Arunachalam briefing him in 1989 that "India could then only assemble nuclear weapons but not deliver them."[71] As he put it, "we could laboratory test everything…but the bomb delivery was still in progress."[72]

More evidence of the lack of a delivery capability comes from then Chief of Air Staff S. Mehra who used the occasion of the 1989–1990 Kashmir Crisis and the prime minister's concerns about a potential Pakistani surprise nuclear strike to lobby for the removal of internal firewalls between the civilian research and development and the military user agencies.[73] The prototype Indian nuclear device under development had until then not been shown to the air force.[74] However, because no positive response was forthcoming, he and the two other service chiefs concluded that India did not possess a ready arsenal at the time.

The modification of aircraft for nuclear delivery reliably and safely turned out to be a huge technical and managerial challenge that consumed the DRDO's attention for six years and perhaps more. It is a telling reminder of the hurdles proliferating countries face when transforming crude capabilities into operable systems. But it is an even more pointed reminder of the pitfalls of weak inter-agency planning and coordination. There was a major problem interfacing the nuclear weapon with the Mirage. Senior Indian air force officials recall that DRDO's original intent may have been to arm ballistic missiles with nuclear warheads and circumvent the air force entirely. However, the warhead developed was too large and heavy for ballistic missile carriage at the time.[75]

Resolution of these technical bottlenecks took between 1989 and 1994 to resolve. However, the problem as senior Indian air force officials at the highest levels viewed it was not one of technical challenges alone but of the compartmented system of information flows, planning and management. The government did not issue specific nuclear tasking for the Mirages when they were acquired from France in the mid-1980s. Likewise, the air force was neither given nor asked for inputs on the size, weight and dimensions of the proposed nuclear weapon. A senior individual with insider knowledge of the program volunteered to the author that one should assume that "India could have acquired an air delivery capability by 1996." Prior to that date the deterrent was a "paper tiger." To be sure nuclear weapons existed. However, he emphasized, "capability is a function not just of the weapon but what you can actually do with that weapon." If a nuclear emergency had arisen in 1994–1995, the air force "may have been forced to do something." However, "given the large number of unresolved issues…the so many imponderables," it was difficult to estimate the likelihood of success.[76]

Optimizing decision-makers, after electing to weaponize India's nuclear capability in the spring of 1989, would have ordered policy planners to simultaneously think through command control procedures and operational planning. However, due to the compartmentalized and sequential nature of planning, political leaders did not think it necessary to think through these institutions and procedures. During the Kashmir Crisis with Pakistan in 1989–1990, for example, the Indian government found itself without a nuclear command-and-control system. Worse, it found itself without guidelines and procedures to respond to a nuclear emergency.[77] At the time, command and control just consisted of the prime minister, his principal secretary, and the scientific advisor to the defense minister.[78] The ruffled prime minister conveyed his concerns to his principal secretary saying, "[T]his is scary. This matter cannot just be between the prime minister and the scientific advisor. Supposing someone attacks Delhi, there is no formal procedure as to who then decides what to do. We have to institutionalize it."[79]

Arun Singh, the former minister of state of defense whom the prime minister appointed in the wake of the crisis to review India's nuclear preparedness and make recommendations for a command control system found himself aghast at the bureaucratic chaos inside government. He thought "it...crazy that BARC[80] didn't know where DRDO stood or vice versa. Nothing had been worked out as to who was to control the weapons and under what circumstances and time frame we would strike back."[81] The Arun Singh Committee subsequently prepared emergency response procedures and command-and-control mechanisms, but it did not delve into operational planning.[82] Further, neither the armed services in general nor more specifically the air force found representation on the committee. Retired army chief General Sundarji served on the committee as a token representative from the services.[83] However, the sitting service chiefs knew neither of the committee's existence nor of the specific nature of the general's inputs.

Indian decision-makers' obsessive desire for opacity therefore resulted in a skeletal and tenuously institutionalized command-and-control system and the near total absence of operational planning between the scientific and military agencies. What this meant was that although India possessed nuclear weapons, its institutional and organizational capacity to press them into military operations was far from assured. A senior official who served at the highest levels of the Indian government at the time claims that it would be reasonable to assume that the government had prepared emergency action and coordination protocols by the mid-1990s. If a nuclear explosion occurred, it would be the DAE's task to make an assessment. The DAE, which held custody of the fissile cores, would then pass them on to DRDO, which would in turn assemble nuclear weapons and turn them over to the air force. The planners believed 72 hours would be a reasonable time frame to constitute a nuclear force and launch retaliation.

In the event of the prime minister's incapacitation, power would devolve upon the Cabinet Committee on Security (CCS).[84] But the likelihood of that event happening was considered low. A Pakistani nuclear attack, the officials surmised, would be limited and symbolic and leave the functioning of the federal government relatively intact. However, in the worst-case "bolt-out-of-the-blue" scenario that Delhi did indeed go up in a mushroom cloud, power would devolve upon a hierarchy of state governors and principals in the state civil service who would assume responsibilities of the federal government. And the military would function under a reconstituted civilian authority. India, the leaders of the nuclear network believed, was a "...big country. It would survive!"[85]

The trouble with the above protocols was that they remained a secret even within the loose network of scientists who constituted India's principal policy planners during that time. Above all, they remained "paper exercises."[86] There were no written standard operating procedures, a Red Book for individuals to follow. Barring one or two officials at the very top who knew of the protocol principles in their entirety, other members of the nuclear network, never more than a dozen senior officials in any case, knew only fragments of them. Because little was committed to paper, the institutional memory of the state beyond this network of officials remained a blank state.[87] Furthermore, the DAE and DRDO did not practice any emergency drills on the ground to test their coordination and emergency responses.[88] From the mid-1990s onward, the air force chiefs inferred that such protocols likely existed.[89] But they were not informed of their content.

The president as the constitutional head of state was privy to some of this knowledge.[90] Similarly, a spare oral brief was made to new holders of the prime minister's office. However, if they were deemed disinterested, and at least three incumbents in the 1990s were,[91] their principal secretaries were briefed instead.[92] Beyond the prime minister and his secretary, no information was shared with ministers on the CCS or with federal governors in provinces, and provincial civil service heads who might be called upon to assume responsibilities of government. The military leadership was equally clueless about how it was to function under a new civilian dispensation. As the senior government official with the God's eye view of the program at the time put it to the author: "command and control essentially meant gathering all the members of the group (nuclear network) under one roof as quickly as possible."[93]

The accounts of senior Indian policy planners from this period also reveal how secrecy, compartmentalization and monopolist decision-making, freight policy with faulty analogies and cognitive biases. According to India's coordinator for nuclear planning, Ambassador Naresh Chandra, decision-makers' fear of compromised secrecy was the greatest factor that prevented them from institutionalizing the nuclear program and developing operational plans and procedures. They believed the "government was porous" and given the "fundamental inefficiency and sloppy approach of the bureaucracy...the latter could not be relied upon to keep matters secret."[94]

In their minds, the consequence of that discovery would be a new round of US-led sanctions, analogous to the one Washington imposed on India's civil nuclear power sector in the wake of the 1974 nuclear test. But this time around the "sanctions regime would be harsher" and "India's relative capacity in the 1990s to withstand sanctions...much lower."[95] Hence the "emphasis was on developing weapons" alone. As Chandra put it, "...operations would follow at some later point."[96] The former Indian Deputy National Security Advisor Satish Chandra justified Indian decision-makers' actions similarly: "remember, India was already under sanctions...technology denial regimes...and threat of further sanctions was always there. If the military were involved in a more substantial way, the game would be up...external powers would pick up the scent of India's nuclear weaponization at once…and sanctions would have followed."[97]

The evidence therefore suggests that decision-makers' fear about the repercussions of their actions and not optimization was the key determinant that shaped the scope of India's operational posture in the 1990s. The statements above are also revelatory of the cognitive biases that pervaded their operating assumptions. Consider the belief of Indian decision-makers that weaponization could be held a secret if most information concerning it was left disaggregated within the state. This belief belies common sense as the direction in which India's weaponization program was headed, if not its scale and scope, was an open secret. From the early 1990s on, India and Pakistan were presumed *de facto* nuclear weapon powers. Scholars[98] and US government officials[99] believed both countries capable of assembling and exploding nuclear weapons. A 1993 US National Security Council report to Congress for example clearly states, "we believe India maintains a nuclear weapons development effort along with its active program to develop delivery systems for those weapons."[100] A 1996 US Department of Defense report was similarly blunt in its assessment: "India is believed to have a stockpile of fissile material sufficient for fabricating several nuclear weapons and could probably assemble at least some of these weapons within a short time of deciding to do so."[101]

Following on the heels of such assessments, the idea that a regime of "tacit" nuclear deterrence had come into existence in South Asia after the 1990 Kashmir Crisis became the received wisdom.[102] Many US government entities and private think tanks in the early 1990s turned their entrepreneurial attention to promoting arms control and nuclear best practices drawn from US–Soviet Cold War experiences to prevent a potential nuclear war in South Asia, the region which then US President Bill Clinton described as the "most dangerous place on earth." In light of all the attention Indian and Pakistani proliferation received at the time, the belief among Indian decision-makers that this nuclear reality could still be denied bespeaks of cognitive dissonance, the psychological condition in which individuals mitigate the dissonant aspects of their belief systems by altering them or adding new elements to make them more harmonious.

Their further belief that foreign discovery of the weaponization program would trigger consequences far worse than those that emerged in the wake of the 1974 nuclear test is also an example of erroneous analogizing. It follows the bias train of the "availability" heuristic, a condition in which decision-makers make judgments of the probability of an event occurring and imagining its consequences not on the basis of any systematic thought process but on the vividness of a prior event or events lodged in their memory.[103] In India's case, that event was the 1974 nuclear test. Its consequence was US-orchestrated international sanctions against India's nuclear power sector.[104] As a consequence of those sanctions, India's nuclear power sector stalled. Electricity generation from nuclear power never exceeded 3% of India's total power generation.[105] It was this memory and the presumed viability of the threat of economic and technological sanctions, which deterred successive Indian prime ministers from conducting further nuclear tests until 1998. However, the analogy they drew between the 1974 test, weaponization and weaponization-related operational planning was biased on three counts.

First, the consensus in the US policy community by the early 1990s was that India was capable of building and deploying nuclear weapons even if it had not done so already; and that a recessed capability probably existed in the bowels of the state. Second, examples of triggering events under US sanction laws at the time particularly the Nuclear Nonproliferation Act, were nuclear testing, the violation of IAEA safeguards agreements, and cooperation agreements with the US.[106] Doctrine, procedures and operational plans, all intangibles, did not qualify as triggering events.[107] No doubt, existing laws could be read more expansively to fit the situation. Nevertheless, compared to stark events such as nuclear testing, the development of doctrines, procedures and operational plans are a relatively ambiguous phenomenon. These are relatively harder to detect and it is generally more difficult to make determinations concerning them. Third and perhaps more significantly, since 1974, Indian nuclear, space and missile entities were already the target of US nuclear and other high-tech technology denial regimes.[108] Furthermore, the US' threatened denial of Eximbank financing and loans from international financial institutions were indicative of limited and not blanket economic sanctions.

When questioned by the author, India's former Deputy National Security Advisor Satish Chandra rationalized the analogizing between the 1974 test and weaponization-related operational plans and procedures on grounds that "...there are laws on the books and then there are informal sanctions. The US has considerable discretionary power regarding sanctions...such as denial of aid, multinational loans, funds and so forth. India had to keep that in mind, when deciding how to deal with its covert nuclear status."[109] However, it remains doubtful if these rationalizations were ever subject to "truth tests" within India's secretive and monopolistic decision-making enclave at the time.

The Indian decision-makers' belief in the credibility of US sanctions threats is further evidence that their judgments were clouded by the "representative" heuristic to the extent those threats were deemed representative of Washington's general population of proliferation-related sanctioning acts. The venerable K. Subrahmanyam pointed out the logical fallacy of Indian economists and policy planners when he said, "...the perception was mostly based on what they heard from their American counterparts, and not comprehensive analysis of US behavior pattern when their interests clashed with their declaratory nuclear policies."[110]

Indeed, had Indian decision-makers investigated the universe of US proliferation-related sanctioning behavior, they would have discovered a history of US opposition and then grudging acceptance of most proliferating countries.[111] The list of states included Britain, France, China and Israel.[112]

During the 1980s and 1990s, Washington turned a blind eye to Pakistan's nuclear program and proved helpless in stanching Chinese nuclear and missile assistance to Pakistan.[113] Indian decision-makers would have also discovered that US decision-makers used sanctions selectively, applied them narrowly to specific entities, often issued waivers and at other times declined to make determinations at all.[114] Above all, they would have found that US policy makers constantly weighed the restraining effects of sanctions against the loss of leverage on a targeted state.[115] Indeed the limited US sanctioning of Pakistan under the Symington Amendment in the 1990s signaled the floor for punishment.

In this regard, one of the most dramatic instances of unstructured decision-making comes from India's former National Security Advisor (NSA) Brajesh Mishra. When asked by the author if the threat of sanctions weighed on his mind before the BJP government ordered tests in 1998, his response was: "I was never bothered...I didn't even consult anyone. My gut feeling was that once you tested and you were clear about your economic reforms then you will begin to have dialogue with all the countries...I was quite clear that India being such a big country, if you only had the guts at the decision-making level, had that bent of mind...you could do it."[116] Most of the evidence therefore demonstrates that Indian decision-makers were not rational optimizers. If anything, they were cognitive misers.

The impact of limited agent competition and weak monitoring on operations

Secrecy, compartmentalization and low information turnover also had the combined effect of creating a weak nuclear weapons–related knowledge market within the state. The regime of opacity not only made the program less transparent but it also reduced the ability of Indian decision-makers to monitor its performance. Leaders in organizations generally use three mechanisms to reduce the cost of obtaining information pertaining to their subordinates and their performance. The first is visibility, which renders actions easily observable. The second is agent competition, a process that allows rival streams of information to percolate up the management chain. And the third is the institutionalization of bodies of epistemic actors to vet the quality of programs and their progress. All three conditions were absent from the weaponization project with deleterious consequences for both hardware development and operational aspects of policy.

Historically, India's nuclear, space, and defense research and development agencies have enjoyed a high degree of autonomy. Due to the pursuit of "strategic autonomy" Indian leaders have institutionally exempted then from the normal oversight of the state's audit authorities. In cases involving special projects of national significance, the heads of agencies such as the DRDO, BARC and ISRO typically interact with prime ministerial incumbents or senior cabinet ministers directly, circumventing existing constitutional and administrative channels of authority. The state extends generous budgetary support and fast-tracks most projects pursued by these agencies. Although prime ministerial representatives such as the cabinet secretary and the principal secretary sit on the governing boards of these agencies, in the absence of independently instituted monitoring bodies and the vast information asymmetries that prevail in technical settings, political oversight is limited. This remarkable degree of autonomy in India's otherwise over-regulated state has earned this group of agencies the title of "strategic enclave."[117]

Most observers of the "strategic enclave" agree that its unique institutional circumstance is responsible for many management-related project failures in the past. The DRDO in particular has acquired a reputation for being high on promises and low on delivery. High costs, time overruns and shoddy workmanship have characterized many of its ambitious defense projects among others such as the main battle tank (MBT) and the light combat aircraft (LCA) among others.[118] Political and civilian bureaucratic oversight of the DRDO is weak. As a senior defense official put it to the author, "the civilian defense research and development bureaucracy prioritizes ideological goals when conceptualizing and planning projects. They favor indigenization and self sufficiency and this is what the politicians love to hear...a situation made worse because the politicians largely rely on inputs from their civilian advisors and lack independent means to appraise programs."[119]

Nonetheless, the armed services as the end users typically play the role of the external monitoring agents. The services critique projects at the conception stage, issue general services quality requirements (GSQR), depute representatives to the labs, conduct field trials, and ultimately resist accepting weapon systems until performance issues are resolved. Prominent among examples of such successful interventions is the case of the navy's technical audit in the 1980s, which persuaded two prime ministers to kill three reactor designs prepared by BARC for the top-secret nuclear submarine project.[120] Thereafter, India sought Russian assistance in the design and integration of the submarine's nuclear power plant.[121] Similarly, the services' critique of the short-range air defense missile project, first launched as part of the IGMDP in the 1980s, led to its subsequent cancellation[122] and procurement of the Barak missile system from Israel instead.[123] Technical audits by the armed services have also forced DRDO to markedly improve its main battle tank and light combat aircraft prototypes.

However, secrecy and compartmentalized planning on nuclear weaponization precluded agent competition between DRDO and the air force. Between 1987 and 1990, as a senior air force official disclosed to the author, the DRDO did not share details concerning the "hardware" or "drawings" with the air force's testing establishment.[124] As a result, the "boffins" who developed the weapon, recalls another senior air force officer who served at the time, "developed it independently without reference to the delivery platform."[125] There was a problem with carriage because the weapon was too long."[126] This was cause for concern especially during the "rotation maneuver[127] during take-off stage. A skilled Mirage pilot could have pulled it off...but not just any pilot," a senior air force officer with a ringside view of the program told the author.[128] The "...size of the weapon itself, its length and weight upset the aerodynamics and center of gravity of the aircraft."[129]

After 1990, recalled another air force official, "the only details shared [with the air force] concerned the size and dimensions of the weapon container and its weight in general...so that DRDO would be assured that the bomb could be slung beneath the aircraft and there would be sufficient ground clearance. But no additional information was shared with the air force at this stage."[130] However, there were other aspects that needed resolution such as the aircraft's electronic interface and sighting systems to enable the arming and release of the weapon.[131] The electronic interface could not be reconfigured without what one air force officer described as access to the "manufacturer's database" and computer source codes. The aircraft also required extensive rewiring for electrical connectivity to enable the bomb's functions.[132] The Mirages India had acquired from France in the mid-1980s were not nuclear-certified. There were concerns that a post-detonation electromagnetic pulse (EMP) could interfere with the aircraft's computer-controlled fly-by-wire, communications and other electronic systems. According to one senior air force official, "...in the early 1990s, the air force was thinking of one-way missions...it was unlikely that the pilot deployed on a nuclear attack mission would have made it back."[133]

Prior to 1990, an air force officer explained, "DRDO thought they could do the project all by themselves...except that they needed an aircraft. But when DRDO couldn't manage or understand things, they came to the air force."[134] Eventually a team from the air force was roped into the project. Another air force officer from Air Headquarters disclosed that "the air force core team likely included a flight test engineer and three or four assistants, an air frame man, an electrical and electronics man, and a mechanical engineer... besides the test pilot. The DRDO would have had its own team...there are some tasks that DRDO could not have done without the air force." [135] Nevertheless, despite partial cooperation between the two agencies, the air force's test establishment was excluded from the certification process. As a result, the air force did not know the methodology DRDO used to certify the integration of the weapon with the delivery platform.

A senior air force officer who debriefed the test pilot involved in the DRDO's certification trials emphasized that the air force has a clear system for designing, developing and accepting weapon systems. It maintains a vast and varied test establishment with highly specialized and experienced personnel to integrate weapon systems with various platforms. However, in the case of the weaponization program, the air force could not adhere to its organizational rules. It was forced to "break rules" which from an end-user perspective is unacceptable. As he put it, "the need for secrecy is understandable as long nuclear weapons are treated as symbolic...but once requirements shift to operations, it is absurd to keep the user service on the sidelines." In his words,

> when I say I have a test establishment...it starts with a project engineer of a particular project, and this project engineer will work under a chief project officer who is a senior test engineer...so every project that this project engineer is doing, there is a project engineer on top...there is a parallel branch comprising of flight test engineers...each involved in the project...and everything they do is overseen by senior flight-test engineers...and there are test pilots doing projects working with these engineers. Senior test pilots and so forth oversee the test pilots themselves. So it is a team effort...and it is the experience of the entire system that is bearing down on the team. So you can certainly pick out individuals from these institutions...but you will not get the institutional backing...the institutional strength. I as a test pilot can do nothing unless I have access to the test establishment's computer databanks and engineers.[136]

Until 1994, DRDO conducted experimental modifications on just one Mirage 2000 with a single test pilot. There was no backup.[137] But even after that date the internal feedback Air Headquarters received from its "boys" was that the plane's modified systems had not achieved the degree of reliability considered *de rigueur* for performing sensitive nuclear missions.[138] The whole project, senior air force officers claim, would have been better executed if the service had been involved in the planning from the beginning to the end. An observer of the DRDO's certification of the air platform asserted that there was a "hand hammered quality" to the aircraft that were modified for nuclear missions. There were several failures. But with passage of time and some introspection, the system was further refined. However, there were "limitations" in the final product. It was "less capable, less reliable, and generated less confidence."[139]

This same individual with insider knowledge of the program volunteered to the author that "...the conceptualization of any weapon system must be based on ground reality requirements...you don't create weapons and platforms in isolation...[they] must be based on quality requirements of the user service. The political climate must also be very clear...can the weapon that is being developed be used? And if not...why was it developed? The scientists and weapons development agency might have a good idea...but to transform it into a usable weapon...the user must be in the loop...must have a total picture."[140]

Politicians, he continued, "get carried away by stories of India's apparent progress...stories that make banner headlines...but they lack the expertise and time" to appraise technical details.[141] Hence the appraisal process devolves upon senior civil servants. In the case of weaponization, even that process was "hijacked" by DRDO and BARC. The politicians relied on a civilian nuclear coordinator to keep a tab on the scientific agencies. However, in the absence of independent review boards and auditing processes, civilians received no independent feedback. Only the "end-users can provide independent feedback...but their inputs were not sought."[142]

The lack of agent competition between the scientific agencies and the military also stymied the process of operational planning once weapons became available. Without doubt, the fear of US sanctions was the major cause for the political paralysis on this front. Senior military leaders who spoke to the author were unanimous that neither the scientists nor the political decision-makers understood the complexities of operational planning. In the case of conventional war planning, for example, the military has acquired almost exclusive monopoly over operational plans due to the lack of civilian bureaucratic expertise. Civilians tend to set political goals and leave it to the services to work out the logistics of operations.[143] However, in the nuclear domain, the military's direct lack of access to political decision-makers and limited technical knowledge of the nuclear weaponization project created institutional blocks where it was unable to disabuse them of the simplistic belief that the technical capacity to deliver weapons was roughly tantamount to an operational capacity.

Former DRDO Chief V.S. Arunachalam summed up the scientific agencies' technical understanding of operational readiness to the author by arguing,

> If you are saying that the air force didn't have the aircrafts ready...then you are wrong. This is not a situation where we say: we are going to use a nuclear weapon...get an aircraft ready...so that it can carry it...make it ready so that it can withstand the EMPs...nothing of the kind. It's ok... now I get ready...now it can take it on the wings or it can take it on the fuselage...nothing of the kind. I am sure that there was a reasonable amount of information that had been worked through...no pilot would have carried the weapon without knowing what he was carrying. No pilot would have gone there without knowing how to drop it...how to fuse it.[144]

For the air force planners however, weapon delivery and pilot training were only the tip of the spear. To bring that spear tip into action, the resolution of three other conditions was necessary. The first consisted of procedures to coordinate action among the scientific and user agencies. To this category belong timelines for the movement of aircraft, the identification of weapon storage sites, the training of ground crew in weapon storage, weapon movement and loading procedures. Other routines would concern safety and security checks on the aircraft and the weapon. As one senior air force planner explained to the author:

> The pilot learns how to handle the weapon, and its impact on the platform during flight...vibration characteristics etc. It's fine to give the air force dummy weapons to train with. We are now talking about pilots

being trained to handle the weapon system in flight, the ground crew being fully trained to handle the weapon on the ground...the safety standards have to be very high. All instructions have to be written down precisely. Where do you arm the aircraft? You have to arm the aircraft in relative isolation...because if you have an accidental explosion, you don't just lose one aircraft, but you lose 20 aircraft...these are all practices that have evolved over the years...especially on how to handle weapon systems...[145]

In the second category would come target identification and mission planning. Geography, meteorology, demography and cultural factors all go into target selection, a political decision. Among other things, the air force would have to identify air bases for potential deployments, and experiment with combinations of electronic jamming and escort aircraft for different mission targets. It would also have to plan decoy missions to divert attention and increase the chances of penetrating a heavily defended airspace in a country on high alert in anticipation of a second strike. For example, an Indian Air Force study conducted in the early 2000s highlighted the logistical challenges of planning nuclear missions against Pakistan. It showed that a single mission alone could possibly tie up as many as 60 aircraft to assist the penetrating nuclear vectors.[146]

In the third category are pilot communications protocols to abort missions due to geostrategic changes and technical emergencies, as well as procedures for weapon jettisoning and retrieval in the event of an accident or flight diversion. Also included in this category would be protocols to fuse and arm the weapon in the time just before release over a target to minimize the risk of explosion over friendly territory or off-target.[147] Senior Indian air force officers point to three major challenges of nuclear mission planning that were left unaddressed prior to 1999. First, a nuclear mission would have involved a "nap-of-the-earth" flight profile. During such missions attacking aircraft typically hug the ground to escape detection by enemy radar. But the Indian Mirages at the time were not equipped with terrain clearance radars.[148] Hence targets and mission routes would need careful identification and mapping in advance. However, no target lists were provided to the air force.[149] Second, real-time communications are difficult when combat aircraft execute "nap-of-the-earth" flight profiles because the earth's curvature renders the aircraft invisible to both enemy and friendly radar. Advanced air forces typically overcome the problem of command and control by communicating with pilots via satellite or airborne surveillance and command posts perched at high altitudes. Since India lacked both at the time, it would have had to rely on relay aircraft to keep the political leadership in constant touch with the pilot during the length of a nuclear mission. However, the use of relay aircraft complicates logistics and mission planning.

More problematic, the process would require written procedures to enable all parties share a common understanding of what those procedures are.

If such procedures existed at all prior to 1999, the air force did not know them.[150] Third, prior to 1999, the air force did not know who possessed the codes for arming nuclear weapons and how those codes were to be deployed during a mission. Indian weapons at this time did not incorporate permissive action links (PAL) that would permit arming the weapons at will. The assumption in the air force was that the task of arming the weapon would fall on the pilot at a designated time during flight. However, the air force and the scientific agencies did not conduct practice drills to test the communications and weapon arming protocols during a potential nuclear mission.[151]

A number of senior air force officials, including those who served at the highest levels, are unanimous in their account that operational plans and procedures to execute nuclear missions are a post-1998 phenomenon. They concede that civilian officials and the scientific agencies had likely thought through some of these issues prior but did not share them with the air force. For example, Arunachalam insisted to the author:

> …yes…yes…call it the 'Red' book or 'Blue' book…or something…they were clear…at no time a weapon was orphaned out…the weapon systems came with detailed instructions…when to use it, where to use it, how to use it…and all this would have been determined at the prime ministerial level…[152]

However, a senior air force official who served during the 1990s recalls querying Naresh Chandra, the government's coordinator on nuclear planning since 1989, on some of the mission planning procedures. But Chandra, claims the official, "behaved like the typical bureaucrat…he sat like a frog…maintained silence…remaining in an information denial mode."[153] Nor was the air force given tasking orders to prepare internal procedures to program its own response to a nuclear emergency. Arunachalam's view was "…the numbers are so small…the system could be beautifully worked out…"[154] But a principal staff officer at Air Headquarters estimated the chances of mission success in the first half of the decade "at less than 50 percent."[155] Another senior air force officer from the 1990s who participated in the air delivery platform's certification trials and demitted office in the latter half of the 1990s, demurred from even speculating on the probability of mission success. According to him, nuclear missions were the "nightmare scenario" because so little was "…shown to the air force on the ground."[156]

Conclusion

What all this data tells us is that India's capacity to explode a nuclear weapon during the 1990s was not in doubt. However, its institutional capacity to explode nuclear weapons instrumentally over a target in pursuit of political goals remained very much so. Between 1989 and 1999, Indian decision-makers responded to structural pressures and ordered the building of nuclear weapons. But they did not seek to embed those weapons inside organizational and procedural frameworks that would give them operational significance. In the process they opened a vast operational gap, which left the Indian state vulnerable.

India's case provides a window to observe some of the technical, institutional, organizational and procedural challenges of developing operational capabilities in secrecy. Its takeaway point is that a state may be generally good at adapting to environmental pressures. But a state may be simultaneously weak at organizational learning, something that Neorealism takes for granted. Adaptation means tactical adjustments to environmental pressures without an overarching alignment between means and ends. Learning instead implies strategic changes in the ways states apply themselves to problems and seek solutions. The Neorealist assumption that substantial changes in institutional and organizational thinking automatically follow in the wake of technological breakthroughs is therefore questionable.

The other takeaway point of this chapter is that rational decisions, which structural theories assume, are difficult in highly restricted and monopolistic decision-making environments. Problem decomposition, parallel processing and institutional oversight are the precursors for optimization. But this is precisely what decision-makers in the executive cone of proliferating states strive to avoid. Their primary reason for this avoidance behavior is to escape the hostile scrutiny of the nonproliferation regime. However, the price of secrecy is suboptimality. As with firms in the marketplace, decision-makers and states cannot learn without rapid information turnover, "truth tests," the "wisdom of the crowds" logic of multiple agency scrutiny and structured thinking. Indeed, the Indian decision-makers' non-systemized nuclear decision-making, as this chapter process traces at considerable length, is a testimonial to these theoretical findings.

The empirical evidence in this chapter also undermines the moral and cultural explanations that are advanced to explain India's nuclear restraint between 1988 and 1998. It is evident that Indian prime ministers during the 1990s followed a Janus-faced strategy that coupled moralism with an insurance strategy of allowing work on the weapons program to proceed. At least three among six prime ministers during this period, V.P. Singh, Narasimha Rao and Deve Gowda cited economic and not moral reasons for not making India's nuclear capabilities overt. The historical evidence thus shows variation between decision makers' public statements and private actions. The related argument that a unique Indian strategic culture and normative understanding of nuclear weapons as symbolic instruments was the source for operational restraint during the 1990s is also disabused by data on the exacting efforts made by India's research and development agencies and military to perfect the technics of delivery. Finally, a nuanced reading of the data shows that secrecy borne out of fear of economic sanctions and not institutional distrust between civilian and military authorities was the cause for restricted information sharing between the scientific civilian agencies tasked with weapons development and the military agency tasked with operational use.

Notes

1 A version of this chapter appeared in *International Security* in spring 2014. Gaurav Kampani, "New Delhi's Long Nuclear Journey: How Secrecy and Institutional Roadblocks Delayed India's Weaponization," *International Security*, Vol. 28, No. 4 (Spring 2014), pp. 79–114.
2 Perkovich, *India's Nuclear Bomb*, p. 293.
3 George H. Quester, "Nuclear Pakistan and Nuclear India: Stable Deterrent or Proliferation Challenge," *Strategic Studies Institute* (Carlisle: US Army War College, 1992), pp. 5, 7–10.
4 Perkovich, *India's Nuclear Bomb*, p. 295.
5 Leonard Spector with Jacqueline R. Smith, *Nuclear Ambitions: The Spread of Nuclear Weapons 1989–1990* (Boulder: Westview Press, 1990), p. 79.
6 Steve Coll, "South Asia Retains Its Nuclear Option: India and Pakistan Post Dual Risk as Potential Flash Points," *Washington Post* (Washington, DC), September 30, 1991, p. A1.
7 The Kashmir Crisis between India and Pakistan erupted during the winter of 1989 and dissipated by the end of spring 1990. The trigger for the crisis was a domestic insurgency in Indian-administered Kashmir, which broke out in the winter of 1989. Pakistani military and intelligence services gave material and moral support to Kashmiri insurgents on the model of the Afghan insurgency against the Soviets in the 1980s, though on a far lesser scale. In January 1990, the Pakistani foreign minister Shahabzada Yakub Khan traveled to Delhi and delivered what Indian political leaders perceived as a veiled nuclear threat. The crisis was ultimately defused with the help of American diplomatic intervention. But during the crisis, the US believed that Pakistan may have assembled and possibly deployed a nuclear weapon. See, *The Kargil Review Committee Report*, pp. 65, 204; P.R. Chari, Pervaiz Iqbal Cheema and Stephen P. Cohen, *The Compound Crisis of 1990: Perception, Politics and Insecurity* (London: Routledge, 2003); Seymour M. Hersh, "On the Nuclear Edge," *New Yorker* (March 29, 1993), http://www.newyorker.com/archive/1993/03/29/1993_03_29_056_TNY_CARDS_000363214 (July 2012); Robert Burrows and Robert Winderm, *Critical Mass: The Dangerous Race for Superweapons in a Fragmenting World* (New York: Simon & Schuster, 1994).
8 James Adams, "Pakistan Nuclear War Threat," *Sunday Times* (London), May 27, 1990, p. 1.
9 Michael R. Gordon, "South Asian Lands Pressed on Nuclear Arms," *New York Times* (New York), March 23, 1994, p. 5.
10 R. James Woolsey, testimony before the US Senate Committee on Governmental Affairs, *Proliferation Threats of the 1990s: Hearing before the Committee on Governmental Affairs: United States Senate*, 102nd Cong., 1st Sess. (Washington, DC: US Government Printing Office, February 24, 1993), pp. 14–15.
11 George Perkovich, "A Nuclear Third Way in South Asia," *Foreign Policy*, No. 91 (Summer 1993), pp. 96–98.
12 Perkovich, "A Nuclear Third Way in South Asia," pp. 102–104.
13 Ibid., p. 90.
14 Rosalind Reynolds, "The Diplomatic Role of Non-Weaponized Programs," *INSS Occasional Paper 7*, Proliferation Series, USAF Institute for National Security Studies (January 1996), https://www.fas.org/irp/threat/ocp7.htm (November 2012).

15 Jasjit Singh, "A Nuclear Strategy for India," in Jasjit Singh ed., *Nuclear India*, pp. 310–311.
16 The concept of "recessed deterrence" shares similarities with Cohen and Frankel's definition of "nuclear opacity." In a regime of opacity, emerging nuclear powers compartmentalize the nuclear weapon program within the state. The also maintain strict internal secrecy. However, the difference between these two concepts lies in their motivational drivers. In opacity, the causal driver is a commitment to nonproliferation norms.
17 According to Scientific Advisor to the Defense Minister APJ Abdul Kalam's testimony before the Kargil Review Committee, weaponization was completed during 1992–1994. The records of this and other conversations pertaining to India's nuclear weapons program from the early 1980s until 1998 are contained in the annexure to the report, which has not been declassified. See, *The Kargil Review Committee Report*, p. 205. The author's interviews with several senior retired Indian Air Force officers at the highest levels suggest that India achieved an air deliverable capability sometime in 1995–1996; also see Chengappa, *Weapons of Peace*, pp. 382–383.
18 Chengappa, *Weapons of Peace*, pp. 332–333.
19 Ibid., p. 406.
20 The Kargil War between India and Pakistan was triggered by the latter's incursion and occupation of mountain ridgelines on the Indian side of the line of control (LoC) in Kashmir. The war lasted between May and July 1999 and ended with a Pakistani withdrawal from all positions on the Indian side of the LoC. See, Jasjit Singh ed., *Kargil 1999: Pakistan's Fourth War for Kashmir* (New Delhi: South Asia Books, 1999); Peter R. Lavoy ed., *Asymmetric Warfare in South Asia: The Causes and Consequences of the Kargil Conflict* (Cambridge: Cambridge University Press, 2009).
21 Interviews with senior Indian defense official (retd.) "X," New Delhi, India, October and November 2009.
22 *Kargil Review Committee Report*, pp. 187–189.
23 Ibid., pp. 187–193.
24 Deshmukh, *From Poona to the Prime Minister's Office*, pp. 170–171.
25 Interview with Arunachalam; interview with K. Santhanam, Chief Technology Advisor to Science Advisor to Defense Minister (retd.), New Delhi, India, May 2009.
26 Interviews with senior air force officer (retd.) "S," New Delhi, India, December 2009 and January 2010.
27 Interviews with Air Marshal (retd.) "N."
28 Chengappa, *Weapons of Peace*, p. 304.
29 Ibid., p. 335.
30 Ibid.
31 Ibid., pp. 332–333.
32 Deshmukh, *From Poona to the Prime Minister's Office*, p. 171.
33 Interview with Arunachalam.
34 Interviews with Ambassador (retd.) Naresh Chandra, New Delhi, India, October and November 2009.
35 Ibid.
36 Ibid.
37 Interviews with Chandra; Interview with Brajesh Mishra, National Security Advisor/Principal Secretary to Prime Minister (1998–2004), New Delhi, India, October 2009.
38 Chengappa, *Weapons of Peace*, pp. 294–295.
39 Ibid., 299–302; Perkovich, *India's Nuclear Bomb*, pp. 273–276.
40 Perkovich, *India's Nuclear Bomb*, p. 275.

41 Chengappa, *Weapons of Peace*, pp. 253–255.
42 Deshmukh, *From Poona to the Prime Minister's Office*, pp. 164–167.
43 Ibid.
44 Interview with Arunachalam.
45 Interviews with Chandra.
46 Interviews with Subrahmanyam.
47 Interviews with Chandra.
48 Ibid.
49 Interview with senior air force officer (retd.) "S."
50 Interview with Air Chief Marshal (retd.) S.K. Sareen, Chief of Air Staff (1995–1998), Gurgaon, India, January 2010.
51 Interview with Air Chief Marshal (retd.) "O," Chief of Air Staff, New Delhi, India, December 2009.
52 Interview with Iyengar.
53 Interview with senior army officer "Q," NBC Warfare Directorate: Army Headquarters, New Delhi, India, May 2009.
54 Interviews with Subrahmanyam.
55 Ibid.
56 Admiral (retd.) Arun Prakash, "9 Minutes to Midnight," *Force* (July 2012), p. 4.
57 Interviews with senior Indian defense official (retd.) "X."
58 Perkovich, *India's Nuclear Bomb*, pp. 313–314.
59 Interviews with Subrahmanyam.
60 Perkovich, *India's Nuclear Bomb*, p. 313.
61 Chengappa, *Weapons of Peace,* p. 391.
62 Interviews with Senior Indian defense official (retd.) "X."
63 For career trajectories of these officials see, Chengappa, *Weapons of Peace*.
64 Deshmukh, *From Poona to the Prime Minister's Office,* p. 171; Chengappa, *Weapons of Peace,* p. 335.
65 Interview with Air Chief Marshal (retd.) "O."
66 Interviews with senior Indian Air Force officer (retd.) "Z," New Delhi, India, December 2009 and January/February 2010.
67 Interview with Arunachalam.
68 Hansen, *U.S. Nuclear Weapons,* p. 13.
69 Ibid., p. 17.
70 Subrahmanyam, "Indian Nuclear Policy," in Subrahmanyam and Monteiro, *Shedding Shibboleths,* p. 44.
71 Chengappa, *Weapons of Peace*, p. 354.
72 Ibid.
73 Perkovich, *India's Nuclear Bomb*, p. 305; Gupta, "Know What They Did That Summer."
74 Gupta, "Know What They Did That Summer."
75 India began developing the short-range Prithvi ballistic missile as part of the Integrated Guided Missile Program (IGMDP) in 1983. The maiden launch of the missile occurred in 1987. Flight trials or the Prithvi continued until the late 1990s. There is evidence to suggest that Indian defense agencies were able to modify warheads for ballistic missile delivery by 1996–1997. However, it is uncertain if the systems met operational standards of reliability and safety. According to a former C-in-C, Strategic Forces Command, who spoke to the author on the condition of anonymity, even as late as 2003–2004 combat aircraft were the most flexible and reliable nuclear delivery systems India possessed. Interview with C-in-C, SFC, "P," New Delhi, India, April 2009; also see, Chengappa, *Weapons of Peace,* p. 418
76 Interview with Air Chief Marshal (retd.) "O."

77 Chengappa, *Weapons of Peace*, pp. 353–356.
78 Ibid., pp. 354–355.
79 Ibid.
80 The Bhabha Atomic Research Centre (BARC) is India's premier nuclear weapons research, design and development agency.
81 Chengappa, *Weapons of Peace*, p. 356.
82 Interviews with Subrahmanyam.
83 Ibid.
84 The Cabinet Committee on Security (CCS) comprised of the ministers of external affairs, defense, home, and finance.
85 Interviews with senior Indian defense official (retd.) "X."
86 Ibid.
87 Ibid.
88 Interviews with senior Indian Air Force officer (retd.) "Z."
89 Ibid.
90 Interviews with senior Indian defense official (retd.) "X."
91 The three prime ministers were Chandra Shekhar, I.K. Gujral and H.D. Deve Gowda. Interviews with Arunachalam and senior defense official (retd.) "X."
92 Perkovich, *India's Nuclear Bomb*, p. 377.
93 Interviews with senior defense official (retd.) "X."
94 Interviews with Naresh Chandra.
95 Ibid.
96 Ibid.
97 Interview with Satish Chandra, Deputy National Security Advisor (1999–2005), New Delhi, India, May 2009.
98 Perkovich, "A Nuclear Third Way in South Asia," pp. 85–104.
99 For examples see speech by John M. Deutch, Director CIA, "Proliferation is Key Security Challenge for US and Allies," December 14, 1995; retrieved from *Federation of American Scientists,* http://www.fas.org/irp/threat/951027_dci.htm (May 2012).
100 National Security Council (1993), *Report to Congress on Status of China, India and Pakistan Nuclear and Ballistic Missile Programs* (F94-1392) (Washington, DC); retrieved from http://www.fas.org/irp/threat/930728-wmd.htm (May 2012).
101 Office of the Secretary of Defense (April 1996), *Proliferation Threat and Response* (Washington, DC); retrieved from http://www.fas.org/irp/threat/prolif96/ (May 2012).
102 Devin Hagerty, "Nuclear Deterrence in South Asia: The 1990 Indo-Pakistani Crisis," *International Security,* Vol. 20, No. 3 (Winter 1995/1996), pp. 79–114.
103 Gilovich and Griffin, "Introduction – Heuristics and Biases: Then and Now," pp. 2–3.
104 Perkovich, *India's Nuclear Bomb*, pp. 190–225.
105 See M.V. Ramana, *The Indian Nuclear Industry: Status and Prospects*, Nuclear Energy Futures: Paper No. 9 (Waterloo: The Center for International Governance Innovation, 2009), http://princeton.academia.edu/MVRamana/Papers/405419/Indian_Nuclear_Industry_Status_and_Prospects (May 2012).
106 Richard H. Speier, Brian G. Chow and S. Rae Starr, *Nonproliferation Sanctions* (Santa Monica: Rand, 2001), pp. 12–13.
107 Ibid.
108 Perkovich, *India's Nuclear Bomb*, pp. 190–225.
109 Interview with Satish Chandra.
110 Subrahmanyam, "India's Nuclear Quest," p. 142.
111 Or Rabinowitz, *Bargaining on Nuclear Tests: Washington and Its Cold War Rivals* (Oxford University Press, 2014).

112 Subrahmanyam, "Nuclear Realities," in Subrahmanyam with Monteiro, *Shedding Shibboleths*, pp. 94–107; also see, Maria Zaitseva, *When Allies Go Nuclear: The Changing Nature of the American Response to 'Friendly' Nuclear Programs*, PhD Dissertation (Ithaca: Cornell University, 2011).
113 Subrahmanyam, "India's Nuclear Quest," pp. 138–140.
114 Speier, Chow and Starr, *Nonproliferation Sanctions*, pp. 16–23.
115 Ibid., pp. 23–29, 35–52.
116 Interview with Mishra.
117 Abraham, "India's Strategic Enclave: Civilian Scientists & Military Technologies," pp. 231–252.
118 "Arjun Main Battle Tank," *Government of India Press Release*, May 5, 2008, http://pib.nic.in/newsite/erelease.aspx?relid=38445 (May 2013); Ajai Shukla, "Armed Forces Prefer Russian Armor," *Business Standard* (April 19, 2008), http://web.archive.org/web/20110607132933/http://www.business-standard.com/india/storypage.php?autono=320574 (May 2013); Manu Pubby, "Arjun Tank Fails Winter Trials, Army Chief Writes to Antony," *Indian Express* (April 17, 2008), http://www.indianexpress.com/news/arjun-tank-fails-winter-trials-army-chief-writes-to-antony/297768/ (May, 2013); Amitav Ranjan, "Arjun, Main Battle Tanked," *Indian Express* (November 27, 2006), http://www.indianexpress.com/news/arjun-main-battle-tanked/16589/1 (May 2013); "Perform or Perish: Antony Tells DRDO," *Zee News.com* (May 29, 2013), http://zeenews.india.com/news/nation/perform-or-perish-antony-tells-drdo_851697.html (May 2013); "Don't Extend Tejas Deadline, Antony Tells DRDO," *Zee News.com* (March 24, 2013), http://zeenews.india.com/news/nation/don-t-extend-tejas-deadline-antony-tells-drdo_837460.html (May 2013).
119 Interview with senior Indian defense official (retd.) "F," New Delhi, India, December 2009.
120 "Victimized By the Official Secrets Act: The Story of Dr. B.K. Subbarao," *Manushi* Issue 108, http://www.indiatogether.org/manushi/issue108/subbprof.htm (May 2013).
121 Rear Admiral (retd.) A.P. Revi, "Arihant: The Annihilator," *Indian Defense Review*, Vol. 24, No. 4 (October-December 2009), http://www.indiandefencereview.com/spotlights/arihant-the-annihilator (May 2013).
122 "India Shuts Down Trishul Missile Project," *Rediff on the Net* (February 27, 2008), http://www.rediff.com/news/2008/feb/27trishul.htm (May 2013).
123 "India and Israel's Barak SAM Development Project(s)," *Defense Industry Daily* (January 24, 2013), http://www.defenseindustrydaily.com/india-israel-introducing-mr-sam-03461/ (May 2013).
124 Interview with senior Indian Air Force officer (retd.) "M," New Delhi, India, December 2009.
125 Interviews with senior Indian Air Force officer (retd.) "Z."
126 Ibid.
127 Rotation maneuver is the formal term for aircraft liftoff from the runway. If executed improperly, it can cause the aircraft's tail to strike the runway. If the weapons slung beneath a combat aircraft are too large or long, they can strike the runway during take off and cause an accident. According to a senior Indian air force official, the casing of the bomb first flight tested in the early 1990s was so long that the distance between the tail of the bomb and ground clearance was a mere a "three inches." Interviews with Air Marshal (retd.) "N."
128 Ibid.
129 Interviews with senior Indian Air Force officer (retd.) "S."
130 Interview with senior Indian Air Force officer (retd.) "L," New Delhi, India, December 2009.

131 Ibid.
132 Interviews with senior Indian Air Force officer (retd.) "Z."
133 Interviews with senior Indian Air Force officer (retd.) "S."
134 Ibid.
135 Interview with Air Marshal (retd.) "K," New Delhi, India, July 2010.
136 Interview with senior Indian Air Force officer (retd.) "M."
137 Interviews with senior Indian Air Force officer (retd.) "Z."
138 Ibid.
139 Ibid.
140 Ibid.
141 Ibid.
142 Ibid.
143 Srinath Raghavan, "Soldiers, Statesmen and India's Security Policy," *India Review,* Vol. 11, No. 2 (May 2012), pp. 116–133.
144 Interview with Arunachalam.
145 Interview with senior Indian air force officer (retd.) "M."
146 For example, a typical nuclear task force would include two nuclear-armed aircraft, three to four electronic counter measures escort aircraft, another three to four aircraft for air defense, and a similar number to suppress enemy ground defenses. A single mission would comprise 15–20 aircraft and at least two or three decoy missions would be planned simultaneously. See, Pravin Sawhney, "Bombed," *Force* (February 2004), p. 8.
147 Interviews with senior Indian defense official (retd.) "'A," New Delhi, July and August 2010.
148 Interviews with Air Marshal (retd.) "N."
149 Interviews with senior Indian defense official (retd.) "A."
150 Interviews with Air Marshal (retd.) Ajit Bhavnani, C-in-C, Strategic Forces Command (2004–2005), New Delhi, India, April 2009 and February 2010.
151 Ibid.
152 Interview with Arunachalam.
153 Interview with senior Indian defense official (retd.) "F."
154 Interview with Arunachalam.
155 Interviews with Air Marshal (retd.) "N."
156 Interviews with senior Indian Air Force officer (retd.) "Z."

5 The challenges of nuclear operationalization (1999–2010)

Post-1998, Indian decision-makers have become more socialized into the operational logic and practices of nuclear deterrence. The reasons for this have to do with the following: (a) the strength of nuclear epistemic actors' institutionalization within the state; (b) the increased openness of the state's decision-making structure; and (c) greater inter-agent competition, especially within the scientific community and between the scientific community and the military. All three developments are related to decision-makers' formal commitments to transforming India's nuclear capabilities into a realizable force on the ground. The latter goal, particularly the commitment to transform symbolic into operable forces, has forced political principals to expand the mobilization of India's nuclear epistemic actors as well as to institutionalize them in the form of the military's Strategic Forces Command (SFC) and the Strategic Program Staff (SPS) to manage and oversee the nuclear force.

The end of the internal regime of nuclear opacity has also begun to transform the pre-1998 organizational pattern of nuclear decision-making within the state. The earlier pattern prized compartmentalization and disaggregation of information. These organizational conditions aggravated the scope for heuristics and cognitive biases in decision-making. Nuclear decision-making in India still remains secret and compartmentalized. Yet, the new structures and institutions of decision-making incorporate more lateral information sharing, institutionalized review processes, and inter-agent competition. Also visible are the first shoots of independent referee institutions capable of overseeing "truth tests" by rival claimants of knowledge. These processes have partially injected a semi "wisdom of the crowds" logic into the decision-making process producing outcomes that are more rational and optimal.

The process of formal socialization and institutionalization, however, only began to take shape in the mid-2000s. Between 1998 and 2004, the time it took for India to normalize its status as a nuclear weapons power, Indian decision-makers retained most of the legacy institutions and practices of the past: weakly institutionalized epistemic networks, compartmentalized information, the absence of review processes, and minimal agent competition. For these reasons, until at least 2004, there was a considerable slack in the operationalization of the Indian nuclear force. Many informal decisions made in the first half of the decade stemmed from the absence of structured thinking. These decisions, insofar as force lethality is concerned, have produced a negative path–dependent lock in effect. Little further optimization is possible on the latter end short of completely overturning the status quo.

From the mid-2000s, the military's institutionalization in operational planning coupled with more structured decision-making in the PMO, especially in the aftermath of the institution of the SPS, have helped streamline intra- and inter-agency coordination. Standard operating procedures and routines to manage the nuclear force have taken root. Technical controversies pertaining to the nuclear force are now partially subject to an inter-agency review process. Likewise, an inter-agency SPS now oversees long-term planning of the nuclear force pertaining to force structure and acquisitions. It also provides independent advice to India's National Command Authority (NCA) on technical issues and subjects ranging from arms control, disarmament, technology controls, nonproliferation or any other nuclear force related subject deemed significant by the NCA. These institutional changes have had a net positive effect on India's operational posture.

No doubt, there are many technical and institutional anomalies that remain unresolved. The late institutionalization of the SFC has meant that it has to compete against legacy institutions such as the scientific agencies, which have historically controlled the nuclear weapons program. The military's feeble epistemic base in technical nuclear matters, itself an institutional legacy of the past secrecy and compartmentalization, limits the degree of independent oversight that it can immediately exercise over its scientific counterparts. Nonetheless, the military has succeeded in increasing India's operational readiness. It has forced internal debates on nuclear use doctrine[1] and persuaded political principals to initiate the process of changing India's "negative" command-and-control institutions based on organizational divisions to "positive" ones that rely on technology and procedures. Cumulatively, these amount to a slow but tectonic shift in India's approach to nuclear operations.

Likewise, the institution of the SPS represents the first serious attempt by India's leadership toward the creation of a nuclear "system" to ensure that various parts of the arsenal function in a coordinated manner. The SPS serves as an oversight mechanism. It provides India's NCA independent feedback on the SFC and the scientific agencies developing various weapon systems. But it is also a closed and self-referential system albeit with lesser secrecy constraints on internal information sharing than the one that prevailed on policy planners during the former regime of opacity. As with any closed system, the inability of decision-makers to refer to outside sources for information and knowledge imposes structural constraints on learning. Senior Indian national security managers at the highest levels understand this dilemma. Their hope remains, however, that the system will mature over time and become capable of organic growth in response to challenges.[2]

In this chapter, I compare the process of an operationally centric nuclear epistemic community's institutionalization within the state between the first and second halves of the decade 2000–2010. I present evidence to show that weak institutionalization of new epistemic actors and monopolistic decision-making processes in the first half of the decade produced suboptimal outcomes, whose effects are now almost irreversible. These outcomes were the path-dependent legacy effects of the past and not the consequence of prestige-seeking, arms-control norms, or civil-military distrust. Changes in the state's institutional and organizational practices in the second half of the decade have produced operational outcomes that not only bespeak of organizational learning but also disabuse scholarship that pronounced India as unlikely to develop operational nuclear forces. I finally conclude by offering an assessment of the effects of the stronger institutionalization of epistemic actors, structured decision-making and agent competition on India's current operational nuclear posture.

Deepening institutionalization of new epistemic actors and learning

India's decision to claim formal nuclear status in 1998 punctured the regime of internal secrecy. It was the stringent demands of secrecy that prevented Indian decision-makers in the 1990s from broadening the program's focus from narrow technical aspects to operational ones. The new political freedom from secrecy enabled the transplanting of an erstwhile technical program into a more fertile soil of institutions, organizations and procedures that gave substance to operationalization.[3] This new set of "expanding" and "interconnected" goals in turn generated demands for a wider mobilization of the epistemic actors: the strategic analysts, the civilian bureaucrats, the military and independent oversight bodies. Above all, it created the context for political principals' to institutionalize the military's role in nuclear policy development and operational planning.

Initiatives for institutional reforms came in the form of the 1999 Kargil Committee Report,[4] and subsequently the Group of Ministers (GoM) report in 2000.[5] Both proposed reforms in national security planning, intelligence collection and collation, and joint operations among the armed services. They also recommended a significant realignment in civil-military relations and addressed the operationalization of India's fledgling nuclear force.[6]

However, political decision-makers gave preference to the immediate political goal of India's gaining international acceptance as a normal nuclear power, particularly negotiations to normalize India's nuclear status with the United States. They did not prioritize nuclear operational planning. As a consequence, it was not until 2003–2004 that the military gained institutional authority in nuclear force planning and management alongside the scientific agencies.[7] Further, as is often the case with the inception of new institutions, the military's imprint on force management took time to cement.

In the aftermath of the 1998 nuclear test-series, India's national security managers were primarily concerned with addressing the question of New Delhi's role in the post–Cold War world order. As India's then NSA Brajesh Mishra recalls, he was most affected by the Soviet Union's collapse in the early 1990s, the absence of any specific role for India in the new US-led global order and the Indian economy's structural weaknesses in staking India's nuclear claims. As he put it, the "the new world order...India's defense and economic security...these were the three things on my mind...the justification for the tests, whatever you want to call it...is this."[8] Thus Mishra and Foreign Minister Jaswant Singh devoted most of their attention to managing the fall-out of the nuclear tests, India's relationship with the United States and other great powers, and seeking an end to the sanctions regime.[9]

Between 1998 and the outbreak of the Kargil War in 1999, the NSA and his team in the PMO did not apply themselves to addressing the challenges of operational planning either. They brought with them a political understanding of nuclear weapons and gave insufficient attention to the military's attempts to jumpstart the operational process. The latter process, in their mind, would be sequential. It would follow the resolution of political challenges that consumed the decision-makers' immediate attention.

Within months of India declaring itself a nuclear weapon state in 1998 for example, the Chairman Chiefs of Staff Committee (CCoSC) General Ved Malik proposed the creation of a tri-service command, the National Strategic Nuclear Command, to centralize the "custodial, maintenance and training responsibilities" of India's nuclear forces.[10] However, the government did not act on the proposal. Mishra later explained: "It is always in every country... that the armed forces want to get involved in decision-making etc. etc., even on matters that are strictly political...as far as decision-making is concerned... even there they want to participate... we were very clear about a strict division...that they won't interfere in this process."[11] Nuclear planning therefore remained in the pre-1998 groove, confined to a small network of scientists and bureaucrats.

Which is why when the Kargil War broke out in the summer of 1999, and the spotlight turned to the nuclear issue, the government scrambled to get tactical operational planning with the air force off the ground. A senior Indian defense official privy to this effort disclosed to the author that until then, the air force had no idea (a) what types of weapons were available; (b) in how many numbers; and (c) what it was expected to do with the weapons. All the air force had was delivery capability in the form of a few modified Mirage 2000s. At that point, only the air chief, the vice air chief and two other individuals at Air Headquarters had knowledge of the program.[12] The official went on:

> My educated guess is that a directive to bring the military in the loop may have been issued by the prime minister's office. However, given that nuclear decision making until then was confined to the prime minister

and a small set of officials in BARC and DRDO, the directive may have languished. Or alternatively, the prime minister and his top aides may have been told that the air force was in the know...without their understanding that tactical operational planning requires information sharing, coordination, and planning on an entirely different level. Politicians sometimes focus on the big picture and don't pay sufficient attention to details...[13]

But neither the Kargil episode nor the near war with Pakistan in 2001–2002 prodded senior policy planners into rushing institutional changes. For example, the Arun Singh task force on higher defense management, "Task Force on Management of Defense," completed its report in September 2000. It was submitted to the government as part of the final GoM recommendations on "Reforming the National Security System" in February 2001.[14] Some of the key reforms proposed by the task force concerned reforming the Chiefs of Staff Committee (CoSC), the creation of an Integrated Defense Staff (IDS) and within it the SFC to manage nuclear operations. These recommendations were central to reforming India's higher defense management and creating organizational structures to render the nuclear force operational.

India's higher defense management has historically suffered from the absence of unity of command as well as the lack of joint planning and operations among the three armed services. Each service enjoys substantial autonomy in weapons procurement, doctrine development and operations planning. The sole coordination mechanism between the services is the CoSC, which consists of the three serving chiefs. The senior-most service chief among them serves as the chairman, Chiefs of Staff Committee (CCoSC). But the serving chairman of the CoSC does not have administrative authority to establish unity of command or impose force planning and doctrinal decisions upon his peers. The net result is weak coordination and planning among India's armed services.[15]

The Singh task force's proposed solution to this institutional impasse was the replacement of the CCoSC with a Chief of Defense Staff (CDS), who unlike his predecessor would enjoy power over his peers and establish unity of command. The IDS would serve as the administrative secretariat for the CDS and become the focal coordination and planning agency for all of the services' joint commands including the SFC. The recommendation on the coordination of nuclear operations through the IDS and the SFC was significant because of India's institutional legacy of divided control of the arsenal between the scientific and military agencies. The BARC and DRDO retain separate custody of the fissile cores and the non-fissile warhead assemblies. The armed forces in turn have custody of nuclear delivery systems. The reformers concluded that whereas the disaggregation of the arsenal between the various agencies bolstered peacetime safety, it also undermined operational efficiency. The Singh task force therefore sought to find new institutional means to enable better coordination between the scientific agencies and the military.[16]

The government, however, showed no immediate urgency in implementing the task force's recommendations. Although it did institute the IDS in 2001, and within it, a tri-service SFC in 2002 tasked with operational responsibility for India's nuclear forces,[17] the SFC's authority only began to cement after political principals gave it more serious attention after 2005. The CoSC, however, was never reformed. Intra-service rivalry between the air force and the army, and civilian foot dragging ensured that the institution of the CDS remained stillborn (Figure 5.1).

Learning in any system follows the incorporation of new knowledge into existing institutional routines. The incorporation of new knowledge in turn requires input from professionals who staff organizations. In the nuclear as in the conventional sphere, the military's staffing role is absolutely essential in creating strategic and operational knowledge.[18] In the strategic sphere fall numbers, weapon types, targeting and planned use of weapons, and command control. In the operational sphere fall logistics, SOPs, physical infrastructure, security, personnel training and exercises to test the force's response in the field. Personnel training and field exercises

INDIA'S HIGHER DEFENSE ORGANIZATION

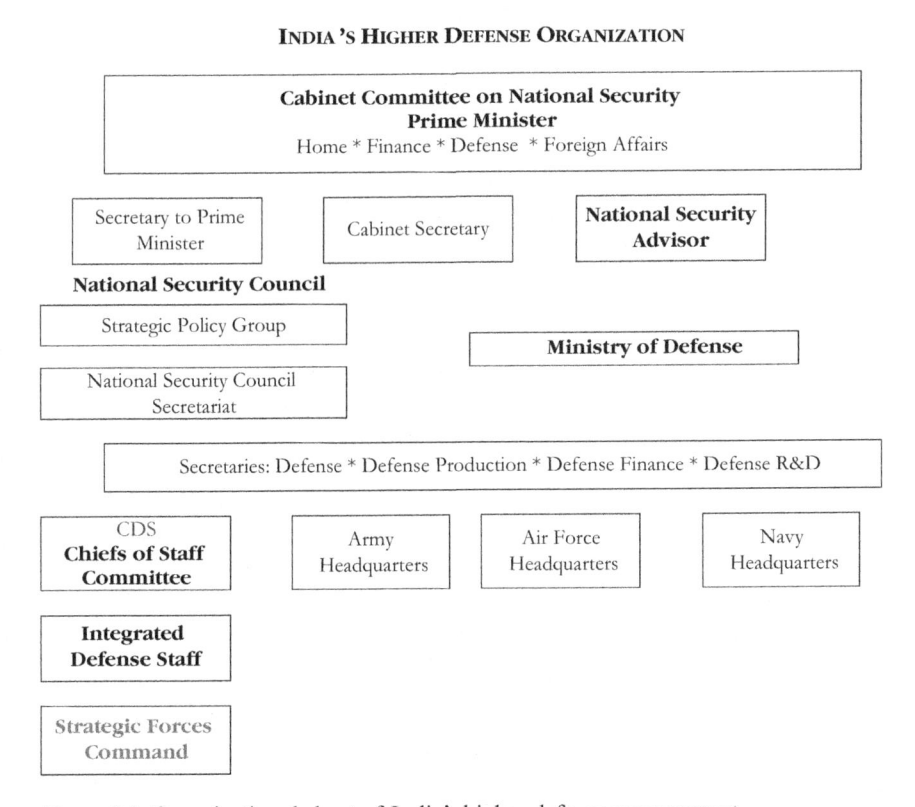

```
┌─────────────────────────────────────────────────────┐
│         Cabinet Committee on National Security      │
│                    Prime Minister                   │
│       Home * Finance * Defense * Foreign Affairs    │
└─────────────────────────────────────────────────────┘

┌──────────────────┐  ┌──────────────────┐  ┌──────────────────┐
│ Secretary to     │  │                  │  │ National Security│
│ Prime Minister   │  │ Cabinet Secretary│  │     Advisor      │
└──────────────────┘  └──────────────────┘  └──────────────────┘

National Security Council
┌──────────────────────┐
│ Strategic Policy Group│              ┌──────────────────┐
└──────────────────────┘              │ Ministry of Defense│
┌──────────────────────┐              └──────────────────┘
│ National Security    │
│ Council Secretariat  │
└──────────────────────┘

┌─────────────────────────────────────────────────────┐
│ Secretaries: Defense * Defense Production *         │
│              Defense Finance * Defense R&D          │
└─────────────────────────────────────────────────────┘

┌────────────┐  ┌────────────┐  ┌────────────┐  ┌────────────┐
│    CDS     │  │    Army    │  │  Air Force │  │    Navy    │
│Chiefs of   │  │Headquarters│  │Headquarters│  │Headquarters│
│Staff       │  │            │  │            │  │            │
│Committee   │  │            │  │            │  │            │
└────────────┘  └────────────┘  └────────────┘  └────────────┘
┌────────────┐
│ Integrated │
│Defense Staff│
└────────────┘
┌────────────┐
│ Strategic  │
│Forces      │
│Command     │
└────────────┘
```

Figure 5.1 Organizational chart of India's higher defense management.

118 *Challenges of nuclear operationalization*

under simulated attack conditions are vital to generate data to assess the viability of existing SOPs and agencies' response under stress conditions. Such exercises are also the means for generating vital data on the user–machine interface, a process that helps identify and eliminate technical and operator errors.[19]

However, India's case suggests that many strategic decisions preceded the SFC's institutionalization. "By that time (the SFC's formation)," the former NSA Brajesh Mishra informed the author, "we had decided how much we were going to do…we had decided…not exactly…but somewhat…approximately…the mix of the two kinds of weapons…nuclear (fission)…thermonuclear…having done that at the political level…then we began to think of a nuclear command authority."[20]

In February 2004, the editor of the Delhi-based *Force* magazine, Pravin Sawhney, reported on the basis of interviews with Air Marshal Asthana, then C-in-C, SFC, that the SFC had been unable to "find a location for its headquarters and role in the employment of nuclear weapons."[21] Asthana also complained that the SFC's staffing requirements were generally unmet and that the government had not made budgetary provisions for technical infrastructure projects such as hardened facilities and bunkers, secure communications, and secure sites for nuclear delivery vehicles.

Among the unknowns at the time was how long it would take India to transition from a peacetime recessed to a force employment mode because the agencies involved – the SFC, the air force, BARC and DRDO – had not practiced drills together. Even as late as 2004, the government had not institutionalized the division of authority and responsibilities among the agencies on general release procedures for the deployment, arming and firing of nuclear weapons.[22] As Mishra put it to the author: "…of course, they (the military) were also very keen about who will give the orders…how will the orders be communicated etc. etc. But…we did not have the time to do anything because we lost the elections and we left."[23]

Soon after it was first instituted in 2002, "SFC postings were considered some of sort of a shit creek…a dead-end career move," according to a Shankar, former C-in-C, SFC. This was partly the result of new tri-service cooperation rules under which officers did not know how they would stand in their parent service after a joint-services stint. But that changed mid-decade. Post-2005, human resource development tasks for the SFC were set at the prime ministerial level. SFC postings were designated upward career moves and officers serving in it started getting paid more than their counterparts in other military commands. The services began assigning senior officers to the SFC who had already completed assignments at Staff College and higher command institutions. Once deputed to the SFC, the officers' focus became exclusively nuclear. They learned "on the job" by doing staff work. Even after officers ended their deputation in the SFC and returned to their parent services, they were "recycled" and returned to the SFC at a later date at more senior levels.[24]

Challenges of nuclear operationalization 119

The process of "recycling" became the means to ensure "continuity." It has become central to consolidating the SFC's epistemic role in India's nuclear planning. Between 2005 and 2010, the SFC's staff strength expanded to a "little below 100," which Shankar emphasized was a "large staff for a command, especially when compared to other conventional operational commands, where staff strength does not exceed 50-60." With organizational expansion, the SFC now has several departments that focus on different aspects of nuclear force development. These include infrastructure, standard operating procedures, general release codes for nuclear weapons, communications and computing, intelligence, and medicine.[25]

The SFC's sustained institutional presence over a decade signifies the formal institutionalization and expansion of a military-centered nuclear epistemic community within the state. However, institutionalization alone says little about an epistemic community's strength or effectiveness. In the case of the SFC, two factors undermined its institutional effectiveness in the immediate aftermath of its inception. First, in the absence of a CDS, the SFC lacked effective administrative authority. In the CDS's absence, the CCoSC was responsible for all command and staff functions. However, the position of CCoSC devolves by rotation on the senior-most serving service chief at any given time. The CCoSC's term can last a year or more or simply a few months. For example, India had a succession of four CCoSC between August/September 2004 and February 2005. Similarly, during 2006–2007 there was a succession of three CCoSC within a span of 10 months.[26] Such rapid rotation brought enormous discontinuity to the task of governing the nuclear force.

Further, the CCoSC is first and foremost a service chief. He is responsible for command and staff functions in his own service (army, navy, air force). According to Admiral (retd.) Arun Prakash, who served as CCoSC for an unusually long 20 months during 2005–2006, the CCoSC is barely able to devote "10-15 percent of his time" to the SFC.[27] Further, despite his seniority, the CCoSC is only nominally the head of the CoSC. The CoSC works by consensus and abides by an informal institutional rule that no service chief will interfere in the functioning of another service.[28]

This created a huge coordination bottleneck for the SFC because the air force and navy each retained independent control over nuclear delivery vehicles. The C-in-C, SFC is a three-star officer and junior in rank to the four-star service chiefs. In India's hierarchical bureaucratic setting, the C-in-C, SFC therefore cannot command the service chiefs to do his bidding. He must operate through the CCoSC, who in the first instance is unable to devote full-time attention to the SFC and in the second is bound by informal institutional rules that favor consensus and noninterference in each service's affairs.[29]

Other problems arose because of the SFC's isolation within the tri-service IDS, the agency in which it is institutionally located. In theory, the IDS was to have responsibility for undertaking all of the SFC's staffing functions and leave its commander with only strategic planning and command duties. However, although the SFC is formally a part of the IDS, civilian principals for political reasons made certain that links between the military's nuclear and conventional commands were minimal, according to a former C-in-C, SFC. The C-in-C, SFC only reported to the CCoSC.[30] As a result, the SFC was unable to delegate staffing duties to the IDS.

As institutional reforms unfolded over the decade, conventional and nuclear commands were divided between the conventional military and the SFC, partly by default and partly by design. The coordinating institutional link between the two was the CCoSC and the IDS.[31] The first was, and still, remains weak. The latter, because of the SFC's insulation within the IDS, is questionable. The resolution of planning and operational problems at the CCoSC-level concerning the SFC therefore became the responsibility of the NSA or his specially designated deputy in the PMO. The PMO in turn lacked the institutional capacity to oversee the scientific and military agents tasked with the development and management of the fledgling nuclear arsenal.

To resolve this institutional logjam, the SFC persuaded the political leadership to create a professional, composite and integrated staff to advise the government on nuclear and related strategic issues within the PMO. This new body, the SPS, came into existence in 2011.[32] Led by a recently retired C-in-C, SFC, the SPS has 25–30 staff members drawn from the ranks of BARC, DRDO, the three armed services and the foreign office.[33] Its staff members include scientific personnel, operations research specialists, a nuclear net assessment specialist, military planners and foreign service officers who advise the NSA and the PMO on developing a ten-year perspective plan on nuclear development, collating intelligence on nuclear adversaries, and ensuring the quality and reliability of nuclear weapons and delivery systems.[34] In addition, a separate Strategic Armaments Safety Authority (SASA) advises the NSA and the NCA on the safety and security of India's nuclear assets.[35] Even prior to 2011, India's NCA informally operated out of the PMO. But the PMO lacked independent institutional means to exercise oversight. The creation of the SPS therefore marks the beginning of an attempt to institutionalize epistemic oversight and deductive control at the level of the NCA.

The deepening institutionalization of a composite set of nuclear epistemic actors within the state notwithstanding, the actors' institutional effectiveness is dependent on a two-step process. First, they must have the ability to generate new consensual knowledge. Next, the actors must have the institutional power to inject that consensual knowledge into the state's existing habitual routines in order to change them. The development of new consensual knowledge depends first and foremost on information turnover and exchange. Information is the fundamental means that professionals use for performing "truth tests" and growing a society's knowledge banks. Making that consensual knowledge part of the state's routines in turn is contingent on the strength of the community's institutionalization and its ability to forge an operating intellectual consensus.

Prior to 1998, both were impossible because information was hived off in a tiny social network consisting of scientists and bureaucrats who even today boast that they will "carry India's nuclear secrets to their grave."[36] But in the post-1998 decade, the Indian military has gained access to sensitive information about the hardware and operational issues. This has provided it the means to challenge both the scientific "strategic enclave" as well as bureaucratic and political decision-makers.[37] With newfound access to critical information and knowledge, the military has had some success in incorporating new consensual knowledge into the nuclear routines of the state, particularly in the realms of force posture, procedures and command control. Consensus, however, eludes India's nuclear epistemic community on the subject of the performance reliability of India's nuclear warhead designs. In its absence and confronted with a technical dead end on the nuclear force's operational effectiveness due to warhead design limitations, the military has sought to remake the consensus on the technical reliability of delivery systems as a means out of the existing dilemma.

The shift from heuristics to structured decisions and planning

Non-institutionalized decision-making and planning in the first half of 2000–2010 and the weak institutionalization of the epistemic actors in this period, once again show why operational outcomes in India exhibit signs of uneven optimization. Without doubt, Indian leaders in the last decade committed themselves to "expanding" and "interconnected" goals. However, they did not immediately match those goal commitments with a simultaneous resolve to building strong institutional capacities. In the latter's absence, their decisions from the first half of the decade corroborate many of the fundamental insights from cybernetics and cognitive theories: sequential actions, loose coupling and the use of simple heuristics. Instead of drawing on blueprints to guide policy, they followed their gut instincts to make determinations. Often, their measures of optimality were not consensually determined scientific or management benchmarks but internally held values and belief systems.

Many early decisions, especially those concerning nuclear warhead lethality for example, have had a path-dependent lock in effect that rule out optimization in the absence of a radical shift in policy. This has had a negative impact on strategic force planning. Barring the complete upending of the status quo, optimization is now only possible through improvements in the design and reliability of delivery systems. The latter is now the focus of the SFC's efforts at force optimization and the evidence suggests that it has had some success is persuading political decision-makers into forcing the weapons research and development establishment to accept this consensus.

Equally germane to the demands of operations, the military's institutionalization in nuclear policy planning and the creation of composite SPS have put in place the organizational foundation for problem decomposition, parallel processing and the substitution of simple heuristics-based assumptions with judgments based on operations research. There is now greater emphasis on inter-agency planning. Actions are more coordinated between them due to new common operating procedures. Military exercises have revealed logistical vulnerabilities in the transition from peacetime to wartime alert. Some procedural modifications have been instituted to address them. Remarkably enough, the military has succeeding in leveraging the logistical demands of the sea leg of the triad to push civilian decision-makers to substitute organizational (negative) for the operationally more efficient procedural (positive) controls, with some success.

When designing a nuclear force, planners think in terms of damage expectancy (DE) to enemy targets. Numerical estimates of nuclear warheads and delivery systems flow from this fundamental calculation. DE is the product of the probability of target kill, air defense penetrativity, pre-launch survivability of the weapon system and its reliability. Among these probabilities, target kill and reliability of the weapon system form the core concerns of professional planners. Target kill depends on the nuclear warhead's yield (lethality) and it reliably producing that yield every time it is exploded.[38] However, evidence from India's 1998 nuclear tests has raised serious concerns about the upper-yield limits and reliability of its warhead designs.[39] Further, the political management of the technical controversy that arose in the wake of those tests compellingly shows that simple heuristics and not rational optimization drove decision-making.

It is now apparent that pre-1998 nuclear weapons design in India was almost the exclusive enterprise of its scientific enclave with minimal direction from the political leadership and none whatsoever from the military. The political leadership approved the development of advanced nuclear weapon designs such as boosted-fission and thermonuclear warheads without understanding the technical implications of what those weapons might mean for any future force design.[40] Similarly, like with many principal-agent dilemmas that arise from conditions of "information asymmetry," the political decision-makers had little understanding of the technical parameters and demands of a field-testing program to validate designs that BARC had on its shelf.

To be sure, the nuclear test window in 1998 was determined on the advice the political decision-makers received from their scientific advisors.[41] However, the nuclear scientists, who after 1974 were frustrated by their inability to persuade the political leadership to authorize hot-tests, offered the political leaders a compressed program of rushed tests to minimize political risk.[42] The political decision-makers' acquiescence of this rapid test series itself rested on a heuristic understanding of the political risk they and India could bear in the ensuing confrontation with the United States.

Among the nuclear weapon designs tested in May 1998 were that of a fission weapon and a two-stage thermonuclear device. The thermonuclear device likely had a boosted-fission trigger in the first stage, the scientists' goal likely being to piggyback the boosted-fission design on the thermonuclear device.[43] According to Indian government sources, the thermonuclear device was deliberately tested at a low yield of 43 kt, but which in the actual weapon could be dialed up to 200 kt. In the immediate aftermath of the first round of nuclear tests on May 11, 1998 itself, the coordinator of the test program K. Santhanam concluded on the basis of preliminary observations of instrumental test data and the crater morphology at the test site that the thermonuclear design had "underperformed."[44] However, the BARC team rejected DRDO's assessments on grounds that the latter's "instrumentation was faulty."[45] BARC, India's principal nuclear weapons design agency, reported to the government after the second round of tests on May 13 that it had achieved all its design and data objectives from the tests.[46] Following this advice, Vajpayee's BJP government declared a moratorium on further testing.

Both these episodes, the scientific and its follow-up political act, exemplify how the absence of strong institutions and structured decision-making produce suboptimal policy outcomes with deleterious consequences. With no institution or agency to monitor the scientific agencies, the principals (political decision-makers) had few means to monitor their agents' (scientists') performance. The disputing scientific agencies themselves, DRDO and BARC, lacked independent institutional mechanisms to subject members of the nuclear cohort to "truth tests" before making consensual claims. The consequence was faulty reporting on one of the most sensitive national security matters to the government.

Absent any institutional processes to weigh down decision-making, Prime Minister Vajpayee claimed the tests a success and declared a test moratorium almost immediately after without awaiting further triangulation of seismic data and crater morphology observations with post-shot radioactivity measurements. The prime minister, as Indian Foreign Minister Jaswant Singh later revealed, "...was by instinct placatory...had from the beginning in his public stance been in support of disarmament...there was no bouncing off of ideas with his confidantes...it [the testing moratorium] was an instinctive reaction. It shows up Vajpayee in bad light. But the fact of the matter is the Indian political leadership does not have the tradition of either great study or reflection..."[47]

Within six months of the May 1998 tests, the DRDO issued a classified report to the government, which raised doubts about the reliability of the thermonuclear design. In response, then NSA Brajesh Mishra summoned a meeting of the DRDO and BARC representatives to discuss the report's findings. But at the end of it, he squelched the debate by saying the "government would stand by Dr. Chidambaram's [BARC] opinion." Mishra's account of the episode is telling. As he put it to the author:

> ...the funny thing is the pressure to test came from these very scientists. So when finally in '98 we said: go ahead and do it...I asked them how long would it take to test...these scientists who had weaponized...they were the ones who were insisting that there must be tests...and we wanted to do it openly...and then declare ourselves as a nuclear weapon state.
>
> So...the scientists...and there must have been many involved...but the five I know are Dr. Chidambaram, Kakodkar...Sikka...from BARC and

Kalam and Santhanam from DRDO...now when they went in for the tests they told me that they wanted to do six. We can't do it one day...we need two days. First day they tested three, and then two days later they wanted to test another three. But after the fifth one, they telephoned me and said we don't need another one. We have all the data that we wanted. They said the tests are successful...the weapon design is proved.

...a couple of months later [after the May 1998 tests] Dr. Kalam and Dr. Santhanam came to see me...and it was Santhanam who said that they had doubts about this...and we need to do something about this. And I asked: we need to do what? We have declared a moratorium...So I said: you have doubts...I will call the people from Bombay...let's sit down and discuss the matter. You raise the doubts and let them reply. So I called a meeting with the five of them...so Santhanam gave his reasoning...The three of them (BARC team) gave their replies. More particularly, Sikka who was the man intimately involved with the design came out with a long explanation... giving this detail...that detail. I said ok...the meeting ended.[48]

When asked why he did not appoint a scientific commission comprising retired nuclear scientists and weapon designers to review the DRDO's findings and render independent advice to the government, Mishra replied:

We tested five times...apart from 1974. In '74 when the test was done... nobody came out and said: we want a review...whether the test was successful or not successful...the point I am trying to make to you is: if we don't trust those very same people who were insisting upon tests....I mean the political leadership never went to them and asked them to test...it was they...the scientists...who for years had been insisting on testing...at least for 10 years...so then you appoint a review committee to verify the results? I mean this is a strange logic....a review committee also means giving up your secrets...whatever you have.[49]

The above account, if accepted literally, is the clearest evidence of the triumph of faith-based politics over any countervailing notions of rationality. In order to maintain the internal simplicity and consistency in their decision-making, Indian decision-makers chose preformed beliefs over institutionalized "truth tests" to resolve uncertainty in an issue area where they lacked credible knowledge. Their approach was, as Santhanam observed years later, "I have made up my mind, don't confuse me with facts."[50]

An alternative explanation is that the political decision-makers simply decided that it was not worth the trouble to validate the thermonuclear design through a program of further tests as the latter decision would further inflame the United States and burn more political capital. Perhaps the politicians decided the 20–30 kt-fission weapon, which Santhanam claimed had "worked like a song,"[51] would suffice for purposes of deterrence. In fact, during the

Challenges of nuclear operationalization 125

thermonuclear weapon controversy, which erupted in 2009 when Santhanam went public with his claims, the former Scientific Advisor to the Defense Minister Dr. V.S. Arunachalam argued that deterrence "is...a mind game" and simple Hiroshima-type devices would be sufficient to kill people in the hundreds of thousands. It therefore would not matter if India lacked a reliable thermonuclear warhead with a scaled-up yield of 150 kt.[52]

If this latter reasoning were the decision-makers' private justification for foregoing any further testing, then it would once again point to the prevalence of satisficing over optimization in Indian policy planning. The thermonuclear design, or the boosted-fission weapon, if part of the mix of warheads that make up India's nuclear force, will always remain dogged by uncertainty.[53] The yield reliability of the thermonuclear device's boosted-fission trigger is also uncertain.[54] Assigning these designs reliability probability estimates in the absence of full-scale "hot" tests carries high risk. This essentially means that the foundation for determining the size of the nuclear force is arbitrary and unscientific because the reliability of the thermonuclear design and its boosted-fission trigger cannot be determined with accuracy.

On the other hand, the alternative solution of building a nuclear force centered on 20–30 kt fission weapons imposes significantly higher performance and reliability demands on weapon carrier systems such as ballistic missiles.[55] The absence of this understanding early on suggests that Indian political decision-makers harbored a simple heuristics-based understanding of nuclear force planning; that the lack of structured planning and oversight in India's nuclear decision-making processes in the first half of the last decade has created negative path dependencies without the policy makers even comprehending the deductive consequences of their decision.

Unlike the United States, India did not have the institutional equivalent of a JASON Committee[56] at the time to independently advise the government on the science and engineering of nuclear weapons. Senior members of India's nuclear weapons design establishment such as former AEC Chairman Dr. P.K. Iyengar have admitted that in the past the federal government's technical and nontechnical proxies who sat on the AEC's board lacked both information and knowledge to undertake any meaningful audit of BARC's performance.[57] Indeed, the 1998 test episode is evidence of the limits of even DRDO's auditing capacity, the one government agency responsible for weaponization and the instrumentation for measuring test yields. Because the military was never part of the nuclear design effort and is a consumer, it remained a vehicle for transmitting scientific dissent and not independent oversight.[58] Thus until the thermonuclear weapon test controversy exploded in public, there were no guards who could exercise effective oversight over India's nuclear guardians, a condition that imposed institutional limits to any nuclear learning in the system.

Warhead yield limitations and reliability concerns also shifted attention to the performance of delivery systems: aircraft and ballistic missiles. Combat aircraft constitute the most "flexible" nuclear delivery vehicles in India's inventory.[59]

126 *Challenges of nuclear operationalization*

But aircraft typically suffer from range and penetrativity limitations, which in India's context confine their use to the Pakistan theater of operations. An Indian Air Force study conducted in the early 2000s highlighted this problem by showing that a single nuclear mission against Pakistan could tie up as many as 60 aircraft to assist the penetrating nuclear vector, a huge resource drain during a conventional war.[60] Reliability is a lesser concern with dual-use aircraft because the bulk of the inventory is imported.

However, aircrafts' range limitations and vulnerability to air defenses means that long-range ballistic missiles, land and sea-based, are India's primary means for targeting China. However, reliance on simple fission devices raised the performance and reliability demands on ballistic missiles. Fission warheads are heavier than their boosted-fission and thermonuclear cousins.[61] Compared to the latter, they also consume more fissile material per unit.[62] Furthermore, their lower yield very likely means that a ballistic missile unit will likely have to deploy multiple reentry vehicle (MRV) bus to achieve the same bang that a single thermonuclear warhead would have achieved. More accurate guidance systems must now compensate for lower yields when targeting large urban centers over long distances.[63] Reliance on fission warheads has generated demands for ballistic missiles with greater throw-weight capacity and the development of other challenging technologies.[64]

As the SFC's gained institutional authority, it identified two problems with India's emerging long-range ballistic missile force. First, the missile systems had been subject to a very small number of tests. In the Indian case, missile tests until then had been few. Prior to 1998, for example, the Agni technology demonstrator (TD) flew only thrice.[65] Between 1999 and 2011, the medium range Agni II underwent five flight tests. Likewise, the Agni III underwent four flight tests in the years 2006–2010. In these tests, the failure rate for the Agni TD was 33 percent. For the Agni II and III, the failure rates were 40 and 25 percent.[66]

Ballistic missiles incorporate a range of critical technologies: boost, post-boost realignment and spin, stage separation, warhead separation, reentry and navigation systems.[67] All subsystems must function flawlessly for mission success. Malfunctions in any one subsystem either separately or in conjunction with others can cause catastrophic failure. An initial successful launch, therefore, is an inadequate indicator of success as systems can subsequently fail during missile flight. In the case of some of the early Indian missile tests, there is data to suggest that although the missiles launched successfully, they suffered subsystem malfunctions later during flight, which caused navigation errors.[68] Thus the failure rate of some Indian ballistic missiles in this period was probably higher than is publicly reported.[69]

In comparison to the Agni for example, the US MX ICBM was tested 80 times. Soviet and Russian missiles on average were put through 10–20 tests to establish reliability.[70] The reliability for US nuclear warheads is estimated between 0.99–0.995 percent. Their overall system reliability drops "sharply to between 0.8 and 0.95" percent when mated with delivery systems. In theory, the combined system failure probability (nuclear warhead plus delivery system) decreases with every percentage drop in a delivery system's reliability.[71]

Another of the SFC's reliability concerns had to do with the specificity of the Indian missile development program. The missile systems flown until then were custom built as test-beds for validating technologies. It is generally a rule of thumb that quality control during the prototype-manufacturing phase is far higher compared to normal assembly line production. From an operational viewpoint therefore, until and unless Indian missile entities mastered the industrial line production process, systems unreliability would dog the nuclear force.[72]

To resolve the reliability gap, the SFC "issued general staff requirements for delivery systems."[73] Using the new inter-agency process, it also demanded a larger number of missile tests under realistic field conditions to establish baselines for reliability. The scientific agencies in turn contested the military's demands for an extensive program of field tests. A scientific panel the government appointed to study this inter-agency dispute subsequently recommended that statistical analysis of component, subsystem and system testing coupled with "three consecutive" successful flight tests were cumulatively a good proxy for reliability.[74]

The military accepted this determination although it preferred full-scale operational tests. Operational commanders regard statistical analysis of component and subsystem testing a weak proxy for total systems reliability. Yet, the stronger institutionalization and accessibility to critical information enabled the SFC to impose "truth tests" on the scientific agencies and helped generate more rational and optimized solutions to problems of force reliability.

In a related and significant shift, the SFC also successfully changed the methodology for nuclear force planning. Prior to 1998, planners very likely projected acquisitions of warheads and delivery systems on fissile material availability and crude calculations of the weapon systems' prelaunch survivability. With the military's co-participation, force planning shifted to statistical DE estimates. The former C-in-C, SFC Air Marshal Bhavnani who oversaw the process during 2004–2006 alluded to this when he complained:

> ...one of these grey areas in India has always been that civilian control has been so strong over security matters on matters related to strategic security etc., the senior military people do not fit into their scheme of things...when calculating, when strategizing, when coming out with solutions for making nuclear strategy. So in that aspect when a person who has less knowledge about nuclear issues, he then feels that perhaps 10 or 15 nuclear weapons are good enough. We do not think so. Whilst we are there making sure that the weapons are ready, the missiles are ready, the platforms are ready...the strategizing is left to somebody else. So in that sense, who decides whether you need a 100 odd weapons or 10 weapons to achieve that deterrence...it is the strategists. The nation's nuclear

strategy...should be decided by a group of people who are well informed in this area...who are not there to make short term decisions, but the long term ones.[75]

Other senior SFC commanders including Bhavnani's successor Rear Admiral (retd.) Shankar insist, "Everything is numbers based...on operations research-based probabilistic analysis. The former is necessary to arrive at facts...in contrast to the intuitive gut-instinct analysis of the nuclear scientists, politicians, and their civilian advisors in the past."[76]

Force posture development in the first half of the 2000s also suffered from the cognitive dissonance among the handful of decision-makers who in 1998 proclaimed India's nuclear status but then did not follow up their act by building the state's organizational agency to leverage that capability. However, changes in organizational capacities since 2004–2005 suggest that considerable optimization has followed the creation of the SFC and the SPS. From 1998 until at least 2003, Indian leaders retained the institutional legacy of the pre-1998 era: the de-mated and distributed posture, which Ashley Tellis summed up as "strategically active" but "operationally dormant" in peacetime.[77]

Control of the arsenal initially devolved upon the pre-1998 network of scientists from BARC and DRDO. Absent the offsetting impact of institutionalized decision-making that enables problem decomposition and parallel tasking, decision-makers fell into the state's habitual mode of resolving problems in the sequence in which they presented themselves. The latter outcome also owed much to the decision-makers' unchallenged heuristic conditioning drawn from the analogy of the superpowers' Cold War nuclear competition, which equated operationalization with higher force alerting and the subsequently greater likelihood of nuclear use due to inadvertence or accident. Thus in the first five years after the 1998 tests, decision-makers remained focused on the first-order political problems stemming from India's overt nuclear status, while inter-agency coordination problems pertaining to operational planning languished. As a consequence, the friction between operational dormancy and operational employment modes proved stickier than policy makers had imagined.[78]

The 1999 Kargil War and subsequently the 2001–2002 military mobilization against Pakistan empirically demonstrated just how hugely complex the task of nuclear force reconstitution and employment readiness was in the absence of well-developed inter-agency management structures and protocols.[79] In 1999, there was no "common knowledge base" to establish a "common operating base" between the scientific agencies and the air force. The scientific agencies had assumed for example that 72 hours was a reasonable time window within which the nuclear force could transition from recessed to employment mode. However, according to a senior participant in the planning process, it took "nearly a week" before the air force and the agencies were able to "make the weapons operational."[80] Members of the nuclear network had to orally ratify all actions in the absence of institutionalized standard operating procedures, a process that added to the logistical friction.[81]

The 2001–2002 standoff with Pakistan similarly demonstrated that the de-mated operational posture while "politically correct" was "operationally hazardous."[82] Due to the SFC's delayed institutionalization, inter-agency operational procedures remained inchoate. The absence of joint drill and training exercises involving all agencies on the ground meant that the alerting procedures and timelines were still paper exercises. The military also found the alerting and readiness procedures put together by BARC and DRDO to be cumbersome and overly optimistic.[83]

Among the military's first tasks post-2002 was to formalize SOPs and institutionalize operational planning with the civilian bureaucratic and scientific agencies. In December 2002, the government adopted the "Red Book," a highly classified document that "contains the nuclear doctrine plus certain additional standard operating procedures…various chains of command, succession lists…and deals with various contingencies…"[84] After its formation, the SFC institutionalized meetings with the scientific agencies to coordinate nuclear planning at regular "two month intervals."[85] By 2004, the SFC submitted for government approval operational plans pertaining to nuclear release codes.[86] It similarly prepared the "Blue Book," a lower order set of classified instructions that detail procedures at the unit level of the armed forces with regards to nuclear weapons.[87]

Subsequent SFC-led military exercises revealed the difficulties of transitioning from peacetime to a readiness posture. A major logistics challenge was the simple movement of missiles and nuclear warhead components to predesignated mating and launch locations because of India's urban congestion and poor road and rail infrastructure. The military concluded that the logistical drag on the force, especially in the aftermath of a nuclear strike, could reach a tipping point sufficient to disrupt any retaliatory response.[88] It also discovered that many of the de-mated force's components were stored in conditions that left them vulnerable to preemptive attacks.[89] The SFC drew on these lessons along with those from the 1999 and 2001–2002 military mobilizations to move out missiles and nuclear ordnance from densely populated urban areas to alternative locations.[90]

Between 2004 and 2008, the SFC's internal studies concluded that infrastructure support for the Indian nuclear force, especially its communications and transport networks, was weak. In several of the SFC's internal war games involving "first-strike" scenarios, the results were grim: the war dead numbering in millions, the losses of nuclear delivery systems and warheads in large numbers and the debilitating impact on command and control.[91] Drawing upon simulation data to determine what it would take to launch successful retaliatory strikes amidst the compressed decision-making time frames, the SFC helped focus the government's budgetary attention to building up the sinews of its nuclear response mechanisms ranging from communication networks, command-and-control nodes, safe storage and launch hideouts, and transportation links to enable the safe passage of the nuclear force.[92]

Steady pressure from the SFC also persuaded the government to authorize new force constitution protocols. The new procedures have apparently compressed the procedural steps between a de-mated and fully constituted arsenal in operational mode from six to four. Under the new procedures warhead reconstitution begins simultaneously with conventional force mobilization. Delivery systems and warheads are to undergo dispersal in the second alerting stage. The mating sequence of warheads and delivery systems will commence in the third stage. In the fourth and final alerting stage, shared control of the arsenal between the scientific agencies and the military will end and firing authority will devolve upon the military.[93]

Subsequent SFC lobbying ensured clear demarcation of dual-use delivery systems and their crews in the armed services to deal with the problem of crosscutting authorities. Under the new procedures, these assets are "quarantined" and placed under the SFC's command during training exercises and wartime alerting.[94] In peacetime, the arsenal still retains its de-mated form. But underneath that broad institutional tent, smaller procedural changes have begun to transform the earlier civilian reticence concerning positive controls.

As the former C-in-C, SFC, Air Marshal (retd.) Bhavnani put it to Bharath Karnad, "it has been time consuming for political bosses to understand what's a de-mated situation, what's a mated situation, why we should have a mated situation. But once they were made to understand, we are now in a good situation."[95] Thus for example, some types of nuclear ordnance are now co-located with delivery systems at air and naval bases.[96] In the navy's case, the separation is more apparent than real. Thus, the two naval warships, which constitute the sea leg of the triad, are designated to sail with ballistic missiles and nuclear ordnance on board during operational alert.[97] The political leadership probably retains institutional separation and control through representatives of the scientific agencies on board the ships. However, for all practical purposes the navy has custody of the nuclear force.

Affirming that political decision-makers had indeed begun to appraise operational postures on land and sea differently on the basis of their logistical and operational demands, the former NSA Brajesh Mishra candidly admitted to the author:

> You have to make a difference between the navy, the air force, and the missiles on land. When the admiral…is out…hundreds of miles away, he must have those weapons with him…but there must be a way of communication between the submarine or the ship and the decision-makers in Delhi whether to fire or not to fire. But in the case of [the] air force, unless they are on an aircraft carrier…that's a different matter. But with land based missiles that is not the same question…[98]

Senior military officials confirmed the tenor of Mishra's comments in subsequent interviews with the author. As the former C-in-C, SFC, Rear Admiral (retd.) Shankar explained:

> the concept of a "force-in-being" with physical separation between vector, the fissile material, and non-fissile assemblies is a thing of the past. Technology has intervened in the process. Consider the nuclear submarine...the missiles will be encapsulated on board the vessel. You can't then separate the warhead from the missile. The implications of all this being that "procedural" separation must replace "physical" separation in the various states of operational readiness.[99]

Even in the case of the land leg of the arsenal, India is moving in the direction of emplacing ballistic missiles in sealed canisters.[100] Canisterization offers several logistical and maintenance advantages. It enables ease of transport and protects both missiles and warheads from hazardous environmental conditions. Some including Narang regard the emplacement of missiles in sealed canisters an indication of the end of India's institutional practice of keeping its arsenal de-mated.[101] There is no firm evidence of this occurrence yet.[102] However, the canisterization of the land-based missile force could in the future enable the SFC to persuade civilian principals to entirely substitute command-and-control institutions based on physical separation with technological-procedural ones.

In the last decade, therefore, there has been a steady stream of operational improvements at the procedural level of force employment. Most of these improvements stem from new institutional approaches that permit a higher volume of information turnover on sensitive nuclear matters within the state, processes that subject that information to multiple and critical scrutiny from strongly institutionalized epistemic actors, and then transform the consensus that emerges from these processes into new habitual routines for the state to follow. Significantly enough, the relaxation of intense secrecy on all matters nuclear has also begun to impart greater visibility to the actions of the epistemic actors who make up India's nuclear estate. It has also created a more permissive environment for greater inter- and intra-agency competition. Both conditions in turn have strengthened the capacity of political principals to exercise better management and oversight over India's nuclear estate.

Evolving principal-agent relationships and operational dilemmas

Overt nuclear status and the relaxation of extreme internal secrecy also has positive implications for institutional conditions that in the past undermined the capacity of political principals to exercise effective oversight over their scientific and bureaucratic agents. Lesser restrictions on lateral information flows and sharing between the various agencies and agents imply

132 *Challenges of nuclear operationalization*

greater transparency. Principals are now more easily able to observe the actions of their scientific, bureaucratic and military agents. Institutionalization of new epistemic actors, especially the military and the composite SPS signifies greater inter-agent competition. The latter's co-participation amplifies dissenting views and increases the chances of the latter rising to the attention of decision-makers. In the abstract, the institution of an independent review body in the form of the SPS also provides principals the institutional means to level information asymmetries between them and their agents.

All of the above are positive institutional developments that help the cause of operational effectiveness. Yet, the legacy effect of the past also dilutes the maximum positive effect of the new institutional changes. Despite increased information availability and inter-agent competition, for example, newly institutionalized epistemic actors including the military lack independent epistemic means to challenge their scientific counterparts. This puts a cap on the quality of inter-agent competition within the state. Similarly, although civilian principals have enacted institutional reforms to manage nuclear force planning and operations, they have not simultaneously undertaken reforms in the conventional military with the same alacrity.

This institutional stasis has compartmentalized the military's nuclear and conventional commands. Its net effects are diminished situational awareness between the two commands, constrained intra-military agent competition, and the potential for operational blind spots on a fluid battlefield. Finally, the institution of an independent SPS in the PMO is one of the most significant developments in the task of guarding India's nuclear guardians. But the robustness with which the SPS is able to exercise oversight authority is still unclear.

India's military is now privy to information about the nuclear weapons program. But the military also lacks the epistemic means to independently appraise that information.

This is in part a legacy of the development trajectory of India's nuclear program since the late 1950s.[103] Prior to 1998 there was no institutional link between the scientific agencies that designed and built nuclear weapons and the armed services, their designated users.[104] Post-1998, SFC personnel have started undergoing training programs at BARC in nuclear safety and use. But the SFC itself has no independent academic-scientific training to challenge its sources of technical information and knowledge.

The controversy over the reliability of India's nuclear warheads provides a vivid illustration of this problem. Privately, senior military leaders express doubts about the reliability of India's tested warhead designs. Their doubts stem from critical open-source data analysis of the 1998 tests[105] as well as dissenting views from within India's nuclear design establishment itself.[106] In 2009 for example, former chairman of the AEC, Dr. P.K. Iyengar, publicly challenged the claim of his former colleagues that the thermonuclear weapon design tested in 1998 was a success. Iyengar, who had played a leading role in the Indian nuclear weapons research, design and development program from the late 1960s until the early 1990s, argued that the tested design very likely did not achieve an "efficient burn." More "hot tests" were therefore necessary to validate it for operational purposes.[107]

Another controversy arose over the two-stage thermonuclear weapon's boosted-fission trigger. Some scientists maintain that the trigger likely performed well during the test and that it would suffice as a weapon by itself. But others contend that yield reliability in boosted-fission weapons is an empirical art that requires extensive testing for precise calibration.[108] Within the military itself other concerns surfaced in the early 2000s regarding the reliability of the height burst fuse in the weaponized fission design.[109]

The nuclear design establishment has sought to assure the military that further hot testing is unnecessary; that warhead reliability is certifiable through a combination of virtual simulations, the physical testing of warhead components and subsystems, and hydronuclear tests involving subkiloton explosions. These are some of the classic methods used by advanced nuclear weapon powers in their warhead stockpile stewardship programs. But Indian military leaders remain skeptical of these claims in light of the vast disparities in the testing histories of India and its more advanced nuclear peers.[110]

However, because of the military's long institutional isolation from the weapons design establishment, military leaders lack independent means to force credible "truth tests" on the scientists. The military "has no choice" in the words of a former CCoSC, but to accept what the scientists certify as reliable.[111] According to at least two former CCoSC who spoke to the author on the condition of anonymity, "...the military can't go public with these things...but it has expressed its views in laid down channels at every opportunity...it has been done at the highest levels...but...the politicians believe that the existing state of affairs is okay."[112]

Technical controversies aside, limited intra-agency linkages between the military's nuclear and conventional commands also stymies civilian principals' cumulative oversight of military operations. Whereas the institutional impasse between the military and the scientific agencies is epistemic, the cause for the latter is the inability or unwillingness of India's civilian establishment to push through substantive reforms in the higher command of the conventional military.

The dichotomization between India's conventional and nuclear commands stems from the impasse surrounding the institution of the CDS and the joint commands within the IDS. The CDS at the head of the IDS was to be the coordinating link between nuclear and conventional commands. But as discussed earlier in this chapter, due to the government's failure to appoint a CDS, these coordination tasks have fallen on the CCoSC and the IDS, both of which are infirm coordinating institutions in the military. Because the institution of the CDS is stillborn and because the CCoSC and IDS lack effective institutional means to perform command and staffing functions for the SFC, those duties have devolved by default upon the NSA, the SPS and the PMO.

134 *Challenges of nuclear operationalization*

Following the bifurcation in commands, the Indian military's service headquarters (army, navy and air force) almost exclusively concern themselves with conventional war planning and operations. They are, as former CCosC, Admiral Arun Prakash explains, "ill prepared for the conduct of operations of this nature and none of them have been asked to create a branch, directorate or even a cell dedicated to [the] conduct of nuclear warfare or for evolution of related doctrine."[113] The military's higher learning institutions likewise also do not impart training to military officers on nuclear strategy and operations.

This institutional development in and by itself may not be a bad thing. Civilian principals could in the abstract justify retention of direct oversight over nuclear forces because the inherent risks of nuclear warfare dwarf those from conventional means. They could also point to the lack of nuclear operational planning in service headquarters as affirming their claim that nuclear weapons are political weapons not meant for war fighting.

However, the problem with such abstractions in command and planning stems from the fluid nature of military operations that may or may not hew to neat dichotomizations. Many senior military leaders in the SFC and the IDS view sub-conventional, conventional and nuclear operations as part of a single spectrum of operations.[114] They believe that Pakistan and China could use low-yield nuclear weapons on the battlefield for political effect. Such an attack could assume the form of a symbolic strike, a demonstration or warning shot against some tactical Indian formation in the field. As a result, a conventional war could rapidly assume nuclear dimensions, at a pace much faster than most political leaders imagine.[115]

Senior Indian military leaders privately suggest that the likeliest Indian response to limited nuclear use by Pakistan or China would be a war termination strategy at the lowest possible rung of the nuclear ladder.[116] The successful execution of such a strategy, however, would demand a high degree of political-military synergy as well as cooperation between India's conventional and nuclear commands. But the current compartmentalization between India's conventional and nuclear war commands does not bode well for either.

A decade after the 1998 nuclear tests, India's former army chief General (retd.) Ved Malik publicly raised the question whether the services "had been able to interface… nuclear capability with conventional capabilities…?"[117] To this question, former C-in-C, SFC, Air Marshal (retd.) Bhavnani replied in private that "this compartmentalization still exists…and…we've tried our best…we've said that it is important for everyone in the military to understand the nuclear issues…all I can say from the time…from 2001 till today there has been an evolutionary change in the understanding of nuclear warfare. Prior to 2001 nobody even thought about it…nobody said it is time to sit down and figure out the implications of a nuclear war."[118]

Senior SFC commanders claim that procedures now exist for coordinating conventional and nuclear operations. When India transitions from peace to wartime, "the relevant command and control authorities will simultaneously move into the SFC's operational command posts and the SFC will retain contact through close physical proximity and real-time communication links."[119] But paper plans and coordinating procedures, they also concede, are poor substitutes for the horizontal integration of the SFC within the IDS. In the absence of a CDS, the SFC remains an orchestra without a conductor.

In any war, the three service chiefs will primarily focus on fighting their own separate conventional wars.[120] This will also apply to the CCoSC, the nominal head of the SFC, who is first a service chief and then the head of IDS.[121] Operational direction of the SFC, in practice, will devolve by default on the NSA, an individual generally untutored in the arts of operational strategy.[122] This situation would be akin to the 1962 border war with China when Prime Minister Nehru and his senior colleagues subverted the military's operational chain of command by literally interfering in troop deployments at the company and brigade levels with disastrous consequences.[123]

However, civilian principals downplay these concerns. They regard the de facto bifurcation in India's conventional and nuclear commands a useful institutional mechanism for agent control. In their minds, the institutional division reinforces the psychological break between conventional and nuclear operations and counteracts the tendency of military commanders to start treating nuclear weapons as a new normal. Senior officials in the PMO also cite the NCA's direct oversight of the SFC as evidence of civilian interest in military affairs.

The civilian principals' confidence in handling their agents, both scientific and military, substantially draws on the institutionalization of the SPS in the PMO. The SPS marks the creation of a "system" to ensure that various parts of India's nuclear estate, "the scientific teams, the military, and the political leadership, function in a coordinated manner." It marks a concerted attempt to end the legacy of "nuclear fence sitting" and "general secrecy" that forced the nuclear system to "operate in bits and pieces," according to a senior national security manager who served in the PMO.[124]

The SPS helps principals perform three oversight functions. First, it oversees the development of long-term strategic plans for the nuclear force. The agency has representatives from the scientific community, the armed services, the intelligence agencies and the foreign affairs ministry. Together, they develop plans that factor in intelligence on nuclear adversaries, global technological trends and progress in arms control.[125] The integrated planning approach is an attempt to dilute the Indian scientific enclave's historic institutional dominance in weapons design and development; and to ensure that weapon programs give purpose to the strategic agency of the state and not the narrow organizational interests of any one scientific agency. Many of India's large technology programs in the past, including those associated with the nuclear arsenal, were characterized by conflict between the scientific and military agencies.[126] The new approach therefore attempts to generate consensual understandings among India's nuclear epistemic actors. More significant, the principals in the PMO use the SPS to monitor weapons' budgets and development timelines.

The second task of the SPS is to ensure that India develops an organic nuclear system.

At the start of the 2000s, India had a few nuclear weapons. It then announced a doctrine. But they lacked integration.[127] There was a poor fit between the weapons, which were vulnerable and unreliable, and the second strike doctrine, which demanded high survivability and reliability in the nuclear force. The prior regime of secrecy and compartmentalization had also inhibited civilian principals from developing the web of ideas, protocols and procedures that are critical to give military hardware operational teeth. The SPS's tasking therefore involves "the development and deployment of tools to implement doctrine and ensure internal consistency in the working of the [nuclear] system."[128]

Above all, the principals view the SPS's role in helping them "guard India's nuclear guardians." India's national security managers at the highest levels acknowledge that this is the greatest challenge policy makers confront. The problem with any highly secret military or intelligence system is that it is "self-referential." It cannot be any other way because decision-makers in highly secret domains "do not have the luxury of turning to outside sources of information and knowledge."[129] They hope therefore that the formation of a composite body drawn from the ranks of the military and scientists among others will provide the NSA and the PMO independent feedback on the SFC and the scientific agencies developing various weapon systems.

Notwithstanding the positive frames of reference surrounding the SPS, its institutionalization is far too recent to draw firm conclusions about its impact on nuclear principal-agent relationships in India. The agency's success, however, will depend on the quality of its human capital, its access to critical information and its ability to independently challenge the agencies it oversees. In all three areas, there are significant red flags, which suggest that oversight institutions in India will take time to mature.

Available evidence suggests that the SPS draws its staff from the agencies it oversees. The personnel deputed to the SPS do not become part of its permanent staff. Rather, the staff members are temporarily deputed to the SPS on a "need basis,"[130] and return to their parent agency at the end of a rotation stint. This staffing mechanism is problematic for two reasons. One, there is a lack of continuity in the SPS as staff members are rotated in and out after short stints. And two, there is an inevitable conflict of interests as staff members have long-term career paths in organizations subject to the SPS's oversight.

Senior Indian officials including former C-in-C, SFC, Vijay Shankar, maintain that the agency follows a meticulous filing and documentation system that preserves institutional memory and mitigates the problem of continuity.[131]

However, the conflict of interests is a more serious hurdle in the path of the SPS's ability to perform its oversight duties. Thus far only the chief of the SPS, who usually is a recently retired C-in-C, SFC, meets the criteria for continuity and independence.

Another problem has to do with information turnover within the SPS. Although there is higher degree of classified information turnover within the agency, most of it is still compartmentalized and shared on a "need to know" basis. As a former official responsible for net assessments in the military put it, "the guy in room 222 does not know who and what is going on in room 224."[132] In India, the pre-1998 regime of secrecy was rooted in the context of keeping the nuclear weapons program hidden from the prying eyes of foreign intelligence agencies. In the present, the justification for the strict information compartmentalization is existing vulnerabilities in the arsenal.[133] Whatever its rationale, such information rationing limits the SPS's capacity for critical scrutiny and agent competition.

Finally, there is no clarity on whether the SPS will assume the role of the JASON committee and perform similar technical oversight functions. Senior Indian officials acknowledge that in the last 15 years the government has appointed several commissions to investigate and advise on technical aspects related to the nuclear arsenal, including warheads and delivery systems.[134] Several of these committees served prior to the SPS's institutionalization and it is uncertain whether the SPS will become the lead authority in the institution and management of such investigations in the future. A technical committee such as SASA, for example, which advises the NCA on safety and security issues pertaining to nuclear warheads, currently operates within the AEC and BARC.[135] Therefore, unless and until the Indian government resolves institutional issues relating to the autonomy of such committees, the capacity of the SPS to offer independent technical advice will remain constricted.

Conclusion

In this chapter, I trace the process of how the Indian state gradually changed its focus from nuclear adaptation to nuclear learning. In adaptation, systems respond incrementally to systemic pressures. They develop new technological programs and add corresponding institutional and organizational routines to older ones without fundamentally questioning the means from ends. In learning, however, systems respond organically to align means with ends. Epistemic actors and organizational decision-making structures help determine whether states simply adapt or learn when confronted with systemic threats.

Prior to 1998, nuclear epistemic networks were weakly institutionalized within the Indian state. Members of the nuclear network were thus unable to extract commitments from their political overlords. Virtually all information concerning the nuclear weapons program in this era was tightly compartmentalized. In the absence of information availability and turnover, peer review of the state's nuclear decisions was nearly impossible. Further, due to the disaggregated nature of policy planning and decision-making within the state, serious gaps in India's operational nuclear capabilities remained unaddressed.

The absence of strong institutions and organizational processes had spillover effects in the post-1998 decade as well. Affairs continued as earlier, at least for six years following the 1998 tests. Decision-makers continued to resort to gut checks and sought to resolve problems in the sequence in which they presented themselves. The path-dependent effects of prior principal-agent relationships also closed off the road to any further optimization in force lethality. Operational planning suffered as the military's role remained noninstitutionalized and decision-makers attended to first-order political problems thrown up by India's formal claims to nuclear power status.

However, substantial optimization in operational planning followed the institutionalization of the SFC since 2002. Beginning in 2008–2009, the Indian state also began to slowly institutionalize a planning and operationally centric epistemic community in the office of the prime minister. Consisting of scientists, technologists, military operations research analysts and net assessment specialists, this group began to superimpose deductive planning approaches on what was earlier an ad hoc and disaggregated policy process.

With greater information availability and turnover within this group, some "truth tests" or peer-review processes are now possible in both technical and organizational domains. The end of the internal regime of nuclear opacity has also created organizational space for problem decomposition and resolution by multiple agencies within the state. These latter conditions have injected competition and oversight over what was once an insulated and black-boxed area of state policy. More significant, the institutional and organizational changes cumulatively hold the promise of transforming what was earlier a heuristics-based approach to nuclear policy into a more structured and rational one.

Senior Indian national security managers at the highest levels acknowledge that India's nuclear system is a work in progress. They candidly admit that in any closed system the problem of self-referential practices will remain a recurring one. Such a system can never work perfectly. But there is scope for improvement and reducing the margin of error. They point out that in the United States it took nearly 20 years before policy planners gained a grip on the dynamics of a functioning arsenal. In India it has taken policy makers about 10 years to achieve the same under less trying national security challenges. Systems, they maintain, are never static. The ultimate hallmarks of a mature system are endurance, sustainability and the capacity for organic growth in response to challenges. Such a system, they aver, is in place in India now.[136]

Notes

1. Lt. Gen. Nagal, "Checks and Balances," *Force* (June 2014), http://www.forceindia.net/Checks_and_Balances.aspx (September 2014).
2. Interview with senior Indian national security official (retd.) "T", May 2015, Cambridge, MA.
3. Gaurav Kampani, "India: The Challenges of Nuclear Operationalization and Strategic Stability," Ashley J. Tellis, Abraham M. Denmark and Traver Tanner eds., *Asia in the Second Nuclear Age* (National Bureau of Asian Research, October 2013), p. 106.
4. The Indian government appointed the Kargil Review Committee in the aftermath of Pakistan's aggression against India in Kargil in the summer of 1999. The committee's brief was: (a) to review events leading up to the events in Kargil; and (b) to recommend national security reforms to prevent such events from recurring. See, *Kargil Review Committee Report*, p. 25.
5. Mukherjee, "Setting the Stage: The Precursor to Reforms," *Failing to Deliver*, pp. 9–22.
6. Admiral (retd.) Arun Prakash, "India's Higher Defence Organization: Implications for National Security and Jointness," *Journal of Defence Studies*, Vol. 1, No. 1 (August 2007), http://www.idsa.in/jds/1_1_2007_IndiasHigherDefenceOrganization_aprakash (May 2009).
7. Sawhney, "Bombed," *Force*, p. 10; Bharath Karnad, *India's Nuclear Policy* (New Delhi: Pentagon Press, 2008), pp. 94–95.
8. Interview with Mishra.
9. See Indian foreign minister Jaswant Singh's account in, *In Service of Emergent India: Call to Honor* (Bloomington: Indiana University Press, 2007), pp. 231–306.
10. Manvendra Singh, "Who Should Control India's Nuclear Button? Armed Forces Have a Proposal," *Indian Express* (September 1, 1998).
11. Interview with Mishra.
12. Interviews with senior Indian defense official (retd.) "A".
13. Ibid.
14. Prakash, "India's Higher Defence Organization."
15. Kampani, "India: The Challenges of Nuclear Operationalization and Strategic Stability," pp. 107–108; also see, Kampani, "India's Evolving Civil-Military Institutions in an Operational Nuclear Context," *Carnegie Endowment for International Peace* (June 2016), http://carnegieendowment.org/2016/06/30/india-s-evolving-civil-military-institutions-in-operational-nuclear-context-pub-63910 (July 2016).
16. Ibid.
17. Sawhney, "Bombed," p. 10; and *Karnad, India's Nuclear Policy*, pp. 94–95.
18. Interview with Rear Admiral (retd.) Raja Menon, New Delhi, India, March 2009.
19. Koithara, *Managing India's Nuclear Forces*, pp. 154–155.
20. Interview with Mishra.
21. Sawhney, "Bombed," *Force*, p. 9.
22. Ibid., p. 10.
23. Interview with Mishra.
24. Interviews with Vice Admiral (retd.) Vijay Shankar, C-in-C, SFC (2006–2008), New Delhi, India, July and August 2010; Wellington, India, July 2015.
25. Ibid.
26. Prakash, "9 Minutes to Midnight," *Force*, p. 4.
27. Interview with Admiral (retd.) Arun Prakash, CCoSC (2005–2006), Dehradun, India, April 2009.
28. Prakash, "India's Higher Defence Organization."
29. Interviews with Prakash, Bhavnani and Shankar.

30 Interview with C-in-C, SFC, "P".
31 Ibid.; interviews with Bhavnani.
32 Interview with Lt. General (retd.) Balraj Singh Nagal, C-in-C, SFC (2008–2010), New Delhi, India, March 2015.
33 Interview with Brigadier (retd.) Arun Sehgal, Washington, DC, June 2015.
34 Ibid.; interviews with Shankar.
35 Shyam Saran, "Weapon That Has More Than Symbolic Value," *The Hindu*, May 3, 2013, http://www.thehindu.com/opinion/lead/weapon-that-has-more-than-symbolic-value/article4681085.ece, May 2013.
36 Interview with senior defense official (retd.) "X".
37 Interviews with Prakash and Shankar.
38 Theodore A. Postol, "Targeting," in Carter, Steinbruner and Zraket eds., *Managing Nuclear Operations*, pp. 379–380.
39 Tellis, *India's Emerging Nuclear Posture*, pp. 498–522.
40 Indian nuclear scientists privately admit that prior to 1998 nuclear weapons design and development was an autonomous enterprise within the Indian state and one generally bereft of political direction. Interview with Iyengar; interview with Srinivasan; also see, Karnad, *India's Nuclear Policy*, p. 76; Karnad, *Nuclear Weapons and India's Security*, p. 321.
41 Interview with Mishra.
42 Interview with Iyengar.
43 Dr. P.K. Iyengar, "Non-Fissile Doubts," *OutlookIndia* (October 26, 2009), http://www.outlookindia.com/article.aspx?262331 (November 2009); Tellis, *India's Emerging Nuclear Posture*, p. 510; Karnad, *Nuclear Weapons and Indian Security*, p. 406.
44 Santhanam, "The Myth Bomber."
45 Ibid.
46 Interview with Mishra.
47 Cited in Karnad, *India's Nuclear Policy*, p. 70.
48 Interview with Mishra.
49 Ibid.
50 Santhanam, "The Myth Bomber."
51 Ibid.
52 K. Subrahmanyam and V.S. Arunachalam, "Deterrence and Explosive Yield," *Hindu* (September 2009), http://www.thehindu.com/opinion/op-ed/article22870.ece (October 2009).
53 According to Dr. M.R. Srinivasan, former Chairman, Department of Atomic Energy (1987–1990): "…without more tests the reliability of the 20kt fission device is 100 percent," the tritium-boosted design, "it will surely work…there will be a bang! But the full performance of the booster part will be subject to less than 100 percent surety…in the case of the full thermonuclear device the confidence will perhaps be less." Cited in Karnad, *India's Nuclear Policy*, p. 68. The Indian Department of Atomic Energy claims that it is capable of building "fission and thermonuclear fusion weapons from low yields up to around 200 kilo tones (kt)." See, "Pokhran-II tests were fully successful; given India capability to build nuclear deterrence; Dr. Kakodkar and Dr. Chidambaram," *DAE Press release No. 52820* (September 25, 2009), http://pib.nic.in/newsite/erelease.aspx?relid=52820 (October 2009).
54 Ibid.
55 Koithara, *Managing India's Nuclear Forces*, pp. 129–130.
56 JASON is an independent advisory panel that provides consulting services to the US Government. It was formed in 1960. For JASON reports see, "JASON Defense Advisory Panel Reports," *Federation of American Scientists*, http://www.fas.org/irp/agency/dod/jason/.

57 Interview with Iyengar. For an excellent analysis of the principal-agent problem concerning the Indian political executive and the Department of Atomic Energy see, Buddhi Kota Subbarao, "The Darkness Surrounding That Day in the Desert," *OutlookIndia*, October 5, 2009, http://www.outlookindia.com/article.aspx?262028 (November 2009).
58 Karnad, *India's Nuclear Policy*, pp. 69–70.
59 Interview with C-in-C, SFC, "P".
60 Sawhney, "Bombed," p. 8.
61 Interviews with Iyengar and Shankar.
62 Ibid.
63 Koithara, *Managing India's Nuclear Forces*, pp. 129–131; also see, Gaurav Kampani, "Is the Indian Nuclear Tiger Changing Its Stripes? Data, Interpretation and Fact," *Nonproliferation Review*, Vol. 21, Issue 3–4 (2014), p. 387.
64 Ibid., p. 386.
65 "Agni (Technical Demonstrator), Missilethreat.com, http://www.missilethreat.com/missilesoftheworld/id.7/missile_detail.asp (May 2012).
66 Kampani, "India's Evolving Civil-Military Institutions in an Operational Context."
67 Militarily Critical Technologies List, Part II, *US Department of Defense* (1998), p. II–1–10.
68 Karnad, *Nuclear Weapons and Indian Security*, p. 430.
69 Kampani, "India's Evolving Civil-Military Institutions in an Operational Context."
70 Ibid., p. 83.
71 Koithara, *Managing India's Nuclear Forces*, p. 131.
72 Ibid., p. 132.
73 Interviews with Shankar.
74 Karnad, *India's Nuclear Policy*, p. 83.
75 Interviews with Bhavnani.
76 Interviews with Shankar.
77 Tellis, *India's Emerging Nuclear Posture*, pp. 367–467.
78 Interview with Prakash; Karnad, *India's Nuclear Policy*, p. 93.
79 Ibid.
80 Interviews with senior Indian defense official (retd.) "A".
81 Ibid.
82 Karnad, *India's Nuclear Policy*, p. 93.
83 Sawhney, "Bombed," p. 10.
84 Interview with Prakash. According to a senior SFC officer who spoke to the author on condition of anonymity, a committee led by K. Subrahmanyam prepared the "Red Book" in September/October 1999.
85 Interview with C-in-C, SFC, "P".
86 Interview with Mishra; Sawhney, "Bombed," p. 10.
87 Interviews with Bhavnani.
88 Interview with Prakash; Karnad, *India's Nuclear Policy*, p. 103.
89 Ibid., p. 97.
90 Ibid., p.103.
91 Interviews with Bhavnani and Shankar.
92 Ibid.
93 Karnad, *India's Nuclear Policy*, pp. 95–96.
94 Interviews with Shankar.
95 Karnad, *India's Nuclear Policy*, p. 99.
96 Ibid.
97 Koithara, *Managing India's Nuclear Forces*, p. 137.

142 *Challenges of nuclear operationalization*

98 Interview with Mishra.
99 Interviews with Shankar.
100 Kampani, "Is the Indian Nuclear Tiger Changing Its Stripes?" pp. 388, 390.
101 Narang, "Five Myths about India's Nuclear Posture," pp. 148–150.
102 Kampani, "Is the Indian Nuclear Tiger Changing Its Stripes?," p. 390.
103 Abraham, *The Making of the Indian Atomic Bomb*.
104 Interview with Iyengar.
105 Admiral (retd.) Arun Prakash, "Riding Two Horses," *Force* (November 2009), http://www.forceindia.net/arunprakash14.aspx (December 2009).
106 Karnad, *Nuclear Weapons and Indian Security*, pp. 431–433; *India's Nuclear Policy*, p. 69.
107 Iyengar, "Non-Fissile Doubts"; also see the public protest note to the Indian government by several senior scientists from India's "strategic enclave." Statement By Deeply Concerned Senior Scientists, "On Thermonuclear Weapon Capability and Its Implications for Credible Minimum Deterrence," *Mainstream*, Vol. XLVIII, No. 1, December 2009, http://www.mainstreamweekly.net/article1865.html (December 2009).
108 Tellis, *India's Emerging Nuclear Posture*, pp. 520–521.
109 Sawhney, "Bombed," p. 8.
110 Karnad, *India's Nuclear Policy*, p. 66. As former CCoSC, Admiral (retd.) Arun Prakash explains it: "I don't think anyone is satisfied. I mean people in the military wonder if five tests are enough for all time to come when other countries have conducted over hundreds of, even thousand, tests of thermonuclear weapons... they needed to do those tests, then are our computer simulations enough?," cited in Karnad, "*India's Nuclear Policy*, p. 69.
111 Interview with Prakash.
112 Interview with Prakash; interviews with CCoSC "R", New Delhi, India, July and August 2010.
113 Interview with Prakash.
114 Interviews with Shankar.
115 Interviews with Prakash and Bhavnani.
116 Interviews with CCoSC "R"; personal communication with Prakash.
117 General (retd.) Ved Malik, Army Chief of Staff (1997–2000), "Operation Shakti: A Decade Later," *USI Journal*, Vol. CXXXVIII, No. 572, April–June 2008, http://www.usiofindia.org/Article/?pub=Journal&pubno=572&ano=337 (May 2009).
118 Interviews with Bhavnani.
119 Interviews with Shankar.
120 Interview with Prakash.
121 Ibid.
122 Interviews with Prakash, Bhavnani and Shankar.
123 Srinath Raghavan, "Civil-Military Relations in India: The China Crisis and After," *Journal of Strategic Studies*, Vol. 32, No. 1 (February 2009), pp. 149–175.
124 Interview with senior Indian national security official (retd.) "T".
125 Ibid. Interviews with Shankar and Sehgal.
126 Gaurav Kampani, "Stakeholders in the Indian Strategic Missile Program," *Nonproliferation Review*, Vol. 10, No. 3 (Fall/Winter 2003), pp. 48–67; Narang, "Five Myths about India's Nuclear Posture," pp. 145–147.
127 Interview with senior Indian national security official (retd.) "T".
128 Ibid.
129 Ibid.
130 Interviews with Nagal, Shankar and senior national security official (retd.) "T".

131 Interviews with Shankar.
132 Interview with Sehgal.
133 Interview with Nagal.
134 Interviews with Srinivasan and senior Indian national security official (retd.) "T".
135 Saran, "Weapon That Has More Than Symbolic Value."
136 Interview with senior Indian national security official (retd.) "T".

6 Conclusion
Variations in practices of secrecy and its impact on nuclear outcomes

In this book I offer a theoretical framework and present evidence to show some of the slack in India's development of an operational nuclear capability. I identify the institutional and organizational pathologies that were responsible for India's inchoate response to an emerging Pakistani threat in the 1980s, its hesitancy in embedding nuclear weapons within soft operational routines during the 1990s and the varying tempo of operational developments in the decade thereafter. I argue that institutional and cognitive decision-making frameworks explain these phenomena better than traditional structural, normative and cultural ones.

Specifically, I tie the Indian state's decision-making pathologies to weak learning among its leaders. I attribute weak learning to poorly functioning knowledge markets within the state, informal and *ad hoc* decision-making processes, and weak institutional oversight. The reason for these prevailing institutional practices until 2004–2005 was the extreme secrecy surrounding India's nuclear weapons program. Cumulatively, the internal regime of secrecy cocooned Indian leaders in an environment of relative information and knowledge scarcity, which produced suboptimal outcomes.

Even in the post-1998 era, the period in which India has gained *de facto* international acceptance as a nuclear weapons power, doubts remain about India's ability to deploy an operational nuclear force effectively. This has as much to do with the lock-in effects of past technical choices as with the difficulties India's national security managers face in sloughing off historical institutional practices. Beginning from about 2004, however, India's nuclear trajectory has aligned more closely with the expectations of structural theories.

Since then, Indian leaders have gradually mobilized a wider range of epistemic actors within the state, institutionalized structured decision-making processes, and established oversight mechanisms to monitor the performance of their scientific and military agents. However, the time it has taken Indian policy to match the rationality and optimality assumed in principle by structural theories points to the stickiness of existing institutions and the path dependencies they engender because of sunk costs.

India's nuclear history raises an intriguing question: is there something specific about the country's institutions, the nature of its bureaucracy or its civil-military relations that set it apart from other nuclear weapon powers? Further, if secrecy and the institutional-organizational pathologies associated with it produce universal distortions, then are similar effects observable in other cases of nuclear proliferation? If they are not, then the inevitable follow-up question is why not? After all, secrecy is a characteristic of all nuclear weapon programs. Is there then some variation in the practices of secrecy that distorts rationality and produces suboptimal outcomes?

As far as bureaucracy is concerned, the Indian nuclear weapons program operated within a sequestered enclave. The state did not establish its standard supervisory controls over it and compensated for that deliberate oversight by placing the enclave under the direct control of the PMO. However, the development history of other nuclear weapon powers suggests that India's practice was not unusual.

In the United States, the Manhattan Project unfolded under the direct oversight of the President and a small council of senior advisors. Through the duration of World War II, Congress, the president's cabinet and other oversight authorities within the US government knew nothing of it. In France, scientists enjoyed significant autonomy in the first seven years of the nuclear program and civilian bureaucrats deferred to their judgments. In Israel as well, Prime Minister Ben Gurion ran the Dimona nuclear reactor project as a state within a state. The examples of China, Pakistan and Iraq were no different. In all states, nuclear enclaves showed characteristics of high centralization and administrative autonomy. The difference between the Indian and the US, French, Israeli and Pakistani cases, however, lies in the treatment accorded to institutional processes and the near total absence versus the existence of some, albeit, weak oversight mechanisms.

The second question concerns civil-military relations. Many attribute the pathologies in India's civil-military relations as the cause behind its odd nuclear behavior. If this were true, however, we would observe manifestations of distrust elsewhere: in conventional war operations and in military aid to civilian authorities. However, we observe contrary trends in both cases. The Indian military enjoys near total autonomy in conventional war operations. Civilians set strategic goals and allow the military autonomy to plan and execute operations.[1] India's civilian leadership has also not hesitated to use the military to manage India's internal crisis of governability. As Shashank Joshi has pointed out, of the 17 major military campaigns the Indian military has conducted in post-independent India's history, 12 were domestic in nature. Between 1982 and 1989 for example, the army deployed 721 times to assist civilian authorities.[2] Over the last decade as well, the Indian military's role has become institutionalized in the nuclear decision-making process. In fact, over the last decade, the SFC has gained significant influence in nuclear force planning, user certification of weapon systems, operating procedures, training, and the development of infrastructure invisibles. Institutional and operational changes in the Indian nuclear force have come without any fundamental changes in the DNA of civil-military relations.

In other nuclear weapon powers as well, governments gradually shared control of nuclear weapons with the military. Decision-makers initially either kept nuclear weapon programs outside the purview of the military as an institution or compartmentalized them within a small section of the services. A prominent example of this policy behavior is the US itself. Although the US allocated nuclear bombs to the air force for use against Japan during World War II, the joint chiefs and the air force were not privy to details about the nuclear weapons until 1949, the year the Soviet Union ended US nuclear monopoly and forced President Truman's administration to take nuclear operational planning seriously.[3]

In France too, with the exception of a small group of military officers, the military as an institution remained more interested in guerilla warfare in the colonies and conventional rearmament, until the Gaillard government signed off on the development of a nuclear device in 1958.[4] In the Israeli case, the 1967 Six-Day War catalyzed the military's institutional participation in nuclear operations planning.[5] The Pakistani program too began as a civilian enterprise. The Pakistani military gained control of the program in the aftermath of a coup in 1977. But until the early 2000s, institutional planning with regard to nuclear weapons was tightly restricted to a small section within the military.[6]

The difference between India and most other nuclear weapon powers essentially centers on the process of weapon development and operational plans and procedures concerning it. In other nuclear powers, it appears the decision to develop nuclear weapons was followed by the mobilization of a highly select but diverse set of epistemic actors. The latter included scientists, civilian bureaucrats, military leaders and political authorities. The epistemic actors had relatively easy access to decision-makers. Once their role was formally or informally institutionalized, the epistemic actors were successful in persuading decision-makers to make political and budgetary commitments to bring the programs to fruition. No doubt, decision-makers reduced the scale and scope of structured decision-making. But they did not abandon structure altogether. Above all, despite the regime of secrecy, the principals ensured agent competition and third-party scrutiny to monitor the performance of the programs.

The institutional difference between the United States, France, Israel and Pakistan and India is one between the degrees of secrecy. Secrecy can be conceptualized as a continuum – low, medium and high – along two axes: internal and external. High external secrecy has a less debilitating impact on the domestic management of the program compared to a corresponding regime of high internal secrecy. The two however are interlinked. A state most concerned with hiding its proliferation effort from external scrutiny will also be inclined to keep it under tight wraps domestically. Correspondingly, a state less concerned with external secrecy will have more breathing room for establishing institutionalized management controls within. A lower degree of domestic secrecy also creates more institutional space for structured

Table 6.1 Variations in institutions of secrecy

		External		
		High	Medium	Low
Domestic	High	India Iraq		
	Medium		Israel	France Pakistan
	Low			

decision-making and parallel problem-solving across multiple agencies across the state.

In this concluding chapter, I undertake a preliminary survey, which also serves as a plausibility probe, of the early proliferation pathways of four other states to compare and contrast them with India's. The four other cases are France, Israel, Pakistan and Iraq.

In this survey, India is classified as a case with high external and domestic secrecy.

France, Israel and Pakistan on the other hand are classified as cases with low external and medium domestic, medium external and medium domestic, and low external and medium domestic regimes of secrecy. The evidence shows that the absence of high external and domestic secrecy in France, Israel and Pakistan were permissive conditions that allowed decision-makers and planners to design better institutional means to manage nuclear weapon programs.

Iraq, the fourth case, closely parallels India because it too followed institutional practices of high external and domestic secrecy (Table 6.1). The Iraqi example reveals many of the institutional pathologies that stymied Indian management. Other examples of states, which instituted regimes of high external and domestic secrecy are Libya and Iran. Both are promising avenues for continuing research.

Regimes of moderate secrecy and proliferation outcomes

The French, Israeli and Pakistani cases represent time-lapse mechanisms that capture institutional variations in the regime of secrecy. Although each state conducted its nuclear program in secrecy, the secrecy was never sufficiently acute to jeopardize institutional controls within the state.

France

In many ways the French route to nuclear weapons shares similarities with India. As in India's case, strong political direction in France was lacking during the duration of the Fourth Republic. The political characteristic that best defined the French Fourth Republic in the aftermath of World War II was a series of unstable governments and rapidly changing cabinets. Prime ministerial direction was sometimes contrary to actual policy suggesting that prime ministerial incumbents were not on top of their nuclear policy game.[7] As in India, a small group of scientists, civil bureaucrats and military leaders worked on the atomic energy program.[8] And yet unlike India, despite the political drift, the French nuclear weapons program proved remarkably successful. Beginning in 1954–1955, it took France just six years to explode a nuclear device.[9] Equally significant, weaponization and deployment followed in the immediate aftermath.[10]

On closer examination, the evidence suggests that similarities between the French and Indian cases are more apparent than real. For one, the secrecy in the French program was not excessive so as to prevent the mobilization of epistemic actors or coordination across multiple agencies, both civilian and military. Prior to World War II, France was one of the leading centers of atomic research in the world.[11] And subsequent to World War II, the French government sought to resume the interrupted research for both civilian and then with greater urgency, for military purposes.[12]

There was little reason for excessive secrecy because there was no major opposition to the French program. The US was indifferent to the French program in its early stages from 1947 to 1955. Even as much as the US opposed the horizontal spread of nuclear weapons in the international system, non-proliferation did not become firmly established as the "third" leg of US grand strategy until the 1960s.[13] Indeed, the French were so open about nuclear weapons development and impending tests in Algeria in the late 1950s that Morocco along with some other African states introduced a General Assembly resolution in the UN concerning the anticipated fallout from those tests.[14]

The difference between the French approach to nuclearization and the one adopted by the US and Britain was the lack of sustained top-down political direction. The lack of such hands on political direction however did not mean that administrative direction was lacking as well. The French civilian bureaucracy wielded great administrative power in the direction and execution of the nuclear program. The lack of political direction and also the relative absence of political constraints allowed the scientists, the civilian administrators and the military free rein to shape policy.

Three characteristics contributed to the successful execution of the French program. The first was the mobilization of an array of epistemic actors. It included scientists, civilian bureaucrats, military leaders and representatives from industry. Second, the French civilian bureaucrats formalized the policy formulation and administrative process. All policy and its execution were subject to scrutiny by independent committees made up of scientists, private industry representatives and civil bureaucrats before formal approval by political leaders. Significantly, the military was roped early into the project.[15] Third, the lateral flow of information between the participating actors and agencies allowed for inter-agency oversight and mitigated principal-agent problems common to all sequestered decision-making environments.

In the aftermath of World War II in 1945, France revived its nuclear research program with the inception of the Commisariat a l'Energie Atomique (CEA) under the leadership of Frederic Joilot-Curie. But the scientists under the leadership of Joilot-Curie dominated the program only briefly in its inception phase from 1945 to 1952. The goals of the scientists and the civilian administrators in this phase were to bring the French program back up to speed from where it had left off in the pre–World War II era, signal French interest in atomic energy, and become included in the US–British strategic partnership. The primary focus of the Commisariat a l'Energie Atomique (CEA) until 1952 was therefore research and competence building.[16] Thereafter, the CEA's goal became industrial. It shifted to the production of electricity from atomic energy and fuel for nuclear weapons. With this change, power also shifted away from the scientists in favor of civilian administrators and the military.[17]

The end of the autistic phase of the research and development program ended in 1952 when it was tied to tangible industrial objectives. This shift invariably led to a wider mobilization of epistemic actors. Scientists came under pressure to accept the judgment of "technicians" and "planners."[18] The need for specialized material and equipment for conducting nuclear experiments, for example, led to the enlargement of connections with the French private industry. In the post-1952 phase of the program, the Industrial Equipment Committee (IEC) advised the CEA on all industrial, equipment and plant matters. The entire membership of IEC, 6–12 members, was associated with the private industry.[19]

There was no pressure from senior military leaders to build nuclear weapons. But the plutonium production program did not go unnoticed within the military. As the plutonium production plan gained momentum within the CEA, Colonel Ailleret, the Commandement des Armes Speciales, conducted studies on the use and effects of nuclear weapons and conditions necessary for their manufacture.[20] The military was subsequently represented on the crucial inter-ministerial committee, which in 1954 advised the Mendes–France government on nuclear weaponry-related development issues.[21] And in the absence of any overwhelming requirement for secrecy, the military also established early representation within the CEA itself. By 1955 for example, General Buchalet formed a secret bureau within the CEA, the Bureau d'etudes generales, which later in 1958 morphed into the Direction des applications militaires, to coordinate and share responsibilities for developing nuclear weapons.[22]

Institutional controls were weak in only the first seven years of the CEA's inception (1945–1952). During these years, the CEA was unique among other French public sector organizations. Typically in France, a ministry would exercise control over a public sector organization. In contrast, the CEA was granted administrative autonomy, placed under the control of the prime minister and removed from the control of the traditional bureaucracy.[23] But the CEA was also structured as a "bicephalous" organization with a scientist high commissioner and a bureaucrat administrative-general at its head. Both were co-equals and in case of a dispute the prime minister arbitrated matters between them.[24]

In the first seven years of the CEA's existence, the scientists enjoyed almost exclusive control of the CEA due to the absence of parliamentary and cabinet guidance. Frequent changes in the cabinet made links with the government tenuous. Due to this lack of political interference, the CEA became used to "freedom of action" and "autonomy." Joilot-Curie's towering personality and the solidarity of the scientists also compelled the administrative branch of the government, the civilian bureaucrats, to defer to the scientific leadership.[25] But even during the CEA's phase of relative autonomy, the civilian administrator did manage to exercise institutional checks on the CEA through an independent Scientific Council, which consisted of 10 scientists who were external to the commissariat and among the most prominent scientists in France.[26]

After the CEA's industrial turn of direction in 1952, institutional controls and oversight authority over it were strengthened. As early as 1950, the high commissioner and *eminence grise* of French nuclear science, Joilot-Curie, was forced to resign his position because of his communist leanings.[27] During this first phase of the nuclear program, a secretary-general served as the link between the high commissioner and the administrative-general. But in 1953, the post of the secretary-general was abolished because it represented a threat to the office of the administrative-general.[28] Subsequent to this, the selection of associates on the governing body of the CEA and the issues brought before the inter-ministerial body in government became the administrative-general's prerogative.

In this second phase of the nuclear program, 1952–1954, the number of associates appointed to the CEA's governing board was increased. The new board included scientists to assist the high commissioner, members of industry, a military representative, the director of the Centre National de la Recherche Scientifique, and three civil servants appointed by the prime minister. This gave the civilian administrators dominant control over the CEA.[29] The independent Scientific Council was also expanded from 10 to 15 members. It was given more formal powers including the power to render advice independent of the CEA on all matters submitted to it. Furthermore, the administrative-general acquired the power to revoke contracts without approval of the science high commissioner in matters of scientific and technical personnel.[30] Such institutional controls and oversight authority mitigated some of the classic principal–agent problems that afflict closed decision-making systems.

Without doubt, the French nuclear weapons program was fragmented within the state. In the early years of the CEA, many scientists in the CEA were opposed to building weapons on moral grounds. They were also concerned that a military program would precede the peaceful uses of atomic energy such as the building of electricity generation reactors; the bomb would siphon off money from such projects.[31] The French military until the mid-1950s was also more interested in insurgent wars in Indo-China and Francophone Africa and in building up its conventional military strength.[32] But despite the absence of overwhelming support for nuclear weapons, as an institution, the military undertook routine steps to acquaint military officers with atomic weapons and energy. Initial studies conducted by the military involved protection from atomic weapons rather than use. The Army also started the practice of sending a small group of officers annually to the CEA and universities for training in the nuclear sciences.[33]

Pressure for a weapons program came from civilian administrators such as Dautry and Lescop who gave it continuity. They, together with a small number of allies in the cabinet and the military, gave it strong central direction. As the nuclear weapons program gained momentum in the mid-1950s, the civilian bureaucrats built a coalition with the armed services and persuaded the army to invest in a plutonium production reactor and the navy to invest in a reactor project for nuclear submarines.[34] The involvement of the armed services in the nuclear project through representation in the CEA, through investments in the CEA's various projects, and through training routines were standard coordination practices in an institutional setting where the nuclear weapons program was a classified project but not one that was subject to external threats, denial or excessive domestic secrecy. Despite the overall fragmentation and lack of political direction, there was an administrative continuity and simultaneity that gave the project technical coherence once political leaders decided in favor of a nuclear weapons program.

Israel

Unlike France, Israel developed its nuclear weapons program under a regime of medium external and domestic secrecy. External secrecy was considered necessary to protect France, Israel's key supplier of the Dimona reactor and plutonium reprocessing plant. It was also a means to deny hostile Arab states the opportunity for preemptive attacks on Dimona and to stave off pressure from the United States. The Israeli program spawned the regime of what we now term "nuclear opacity" under which a state hints that it possesses nuclear weapons but explicitly denies having them.

All this said, however, there was no excruciating international pressure on Israel, either economic or military, to terminate its nuclear weapons program. The United States, despite the absence of strategic convergence with Israel during the years 1953–1968, was ambivalent.[35] After Egypt's military setback in the 1955–1956 Suez Crisis, the threat of a preemptive strike on the Israel's Dimona plutonium production plant became manageable. In the aftermath of the Suez Crisis, the French became even more steadfastly committed to

152 Conclusion

investing in Israel's nuclear weapons effort, and the British defended Israel's nuclear innocence in public.[36]

As with any secret program, institutional controls were weak. The Israeli parliament, the Knesset did not know of it until the project was well underway. The full cabinet did not debate its merits and implications. The program operated under the direct control of Prime Minister Ben Gurion and his principal aides in the defense ministry, Peres and Bergmann. Within the defense ministry itself, the program was fragmented. There was no formal chain of command or standardized procedures and accountability mechanisms. Defense Minister Peres who ran the project on the prime minister's behalf believed in personal relationships. The unusual nature of fund-raising for the project through private donations also injected an element of non-accountability.[37]

But the picture is more complex. Although the nuclear weapons project was not debated within the cabinet at large, leading cabinet ministers and leaders of the ruling MAPAI party leaders knew of it and contested key aspects of the project.[38] The Dimona project was also monitored by a section of nuclear scientists located in the Weizmann Institute outside the state. This group of nuclear scientists acted as an independent institutional check. Third, as the Dimona reactor neared completion in 1963, Prime Minister Eshkol who succeeded Ben Gurion, ended the bureaucratic fragmentation and established institutionalized control along with accountability mechanisms. Finally, the lack of significant international opposition to the program and French role as a supplier of critical technologies, plant and equipment, mitigated some of the internal principal-agent problems and allowed Israel to pursue weapons development and delivery simultaneously.[39]

Between 1955 and the end of the 1960s, Israel was extraordinarily sensitive to the French need for secrecy. Due to the unprecedented nature of the Dimona deal, French politicians were unsure if France should go through with it entirely. For that reason, there were two parts to the Dimona agreement. The first part was political in which French commitments to Israel were left deliberately vague. The second half was the technical agreement that too did not mention sensitive details about the Dimona project such as the size of the nuclear reactor and most importantly, details of the spent-fuel reprocessing plant, the key to producing weapons-grade plutonium. Both governments circumvented roadblocks by dealing with French companies directly.[40]

Within Israel itself, the Dimona project, was not debated in the full cabinet. However, key ministers in Ben Gurion's government including Peres (defense), Eshkol (commerce), and Meir (foreign affairs) – knew of it, if not all the details.[41] Meir in particular contested the project and that conflict became intertwined with her political rivalry with Peres. As foreign minister, Meir resented Peres's direct dealing with France, which she argued bypassed the foreign affairs ministry and amounted to a separate foreign policy.[42] Separately, the ruling MAPAI party's senior leadership resented the secrecy of the project and Ben Gurion and Peres's creation of a state within a state.[43]

Nonetheless, the Dimona project was monitored externally by a body of nuclear scientists housed in Weizmann Institute, which was home to nuclear physicists focused on pure research, separate from the Israel Atomic Energy Commission (IAEC), the state agency responsible for industrial projects. Within the state, Dimona was spearheaded by Bergmann who had a falling-out at the Weizmann Institute over its institutional direction in 1951 after which he left and began his appointment as scientific advisor to Prime Minister Ben Gurion.[44] Bergman found an ally in Mardor in the defense ministry.

A team of nuclear physicists led by Shalit and Ze'ev opposed Dimona for both its scale and audacity. More specifically, they questioned Bergmann and Mardor's competence to execute so complex and immense a project.[45] In response, then Defense Minister Peres formed a special three-man committee comprising Shalit, Ze'ev and Lipkin to plan and monitor the project independently. Further, Bergman and Mardor were removed from direct oversight of the project. Peres also brought in a Colonel Manes Pratt, a military officer from the outside, to execute the construction of the Dimona reactor and plutonium separation plant.[46]

In 1963 Eshkol succeeded Ben Gurion as prime minister. As the Dimona reactor neared completion, Eshkol's government enacted a series of organizational, financial, technical, and strategic reforms within the defense ministry and the atomic energy sector to institutionalize nuclear weapons production and embed it within institutional oversight, organizational coordination, and a web of strategic thought.[47] During Ben Gurion's time, Peres ran the Dimona project out the defense ministry. He subdivided the project into a series of mini-projects and managed them on the basis of personal relationships with individuals who ran them. But there existed no centralized institutional management beyond Peres. Eshkol and his band of reformers changed all that.

As a first step, Eshkol installed the economist and his senior aide Dinstein as deputy minister of defense. As Dinstein recalls, until his time, there was no clear hierarchy, no clear chain of command, no clear-cut division of labor, and no established procedures for order of business in the Dimona project. This is consistent with my theoretical observation that secrecy induces disaggregation and noninstitutionalization within organizations. However, Dinstein ended the fragmentation within the nuclear program and established central oversight.

Between 1955 and 1965, for example, the scientists had assumed oversight role in the program due to the absence of an independent authority. Dinstein brought an end to this practice by strengthening the role of the scientific advisor to the defense minister and institutionalizing his power with an independent advisory body. Similarly in 1965, Dinstein also divested control of the "leading project" from RAFAEL, the defense ministry's scientific research and development body, and shared that authority with a revived IAEC.[48]

The Dimona complex yielded plutonium in 1965. By 1966, Israel had accumulated sufficient plutonium to build a bomb. In November 1966 Israel conducted a critical test, most likely a "cold test" to validate the weapon's design.[49] Parallel with the bomb program, Israel contracted to purchase nuclear-capable combat aircraft and ballistic missiles from France in 1963.[50] The special technical partnership with France and the absence of disruptive US pressure made that feasible.[51] Simultaneously, Eshkol roped in the military to think through how Israel might plan to use nuclear weapons. The composite group consisted of Eshkol, Dinstein, Rabin, Yuval Ne'eman, and Colonels Avraham, Tamir, and Freier. Around 1966, Israel also commenced long-term systematic strategic planning and introduced 5-year plans for developing a force structure alongside a 10-year research and development plan.[52] The 1967 Six-Day War ultimately acted as a catalyst to further the military's participation and institutionalize its role in operational planning.

What all this evidence tells us is that despite the secrecy, Ben Gurion's government did not jeopardize institutional processes entirely. Ben Gurion's senior colleagues in the cabinet were aware of and debated Israel's Dimona project. Like any other classified program, Israeli leaders implemented the nuclear weapons program sequentially. Military leaders were not involved in strategic planning until the completion of the first phase of weapon development. However, many of Israel's problems with disaggregation and sequential planning were mitigated by France's role in the supply of dual-use delivery systems, both aircraft and ballistic missiles. The US decision not to challenge that supply relationship helped prevent schedule slippages. Likewise, the US decision not to disrupt Israel's nuclear quest by cutting off conventional military supplies gave Israeli leaders the structural space to partially institutionalize and coordinate the program domestically despite the secrecy.

Pakistan

Contrary to popular perceptions, Pakistan in the early 1970s was relatively open about its interest in nuclear weapons. The event that launched the Pakistani program was a conference of nuclear scientists that Prime Minister Zulfikar Ali Bhutto called in 1972 to solicit their effort in building a bomb. The conference in the city of Multan was a relatively open one with nearly 400 attendees including westerners and journalists. At the conference, the scientists openly supported the bomb project and Bhutto promised them the resources and political support to do so. Unlike the Indian program where the decision to build a nuclear device in 1972 was reached by the prime minister after consulting three nuclear scientists privately, Bhutto's Multan meeting, according to one observer, had the ambience of a "fish market!"[53]

Unlike India, which diverted fissile material from facilities explicitly acquired for peaceful purposes, Pakistan proposed to import an entire plutonium-based nuclear fuel-cycle, place all the imported plant and equipment under international safeguards, but then use the skills and experience gained from running them to replicate domestic capabilities for a weapons program.[54] To provide the semblance of a peaceful nuclear program, the Pakistan Atomic

Energy Commission (PAEC) drew up an ambitious plan to build 24 nuclear power reactors, which also served as a justification for its proposed heavy water and plutonium reprocessing plants.[55]

Pakistan's relative confidence that its bomb project would not stand thwarted had to do with its strategy and the nature of its alliance relationship with the United States.[56] This gave it the confidence that Washington could be persuaded to accommodate a Pakistani nuclear weapons program.[57] Prior in 1969, Pakistan had facilitated Kissinger and Nixon's "opening" to China. Nixon returned that favor by ordering the famous "tilt" in favor of Pakistan during the 1971 Bangladesh War with India.[58] But when US pressure thwarted the plutonium route, Pakistan brazenly imported an entire gas centrifuge uranium enrichment plant, ancillary equipment and nuclear weapons-related components from Europe and North America, in full view and tacit if reluctant acquiescence on the part of the United States.[59]

Due to the relatively moderate regime of external secrecy Pakistani leaders were able to mobilize a larger array of epistemic actors and took several steps to establish institutional controls. They were not entirely successful as the example of A.Q. Khan's nuclear proliferation network would later show.[60] However, the institutionalization was sufficient for the task of coordination across multiple state agencies. In one manner, Pakistan's institutional arrangements were similar to India's. The PAEC and its chairman reported directly to the prime minister and later president. However, Bhutto realized that he was unable to devote sufficient time on all matters nuclear. He therefore institutionalized the process by setting up the Defense Committee of the Cabinet (DCC) as the inter-ministerial coordination arm for the weapons program within government.

The DCC consisted of the ministers of foreign affairs, defense, finance, information, the three service chiefs, a representative of the PAEC and the secretary to the Pakistan Peoples Party.[61] It decided that Pakistan should pursue the nuclear cycle and the weapon design project simultaneously. Pakistan prepared a test site for the forthcoming nuclear bomb as early as 1979.[62] Further, the weapon design and test of the non-fissile material trigger assembly preceded the availability of fissile material from indigenous Pakistani facilities.[63]

It would be a stretch, however, to argue that Pakistan pursued the development of the weapon and delivery capability simultaneously. The modification of aircraft for nuclear delivery followed the development of the weapon in the mid-1980s. However, due to the integral nature of decision-making through the DCC and the military's institutional representation on that committee, the Pakistan Air Force (PAF) was able to coordinate its efforts with the PAEC and begin tackling the task of modifying F-16s by the late 1980s. That effort did not bear fruit until the mid-1990s.[64] Until then, transport aircraft were Pakistan's delivery weapon of choice. But the PAF drew up contingency plans involving a nuclear demonstration shot using C-130 Hercules transport aircraft as early as 1986.[65] Further, Pakistan's feigned movement of nuclear assets during the 1990 Kashmir Crisis with India to draw US attention is indirect evidence of the existence of planning procedures for nuclear deployment and possibly symbolic use.[66]

Knowledge and material assistance from China also helped Pakistan outsource many of the coordination and parallel tasking challenges that states find difficult to tackle under a regime of secrecy. The Chinese assistance apparently involved the training of Pakistani nuclear scientists in weapon design in Chinese laboratories, the transfer of fissile material, the sharing of an actual weapon blueprint, the design of explosive lenses for an implosion-type weapon, the transfer of a neutron initiator, assistance with underground testing, and possibly the conduct of an actual underground nuclear test for Pakistan at China's Lop Nur test site in 1990.[67]

China and North Korea also transferred complete ballistic missile systems, the M-9, M-11 and the Nodong, to Pakistan in the early 1990s. The Chinese transfer package included training Pakistani missile operators, maintenance and storage procedures. China also built a turnkey missile facility in Pakistan for the manufacture of solid-fuel ballistic missiles,[68] a step that enabled Pakistan to outsource the development of an entire category of delivery vehicles to a legally recognized nuclear weapon state, which was relatively immune to nonproliferation pressures.

Like other organizations where information flow is generally restricted, the Pakistani state and decision-makers also encountered difficulties in monitoring the performance of their scientific agents. Thus, despite Bhutto's enthusiasm for the plutonium fuel cycle between 1972 and 1976, he was unable to accurately assess the claims of the PAEC that it was making progress. One method leaders use to monitor performance within organizations is agent competition. The latter lowers the cost of information exchange and shines the light on problems, successes and failures. Regimes of secrecy however raise the bar for information exchange and thereby compound the problem of management.

Pakistani leaders did not deliberately design agent competition but stumbled upon it by pursuing the plutonium and uranium routes to nuclear weapons simultaneously. The agent competition became institutionalized in the PAEC under Munir Ahmed Khan, the organization tasked with mastering the plutonium fuel cycle and the Engineering Research Labs (ERL),[69] the organization that under A.Q. Khan led Pakistan's centrifuge-based uranium enrichment program. Both entities and their leaders acted as conduits of information for political decision-makers.[70] They also provided institutional oversight and checks over each other. General Zia who succeeded Bhutto after staging a coup realized the benefits of this competition and extended it to nuclear weapon design.[71] Likewise, in the 1990s, the PAEC and the ERL competed against each other in the development of ballistic missiles, with the former pursuing solid-fuel rockets through collaboration with China and the latter with liquid-fuel systems in collaboration with North Korea and Iran.[72]

The agent competition did not address the problem of information asymmetries entirely. Pakistan's dictator General Zia discovered to his unpleasant surprise that A.Q. Khan was prone to manipulating his political masters. Zia subsequently divested control of the weapon development project from ERL and reverted it back to the PAEC's control.[73] Subsequently in the 1990s and early 2000s, Khan peddled centrifuge and nuclear weapon designs to other states including Iran, Iraq, North Korea and Libya.[74] The Pakistani government denied sanctioning these deals and cited the problem of information asymmetries and control in conditions of secrecy.[75]

The agent competition between PAEC and ERL also produced distrust and inefficiencies in the Pakistani program.[76] The PAEC, for example, favored indigenous technologies versus Khan who preferred foreign vendors and refused critical inputs from domestic Pakistani vendors for his uranium enrichment plant. In the larger scheme of things, however, the agent competition between the PAEC and ERL worked to Pakistani decision-makers' advantage. They ultimately benefited from the independent oversight of Chinese entities and scientists who played the role of external consultants in helping Pakistan develop its nuclear arsenal.

Iraq

In the aftermath of the first Persian Gulf War, it became a common assumption that Iraq was on the verge of acquiring nuclear weapons; and that had the war not intervened, Saddam would have acquired them. In the wake of the war, IAEA inspections revealed an extensive Iraqi uranium enrichment program, which encompassed three industrial methods used to enrich uranium: Electromagnetic Isotope Separation (EMIS), gas diffusion and the centrifuge. International inspectors also discovered that Iraqi scientists were working on the design of a nuclear weapon.[77] Together with its possession of biological weapons and toxic nerve agents such as VX, Iraq emerged as the new menace in the Middle East. The discoveries concerning the scale and scope of Iraq's nuclear ambitions came as a shock because so little was previously known about them in the outside world; and also because of the prevailing belief that Israel had ended Iraqi nuclear ambitions in June 1981 by destroying the Osiraq reactor.

But since the early 1990s, more sober reassessments by international inspectors and the accounts of leading Iraqi scientists in the program suggest that initial assumptions about Iraqi nuclear advances were wrong. Not only was Iraq far from producing an actual weapon immediately prior to the 1990–1991 Persian Gulf War, it is also unclear if it would have succeeded in the decade thereafter. US inspector Robert Kelley who was part of the international inspectors' team observed later that Iraq's EMIS isotope separation effort amounted to investments in an industrial project on a gigantic scale, which had little to show for it. The EMIS machines were so poorly designed that each required its own team of operators. Overall 96 machines were required for producing sufficient uranium for a nuclear weapons program. Iraq, overall, did not even possess a fraction of the technical manpower needed.

158   Conclusion

The gas centrifuge project was still in the feasibility stage. Finally, the nuclear weapon design itself, according to Kelley, was more like a student project. The Iraqi scientists and engineers had ploughed through the literature and collected all the theoretical information needed to build a weapon without knowing how to engineer a workable design.[78]

Serious management problems, according to Kelley, stymied the Iraqi nuclear weapons effort. Those problems, as the evidence below shows, had substantially to do with extreme secrecy: vertical compartmentalization of information, weak institutions, sequential planning, information asymmetries between principals and agents, and the lack of agent competition in general.

Israel's destruction of the Osiraq reactor drove the program underground.[79] Prior to this event, the program had relatively strong institutional controls within and enjoyed the benefit of independent French oversight, the external contracting party for the reactor. It had not been Saddam's intent to build a bomb using the Osiraq reactor. Several technical features of the reactor including its size, the nature of the special "caramel" fuel supplied by France and close monitoring by French technicians and international inspectors, rendered that impossible.[80] Iraq's goal in acquiring nuclear weapons through the reactor was probably a long-term one: to use the reactor to train scientific manpower, which could later be re-deployed toward a weapons program.[81]

But in the wake of the reactor's destruction, Saddam ordered Iraqi scientists to develop nuclear weapons. Starting in 1982, the Iraq Atomic Energy Commission's (IAEC) budget saw massive increases. Saddam ended his regime's political vendetta against several nuclear scientists and rehabilitated them. Between 1982 and 1987, the IAEC enjoyed professional autonomy and there was seldom interference by political authorities.[82]

Saddam's decision nonetheless came with the very specific condition that the uranium enrichment program should not arouse suspicion abroad. The IAEC was not to procure sensitive plant, equipment or material from abroad. The entire Iraqi program therefore went underground.[83] This had four deleterious consequences: First, Iraqi scientists settled on vintage technologies that they could not only develop indigenously but also were unlikely to succeed in producing enriched uranium on an industrial scale. Second, intense organizational secrecy forced them to proceed with the development of each technology through the trial-and-error method sequentially, a process that produced lags in the program. Third, because of minimal contact with the outside world and reduced communications within the nuclear scientific and engineering establishment itself, the programs suffered from the lack of independent oversight and scrutiny. Finally, because the scientific teams working on different uranium enrichment technologies were isolated from each other, agent competition was minimal. The result was that Saddam until very late in the game accepted the assurances of progress from his agents without the benefit of independent audits.[84]

Conclusion 159

Iraq initially embarked on two rival paths to uranium enrichment: the EMIS and the gas diffusion methods. For secrecy purposes both teams worked independently of each other.[85] The head of the nuclear program Jafar Dhia drew up stringent procedures for documenting and auditing scientific and technical reports not just to assure technical quality but also to control their distribution within the agencies working on the programs.[86] To further prevent leaks, Dhia settled on an overcentralized method of management. No horizontal communication was permitted between the physics, chemistry and engineering teams working on the projects. Each team communicated its requirements through Jafar who then passed on the design specs for equipment, plant and machinery to specific individuals and agencies. The result was a failure to produce properly working components and program failures.[87] Ultimately Dhia accepted that his management style was cumbersome and accepted the formation of "zumra" or multidisciplinary teams to work on problems.[88] But that occurred in 1987, five years after the program's initiation.

Within the EMIS program, Jafar Dhia also superimposed his ideas on the project. He insisted on a new Penning Ionizing Gauge (PIG) ion source as the heart of the EMIS process instead of relying on the tried and tested calutron technology, which was used during the Manhattan Project and then discarded it because it was considered too inefficient. Many of Jafar's scientific colleagues opposed the PIG process. In 1987, the program failed spectacularly, after which it was abandoned in favor of the calutron method.[89] In the absence of agent competition and the stove piping of all information via Jafar, Saddam and his henchman however were unaware of the dissent within the team until the failures mounted.

The alternative gas diffusion method also proved unsuccessful. The method required highly advanced compressors and machines to push uranium hexafluoride (UF6) gas through metal barriers. These were unavailable domestically and subject to export control laws in the international market. The Iraqi scientists were afraid that attempts to make purchases abroad would alert foreign intelligence agencies to Iraq's nuclear quest. The chief Iraqi scientist Obeidi who was in charge of the program considered the program a scientific exercise and a technology demonstration project at best. Between 1982 and 1987, all his team came up with was a prototype barrier with two compressors.[90] This program, like the EMIS program, was directly under Saddam's supervision. But like with most leaders he could not give sufficient personal attention to the program. In the absence of an independent monitoring body that could provide oversight and redress the problem of information asymmetries, Saddam also remained uninformed about the program's lack of progress until 1987.[91]

Confronted by these multiple failures, in 1987 Hussein Kamal, Saddam's son-in-law, assumed personal charge of the program and tried to revive it through the gas centrifuge uranium enrichment process. But in this program, too, the Iraqi nuclear team tasked with developing centrifuge technology worked in isolation. Without recourse to international assistance, the scientists started with a sequential trial-and-error method involving the World War II–era Beams centrifuge.[92]

Within a few months, the scientists and engineers realized the technology was incapable of yielding weapons-grade uranium. Next, they switched to maraging steel centrifuges and with Kamal's acquiescence ended Saddam's original stipulation of not seeking help from abroad.[93] When this program ran into difficulties, the centrifuge team switched to developing carbon-fiber "super-critical" centrifuge technology.[94] For the latter two programs, the Iraqi team successfully recruited vendors and consultants from Germany, Switzerland and Austria. Thanks to foreign assistance, the program saw some success.[95] Between 1987 and 1990, Obeidi's team that ran the project was successful in demonstrating the technological feasibility of the project.

The problem with the centrifuge enrichment program, like other programs within the Iraqi state, was that it operated in near isolation. Jafar and Obeidi's teams did not talk to each other with highly negative consequences for the program. Thus even while the centrifuge program proceeded apace, there was a lack of coordination between the two teams on the production of uranium hexafluoride (UF6), the critical feed required for the centrifuges.[96] This had highly negative consequences for the weapons program. In 1990 for example, Saddam and Kamal initiated a crash weaponization program in anticipation of the coming war with the United States. To build a weapon, they ordered a grab of the enriched uranium held by Iraq under IAEA safeguards. Their goal was to use a pilot centrifuge facility to enrich the uranium further to weapons-grade. Although Obeidi's team was able to set up a small pilot facility, Jafar's team was unable to produce the UF6 to feed the centrifuges.[97]

There were four groups within Iraq who were working on the nuclear weapons program. Group 1 and 2 worked on uranium enrichment. Group 3 provided administrative support while Group 4 was in charge of the weapon design.[98] By 1990, Groups 1 and 2 had produced 5 g of weapons-grade Uranium-235. The total minimum required for a Hiroshima-type weapon was 18–20 kg.[99] The bomb itself was a paper design. Group 4 had not developed the explosive lenses required to trigger detonation. Neither was any "cold test" performed until then. At that point the delivery system and its guidance system were still under consideration.[100]

Despite the high centralization, the entire program was compartmentalized and suffered from weak intra-institutional linkages. The principals including Saddam Hussein were not only blindsided by the information asymmetries that worked against their favor but were also generally oblivious of the challenges of managing their agents successfully. Such was the compartmentalization within the program that when international inspectors came calling after the Gulf War, Kamal Hussein's Special Security Organization carted and stashed away documents, plant machinery and lab equipment related to the weapons program without consulting the scientists.[101] According to Iraqi scientists, this last act of disaggregation would have made the program extraordinarily difficult to revive, even if Saddam had subsequently decided in its favor.

Revisiting secrecy and decision-making efficiency in India

The above cases suggest that regimes of moderate and low secrecy, both external and internal, have negative effects on the management of large technology projects. Yet, those negative effects do not prevent parallel processing and institutional oversight within the state. Regimes of high external and internal opacity however jeopardize institutional oversight and lead to poor management practices. The logical next questions then are as follows: What causes variation in the regime of secrecy? Why do some states adopt regimes of medium and low secrecy when others follow practices of severe opacity? More pointedly, what caused successive Indian decision-makers and governments to favor extreme versus moderate secrecy? Why did Indian leaders forego the legendary institutional oversight for which the Indian bureaucracy is famous?

There are three hypotheses that potentially explain India's behavior.

The first is variation in external pressure from the US, the chief enforcer of the nonproliferation regime. In this regard, the French, Israeli and Pakistani cases are a timelapse mechanism, which capture the changes in the US approach to proliferation over four decades. Since President Eisenhower first announced the Atoms for Peace program in 1953, US opposition to proliferation in the international system has grown. However, in the case of US allies, nuclear nonproliferation has rarely occupied the top rung of the foreign policy agenda. The evidence shows that although the US sought to lobby and push its allies against the acquisition of nuclear arms, successive US administrations did not exercise sustained pressure to either threaten them militarily or disrupt their economic or security interests. The absence of serious international pressure in turn permitted France, Israel and Pakistan to pursue their nuclear programs with relative ease. Although each state conducted its nuclear program in secrecy, the secrecy was never sufficiently acute to jeopardize institutional controls within each state.

In contrast, US nonproliferation pressure on India was more sustained, especially after India exploited the dual-use technologies route to conduct a "PNE," which contained within it the seeds of a weapon program. Prior to India's test, the US actively assisted India with the acquisition of a complete nuclear fuel cycle. It did not insist on full-scope safeguards as a condition for the supply of critical technologies and equipment. The Indian test, however, caused a sea change in US nonproliferation policy. The test became the trigger for the enactment of tough technology export control regimes – the Zangger Committee and the London Suppliers Group. It also provided the push in the US Congress to enact tough domestic nonproliferation legislation against countries such as India, which did not renounce nuclear weapons and accept full-scope safeguards. In the two decades and a half following the

162   *Conclusion*

1974 test, the US used both measures to effectively cripple India's nuclear power sector. By threatening India's other sectors such as space, computing, electronics and high-tech industry in general and by also threatening to deny India international financial aid and loans through World Bank and IMF, the US became instrumental in forcing India's weapon program underground.

Nonetheless, the US did not threaten India with military action. Nor did it seek to sabotage equipment and facilities, or threaten the lives of Indian scientists working on the weapons program. Compared to Iraq where Israel destroyed the Osiraq reactor and assassinated its scientists or Libya against which the US launched air attacks, the threats to the Indian nuclear program and its economy were relatively moderate. Thus external pressure may not be a complete answer to Indian paranoia and secrecy. There may be other domestic factors that in their interactive effects with external pressure shaped India's institutions of secrecy in the pre-1998 era.

Regional specialists speculate that the Indian state's unusual proclivity toward secrecy is the path-dependent legacy of British colonial rule. During the colonial era, the British classified information in a blanket manner to protect imperial interests. The post-colonial Indian bureaucracy inherited that institutional legacy and has continued it to protect the interests of the ruling regime. Indian government rules mandate routine declassification of documents after fixed time periods. Yet, the government has used arbitrary national security classifications to staunch routine declassification in the areas of foreign policy and defense.

Further, the nuclear weapons program in particular is embedded within India's "strategic enclave," the complex consisting of nuclear, space and defense industries, which operates as a state within a state. At the launch of the nuclear program, the Indian government deliberately institutionalized the program as a semi-autonomous complex removed from collaborating with universities or private industry. This decision was disputed by a section of India's political class and the scientific community who regarded such institutional practices as inorganic and even more draconian than the secrecy laws then instituted in the US and Britain at the time. Successive Indian governments stuck with their initial decision and tightened secrecy laws even further citing dual-use national security reasons.[102]

Among other reasons, the creation of autonomous high-tech enclaves within the state was justified as a means to jump-start Indian science by removing the state's standard bureaucratic oversight mechanisms, which are associated with "red tape" and inefficient outcomes. In the case of India's nuclear sector, as the program failed to keep up its stated promises and as accidents and environmental damage mounted, the atomic bureaucracy raised the barriers to accessing information even further. Eventually, even the weapons program, the jewel of India's nuclear establishment, was left bereft of institutional oversight despite the high centralization and priority that was accorded it.

Finally, secrecy may have normative-reputational roots but not in the manner historically understood in the context of Indian decision-making.

Scholars have generally attributed Indian nuclear hesitancy to the beliefs of its leaders in norms against the acquisition of nuclear arms. Four Indian prime ministers in particular, Nehru, Shastri, Desai and Rajiv Gandhi were opposed to nuclear arms, some more unequivocally than others. However, Indian prime ministers, even those opposed to a nuclear weapons program, also pursued a Janus-faced strategy, publicly opposing India's acquisition of nuclear arms while permitting weapons-related work to proceed in secret. Other prime ministers such Singh, Rao, Gujral and Gowda demonstrated lesser adherence to such normative predilections. But they chose to pay lip service in public to such norms. It is thus possible that Indian prime ministers pursued secrecy out of reputational concerns, because of their own or their predecessors' normative commitments in public.

Whatever the causes of India's institution of extreme secrecy, its consequences should not remain in doubt. Secrecy stymied organizational learning and decision-making efficiency within the state. It cocooned Indian decision-makers in a regime of relative ignorance. Several technical lacunae in India's current operational nuclear capabilities are the legacy of this institution. Short of upending the status quo entirely, they are likely to remain embedded in the operational DNA of India's nuclear force.

Notes

1 Srinath Raghavan, "Soldiers, Statesmen and India's Security Policy," *India Review*, Vol. 11, Issue 2 (May 2012), pp. 116–133.
2 Shashank Joshi, "The Indian Mutiny That Wasn't," *Foreign Policy* (April 5, 2012), http://www.foreignpolicy.com/articles/2012/04/05/the_indian_mutiny_that_wasn_t?page=full (May 2012).
3 Greg Herken, "Diplomacy and Deterrence: The Military Dimension," *The Winning Weapon: The Atomic Bomb in the Cold War* (New York: Knopf, 1980), pp. 195–337.
4 Lawrence Scheinman, *Atomic Energy Policy in France under the Fourth Republic* (Princeton: Princeton University Press, 1965), p. 126.
5 Avner Cohen, *Israel and the Bomb* (New York: Columbia University Press, 1998), pp. 278–279.
6 Khan, *Eating Grass*, pp. 287–355.
7 Gabrielle Hecht, *The Radiance of France: Nuclear Power and National Identity after World War II* (MIT Press, 2009), pp. 28–38; Wilfrid L. Kohl, *French Nuclear Diplomacy* (Princeton: Princeton University Press, 1971), p. 29.
8 Hecht, *The Radiance of France*, pp. 23–47; Scheinman, *Atomic Energy Policy in France under the Fourth Republic*, pp. xvi–xviii.
9 Kohl, *French Nuclear Diplomacy*, pp. 15–16.
10 Ibid., pp. 100–104, 114–115.
11 Bertrand Goldschmidt, *Atomic Rivals* (Rutgers University Press, 1990), pp. 20–284; Wolf Mendl, *Deterrence and Persuasion: French Nuclear Armament in the Context of National Policy, 1945–1969* (Praeger Publishers, 1970), pp. 123–132.
12 Mendl, *Deterrence and Persuasion*, pp. 136–138; Scheinman, *Atomic Energy Policy in France under the Fourth Republic*, pp. 3–9; Kohl, *French Nuclear Diplomacy*, pp. 17–19.

13 Francis J. Gavin, "Strategies of Inhibition: US Grand Strategy, the Nuclear Revolution and Nonproliferation," *International Security*, Vol. 40, No. 1 (Summer 2015), pp. 9–46.
14 William K. Ris, Jr., "Comments – French Nuclear Testing: A Crisis for International Law," *Denver Journal of International Law and Policy*, Vol. 4, No. 1 (1974), pp. 112–113.
15 The military's participation began in 1952, at first tentatively but more definitively after 1954. Kohl, *French Nuclear Diplomacy*, pp. 21–24; Mendl, *Deterrence and Persuasion*, pp. 137–138, 141–144.
16 Bertrand Goldschmidt, *The Atomic Complex: A Worldwide Political History of Nuclear Energy* (The American Nuclear Society, 1982), pp. 121–125; Hecht, *The Radiance of France*, pp. 58–60; Scheinman, *Atomic Energy Policy in France under the Fourth Republic*, pp. 7–8; Kohl, *French Nuclear Diplomacy*, p. 17.
17 Hecht, *The Radiance of France*, pp. 60–78; Mendl, *Deterrence and Persuasion*, pp. 133–138; Scheinman, *Atomic Energy Policy in France under the Fourth Republic*, pp. 58–62.
18 Scheinman, *Atomic Energy in France under the Fourth Republic*, p. 63.
19 Ibid., p. 102.
20 Mendl, *Deterrence and Persuasion*, p. 138; Scheinman, *Atomic Energy in France under the Fourth Republic*, pp. 100–101.
21 Kohl, *French Nuclear Diplomacy*, p. 22; Goldschmidt, *The Atomic Complex*, pp. 130–131.
22 Mendl, *Deterrence and Persuasion*, pp. 141–144; Kohl, *French Nuclear Diplomacy*, p. 23.
23 Ibid., pp. 131–132; Scheinman, *Atomic Energy in France under the Fourth Republic*, pp. 9–12.
24 Scheinman, *Atomic Energy in France under the Fourth Republic*, pp. 14–15.
25 Ibid., pp. 17–18.
26 Ibid., pp. 31–32.
27 Goldschmidt, *The Atomic Complex*, pp. 124–125; Scheinman, *Atomic Energy in France under the Fourth Republic*, pp. 36–48.
28 Scheinman, *Atomic Energy in France under the Fourth Republic*, pp. 50–51.
29 Ibid., p. 52.
30 Ibid.
31 Mendl, *Deterrence and Persuasion*, pp. 136–137.
32 Michel L. Martin, *Warriors to Managers: The French Military Establishment since 1945* (University of North Carolina Press, 1981), pp. 34–38.
33 Mendl, *Deterrence and Persuasion*, pp. 137–138.
34 Kohl, *French Nuclear Diplomacy*, pp. 23–24.
35 Seymour M. Hersh, *The Samson Option* (Random House, 1991), pp. 47–58; Abraham Ben-Zvi, *Decade of Transition: Eisenhower, Kennedy and the Origins of the American-Israeli Alliance* (New York: Columbia University Press, 1998), pp. 93–96, 121–129; Michael Karpin, *The Bomb in the Basement: How Israel Went Nuclear and What That Means for the World* (Simon & Schuster, 2006), pp. 158–161; Maria Zaitseva, *When Allies Go Nuclear: The Changing Nature of the American Response to 'Friendly' Nuclear Programs*, PhD dissertation, Cornell University, 2011, pp. 60–61.
36 Ibid., p. 70.
37 Cohen, *Israel and the Bomb*, pp. 69–70.
38 Karpin, *The Bomb in the Basement*, pp. 120, 122.
39 Ibid., pp. 91–92.
40 Hersh, *The Samson Option*, pp. 68–70; Cohen, *Israel and the Bomb*, pp. 58–60, 73–75.

Conclusion   165

41 Karpin, *The Bomb in the Basement*, pp. 120, 122.
42 Hersh, *The Samson Option*, pp. 59, 65–66; Cohen, *Israel and the Bomb*, pp. 71–72.
43 Cohen, *Israel and the Bomb*, p. 140.
44 Ibid., pp. 27–31.
45 Karpin, *The Bomb in the Basement*, pp. 78–79, 108–112.
46 Cohen, *Israel and the Bomb*, p. 67.
47 Ibid., pp. 223–228.
48 Cohen, *Israel and the Bomb*, pp. 228–231; Karpin, *The Bomb in the Basement*, pp. 258–267.
49 Ibid., pp. 231–232; Ibid., pp. 268–269, 279–280.
50 Ibid.; Ibid., pp. 273–274.
51 Eisenhower was never confrontational with Israel over the Dimona reactor. Kennedy, despite his vehement opposition to nuclear proliferation, accepted Israel's declarations of Dimona's peaceful intent at face value until the spring of 1963. Thereafter, Kennedy intensified pressure on Israel to establish the reactor's peaceful bona fides, but never in a coercive manner or through negative linkages. After Kennedy's assassination, Johnson let the issue fade into the background. See Hersh, *The Samson Option*, pp. 93–128; Ben-Zvi, *Decade of Transition*, pp. 121–129; Karpin, *The Bomb in the Basement*, pp. 178–195, 218–222, 232–239, 250–255.
    There is also evidence to suggest that the Johnson and Nixon administrations may have turned a blind eye to the illegal diversion of enriched uranium from the United States to Israel during the 1960s. See Andrew and Leslie Cockburn, *Dangerous Liaison* (New York: Harprer Collins Publishers, 1991), pp. 71–97.
52 Cohen, *Israel and the Bomb*, pp. 235–239.
53 Khan, *Eating Grass*, pp. 86–87.
54 Ibid., pp. 95–134; David Armstrong and Joseph Trento, *America and the Islamic Bomb: The Deadly Compromise* (Steerforth Press, 2007), pp. 41–45.
55 Khan, *Eating Grass*, p. 131.
56 Husain Haqqani, *Magnificent Delusions: Pakistan, the United States and an Epic History of Misunderstanding* (Public Affairs, 2013); Armstrong and Trento, *America and the Islamic Bomb*, pp. 77–97, 116–120, 138–154.
57 Haqqani, *Magnificent Delusions*, pp. 206–224.
58 Gary J. Bass, *The Blood Telegram: Nixon, Kissinger and a Forgotten Genocide* (Knopf, 2013); Haqqani, *Magnificent Delusions*, pp. 123–170.
59 Steve Weissman and Herbert Krosney, *The Islamic Bomb: The Nuclear Threat to Israel and the Middle East* (Times Books, 1981), pp. 174–194; Armstrong and Trento, *America and the Islamic Bomb*, pp. 47–55, 64–73, 74–77, 98–137; Haqqani, *Magnificent Delusions*, pp. 225–270.
60 Hassan Abbas, *Pakistan's Nuclear Bomb: A Story of Defiance, Deterrence, and Deviance* (Oxford University Press, 2018), pp. 81–149.
61 Khan, *Eating Grass*, pp. 99, 121–123.
62 Ibid., p. 183.
63 Ibid., pp. 174–181.
64 Ibid., pp. 185–186.
65 Ibid., pp. 220–223.
66 Vipin Narang, *Nuclear Strategy in the Nuclear Era: Regional Powers and International Conflict* (Princeton University Press, 2014), pp. 65–69; Khan, *Eating Grass*, pp. 229–232.
67 Reed and Stillman, *The Nuclear Express*, pp. 252–253.
68 Khan, *Eating Grass*, pp. 238–242; Abbas, *Pakistan's Nuclear Bomb*, pp. 121–135.
69 Armstrong and Trento, *America and the Islamic Bomb*, pp. 49–58.
70 Ibid., pp. 56–58; Khan, *Eating Grass*, pp. 147–150, 196–204.

71 Khan, *Eating Grass*, pp. 187–190.
72 Ibid., pp. 238–246.
73 Ibid., pp. 189–190.
74 Armstrong and Trento, *America and the Islamic Bomb*, pp. 158–176; Abbas, *Pakistan's Nuclear Bomb*, pp. 81–149.
75 Ibid., pp. 218–223; Ibid., pp. 183–200; Khan, *Eating Grass*, pp. 359–376.
76 Khan, *Eating Grass*, pp. 151–152.
77 Hymans, *Achieving Nuclear Ambitions*, pp. 84–91.
78 Robert E. Kelley, "The Iraqi and South African Nuclear Weapon Programs: The Importance of Management," *Security Dialogue*, Vol. 27(1) (March 1996), pp. 27–38.
79 Mahdi Obeidi and Kurt Pitzer, *The Bomb in My Garden: The Secrets of Saddam's Nuclear Mastermind* (Hoboken: John Wiley & Sons, Inc., 2004), p. 53.
80 Imad Khadduri, *Iraq's Nuclear Mirage: Memoirs and Delusions* (Toronto: Springhead Publishers, 2003), p. 74; Malfrid Braut-Hegghammer, *Unclear Physics: Why Iraq and Libya Failed to Build Nuclear Weapons* (Cornell University Press, 2016), pp. 53–56.
81 Khadduri, *Iraq's Nuclear Mirage*, p. 82.
82 Hymans, *Achieving Nuclear Ambitions*, pp. 98–99; Braut-Hegghammer, *Unclear Physics*, pp. 46, 48–50.
83 Braut-Hegghammer, *Unclear Physics*, pp. 72–78.
84 Ibid., pp. 80–100.
85 Obeidi and Pitzer, *The Bomb in My Garden*, pp. 53–54.
86 Khadduri, *Iraq's Nuclear Mirage*, p. 83.
87 Hymans, *Achieving Nuclear Ambitions*, p. 99.
88 Khadduri, *Iraq's Nuclear Mirage*, pp. 89–90.
89 Hymans, *Achieving Nuclear Ambitions*, pp. 100–102.
90 Obeidi and Pitzer, *The Bomb in My Garden*, pp. 54–56; Braut-Hegghammer, *Unclear Physics*, p. 91.
91 Braut-Hegghammer, *Unclear Physics*, pp. 95–97.
92 Obeidi and Pitzer, *The Bomb in My Garden*, pp. 67–86.
93 Braut-Hegghammer, *Unclear Physics*, pp. 106–111.
94 Obeidi and Pitzer, pp. 87–98.
95 Ibid., pp. 99–118.
96 Ibid., p. 136.
97 Ibid.
98 Khadduri, *Iraq's Nuclear Mirage*, pp. 90–91.
99 Ibid., p. 121.
100 Ibid.
101 Obeidi and Pitzer, *The Bomb in My Garden*, pp. 139–140.
102 Abraham, *The Making of the Indian Atomic Bomb*, pp. 34–63.

References

Abbas, H. 2018. *Pakistan's Nuclear Bomb: A Story of Defiance, Deterrence, and Deviance*. New York: Oxford University Press.
Abraham, I. 1992. "India's Strategic Enclave: Civilian Scientists & Military Technologies," *Armed Forces & Society*, 18, 2: 231–252.
Abraham, I. 1998. *The Making of the Indian Atomic Bomb: Science, Secrecy and the Postcolonial State*. New York: Zed Books.
Abraham, I. (ed.). 2009. *South Asian Cultures of the Bomb: Atomic Publics and the State in India and Pakistan*. Bloomington: Indiana University Press.
Adams, J. May 1990. "Pakistan Nuclear War Threat," *Sunday Times (London)*, 27: 1.
Adler, E. 1992. "The Emergence of Cooperation: National Epistemic Communities and the International Evolution of Nuclear Arms Control," *International Organization*, 46, 1: 101–145.
Adler, E. and Haas, P.M. 1992. "Conclusion: Epistemic Communities, World Order and the Creation of a Reflective Research Program," *International Organization*, 46, 1: 367–390.
Admiral (retd.) Prakash, Arun. 2007. "India's Higher Defense Organization: Implications for National Security and Jointness," *Journal of Defense Studies*, 1, 1, New Delhi: Institute for Defense Studies and Analyses.
Admiral (retd.) Prakash, Arun. 2009. "Riding Two Horses," *Force*, http://www.forceindia.net/arunprakash14.aspx.
Admiral (retd.) Prakash, Arun. 2012. "9 Minutes to Midnight," *Force*, http://forceindia.net/9Minutestomidnight.aspx.
Admiral (retd.) Prakash, Arun (Chief of Naval Staff: 2004–2006). April 2009. Interview with author. Dehradun, India.
Agni (Technical Demonstrator). May 2012. *Missilethreat.com*, http://www.missilethreat.com/missilesoftheworld/id.7/missile_detail.asp.
Air Chief Marshal (retd.) "O" (Chief of Air Staff). December 2009. Non-attributable interview with author. New Delhi, India.
Air Chief Marshal (retd.) Sareen, S.K. (Chief of Air Staff: 1995–1998). January 2010. Interview with author. Gurgaon, India.
Air Marshal (retd.) "K". July 2010. Non-attributable interview with author. New Delhi, India.
Air Marshal (retd.) Bhavnani, Ajit. (C-in-C, Strategic Forces Command). April 2009/February 2010. Interviews with author. New Delhi, India.

Air Marshal "N". January 2010. Non-attributable interview with author. New Delhi, India.
Albright, D. 2005. "India's Military Plutonium Inventory, End 2004," *ISIS*, http://isis-online.org/uploads/isis-reports/documents/india_military_plutonium.pdf.
Appadorai, A. and Rajan, M.S. 1985. *India's Foreign Policy and Relations*. New Delhi: South Asian Publishers.
Argyris, C. and Schon, D.A. 1980. *Organizational Learning*. Reading: Addison-Wesley.
Arjun Main Battle Tank. May 5, 2008. "Government of India Press Release," http://pib.nic.in/newsite/erelease.aspx?relid=38445 (May 2013).
Arms Control Association. 2012. "The Nuclear Suppliers Group at a Glance," http://www.armscontrol.org/factsheets/NSG.
Armstrong, D. and Trento, J. 2007. *America and the Islamic Bomb: The Deadly Compromise*, Hanover: Steerforth Press.
Arunachalam, V.S. May 19, 2009. Scientific Advisor to Defense Minister/Secretary, Defense Research & Development Organization (1983–1992). Interview with author. Bangalore, India.
Ambassador Chandra Naresh. October and November 2009. Interviews with author. New Delhi, India.
Bajpai, K., Chari, P.R., Cheema, I.P., Cohen, S.P., and Ganguly, S. 1995. *Brasstacks and beyond: Perception and Management of Crisis in South Asia*. New Delhi: Manohar.
Banerjee, I. July 1990. "The Integrated Guided Missile Development Program," *Indian Defense Review* 99–109.
Basrur, R.M. March 2001. "Nuclear Weapons and Indian Strategic Culture," *Journal of Peace Research*, 38, 2: 181–198.
Basrur, R.M. 2006. *Minimum Deterrence and India's Nuclear Security*. Stanford: Stanford University Press.
Bass, G.J. 2013. *The Blood Telegram: Nixon, Kissinger and a Forgotten Genocide*. New York: Knopf.
Bendor, J. and Hammond, T.H. 1992. "Rethinking Allison's Models," *The American Political Science Review*, 86, 2: 301–322.
Bendor, J. 2010. *Bounded Rationality and Politics*. Berkeley: University of California Press.
Bendor, J.B. 1985. *Parallel Systems: Redundancy in Government*. Berkeley: University of California Press.
Ben-Zvi, A. 1998. *Decade of Transition: Eisenhower, Kennedy and the Origins of the American-Israeli Alliance*. New York: Columbia University Press.
Bohren, O. 1998. "The Agent's Ethics in the Principal-Agent Model," *Journal of Business Ethics*, 17, 7: 745–755.
Braut-Hegghammer, M. 2016. *Unclear Physics: Why Iraq and Libya Failed to Build Nuclear Weapons*. Ithaca: Cornell University Press.
Broad, W.J. December 8, 2008. "The Hidden Travels of the Bomb," *New York Times*, http://www.nytimes.com/2008/12/09/science/09bomb.html?pagewanted=all (April, 2013)
Breslauer, G.W. and Tetlock, P.E. (eds.). 1991. *Learning in US and Soviet Foreign Policy*. Boulder: Westview Press.
Brigadier (retd.) Sehgal, Arun. June 2015. Interview with Bharath Gopalaswamy. Washington, D.C., United States.

Burrows, R. and Winderm, R. 1994. *Critical Mass: The Dangerous Race for Superweapons in a Fragmenting World*. New York: Simon & Schuster.

Carter, A.B., Steinbruner, J.B., and Zraket, C.A. (eds.). 1987. *Managing Nuclear Operations*. Washington, D.C.: Brookings Institution.

Chambers, M.R. (ed.). 2002. *South Asia in 2020: Future Strategic Balances and Alliances*. Carlisle: Strategic Studies Institute, U.S. Army War College.

Chandra, Satish (Deputy National Security Advisor 1999–2005). May 2009. Interview with author. New Delhi, India.

Chari, P.R., Cheema, I.P., and Cohen, S.P. 2003. *The Compound Crisis of 1990: Perception, Politics and Insecurity*. London: Routledge.

Checkel, J.T. 2001. "Why Comply? Social Learning and European Identity Change," *International Organization*, 55, 3: 553–588.

Checkel, J.T. 2005. "International Institutions and Socialization in Europe: Introduction and Framework," *International Organization*, 59, 4: 801–826.

Chengappa, R. 2000. *Weapons of Peace: The Secret Story of India's Quest to be a Nuclear Power*. New Delhi: HarperCollins Publishers India.

Cockburn, A. and Leslie, C. 1991. *Dangerous Liaison*. New York: Harper Collins Publishers.

Cohen, A. 1998. *Israel and the Bomb*. New York: Columbia University Press.

Cohen, S.P. and Dasgupta, S. 2010. *Arming Without Aiming: India's Military Modernization*. New Delhi: Penguin.

Coll, S. September 1991. "South Asia Retains Its Nuclear Option: India and Pakistan Post Dual Risk as Potential Flash Points," *Washington Post (Washington, DC)*, 30, A1

Comfort, L.K. 2002. "Managing Intergovernmental Responses to Terrorism and Other Extreme Events," *Publius: The Journal of Federalism*, 32, 4: 29–50.

Comfort, L.K. 2007. "Crisis Management in Hindsight: Cognition, Communication, Coordination and Control," *Public Administration Review*, 67, 1: 189–197.

Congressional Research Service. 1982. *Analysis of Six Issues about Nuclear Capabilities of India, Iraq, Libya and Pakistan, Report Prepared for the Committee on Foreign Relations*. Washington, D.C.: United States Senate.

Davis, Z.S. and Frankel, B. (eds.). 1993. *The Proliferation Puzzle: Why Nuclear Weapons Spread*. Portland: Frank Cass.

Defense Research and Development Organization. 2008. *The Integrated Guided Missile Development Program*. Delhi: DRDO.

Deputy Air Chief of Staff "G". February 9, 2010. Non-attributable interview with author. Gurgaon, India.

Desai. June 3, 1981. "Desai Claims He Has Some Doubts about India's Nuclear Test in 74," *New York Times*, http://www.nytimes.com/1981/06/03/world/desai-says-he-has-some-doubts-about-indian-nuclear-tests-in-74.html (May 2013).

Deshmukh, B.G. 2004. *From Poona to the Prime Minister's Office: A Cabinet Secretary Looks Back*. New Delhi: Harper Collins Publishers India.

Deshmukh, B.G. 2006. "Keep the Faith," *Hindustan Times*, http://www.freerepublic.com/focus/f-news/1698250/posts.

Deutch, J.M. (Director, CIA). 1995. "Proliferation is Key Security Challenge for US and Allies," Federation of American Scientists, http://www.fas.org/irp/threat/951027_dci.htm.

Directorate of Intelligence. 2011. "India's Nuclear Procurement Strategy: Implications for the United States," CIA-RDPS00854R000200120000-0.

Directorate of Intelligence: Central Intelligence Agency. July 1982. "India's Nuclear Program—Energy and Weapons: An Intelligence Assessment," SW 8210056C/SC 00406/82. Approved for release, July 19, 2010.

Don't Extend Tejas Deadline. March 24, 2013. "Antony Tells DRDO," *Zee News.com*, http://zeenews.india.com/news/nation/don-t-extend-tejas-deadline-antony-tells-drdo_837460.html (May 2013).

Fama, E.F. and Jensen, M.C. 1983. "Separation of Ownership and Control," *Journal of Law and Economics*, 26, 2: 301–325.

Frey, K. 2006. *India's Nuclear Bomb and National Security*. New York: Routledge.

Ganguly, S. 1999. "India's Pathway to Pokhran II: The Prospects and Sources of New Delhi's Nuclear Weapons Program," *International Security*, 23, 4: 148–177.

Gartner, S.S. 1999. *Strategic Assessment in War*. New Haven: Yale University Press.

Gavin, F.J. Summer 2015. "Strategies of Inhibition: US Grand Strategy, the Nuclear Revolution and Nonproliferation," *International Security*, 40, 1: 9–46.

General (retd.)Malik, Ved (Army Chief of Staff -1997–2000). 2008. "Operation Shakti: A Decade Later," USI Journal, CXXXVIII, 572, http://www.usiofindia.org/Article/?pub=Journal&pubno=572&ano=337.

George, A.L. and Bennett, A. 2005. *Case Studies and Theory Development in the Social Sciences*. Cambridge: MIT Press.

Gilovich, T., Griffin, D., and Kahneman, D. (eds.). 2002. *Heuristics and Biases: The Psychology of Intuitive Judgment*. Cambridge: Cambridge University Press.

Gilpin, R. 1981. *War and Change in World Politics*. Cambridge: Cambridge University Press.

Goldschmidt, B. 1982. *The Atomic Complex: A Worldwide Political History of Nuclear Energy*. La Grange Park: American Nuclear Society.

Goldschmidt, B. 1990. *Atomic Rivals*. New Brunswick: Rutgers University Press.

Gordon, M.R. March 1994."South Asian Lands Pressed on Nuclear Arms," *New York Times (New York)*, 23: 5.

Government of India. 1999. *The Kargil Review Committee Report: From Surprise to Reckoning*. New Delhi: Sage Publications.

Gowda, D.H.D. May 22, 1998. "Dear Prime Minister Sri Vajpayeeji," *Rediff on the Net*, http://www.rediff.com/news/1998/may/22deve.htm.

Gray, C. 2007. *War, Peace and International Relations—An Introduction to Strategic History*. Oxon: Routledge.

Gupta, S. August 12, 2006. "Know What They Did That Summer," *Indian Express*, http://www.indianexpress.com/news/know-what-they-did-that-summer/10366/.

Haas, E.B. 1990. *When Knowledge Is Power: Three Models of Change in International Organizations*. Berkeley: University of California Press.

Haas, P.M. 1992. "Introduction: Epistemic Communities and International Policy Coordination," *International Organization*, 46, 1: 1–35.

Hagerty, D. 1995/1996. "Nuclear Deterrence in South Asia: The 1990 Indo-Pakistani Crisis," *International Security*, 20, 3: 176–185.

Hall, P.A. and Taylor, R.A.R. 1996. "Political Science and the Three New Institutionalisms," *Political Studies*, XLIV: 936–957.

Hansen, C. 1988. *U.S. Nuclear Weapons: The Secret History*. New York: Orion Books.

Haqqani, H. 2013. *Magnificent Delusions: Pakistan, The United States and an Epic History of Misunderstanding*. New York: Public Affairs.

Hecht, G. 2009. *The Radiance of France: Nuclear Power and National Identity after World War II*. Cambridge: MIT Press.

Herken, G. 1980. *The Winning Weapon: the Atomic Bomb in the Cold War*. New York: Knopf.

Hersh, S.M. 1991. *The Samson Option*. New York: Random House.

Hersh, S.M. March 29, 1993. "On the Nuclear Edge," *New Yorker*, http://www.newyorker.com/archive/1993/03/29/1993_03_29_056_TNY_CARDS_000363214.

Hopkins, R.F. 1992. "Reform in the International Food Aid Regime: The Role of Consensual Knowledge," *International Organization*, 46, 1: 225–264.

Hymans, J.E.C. 2006. *The Psychology of Nuclear Proliferation: Identity, Emotions and Foreign Policy*. New York: Cambridge University Press.

Hymans, J.E.C. 2012. *Achieving Nuclear Ambitions: Scientists, Politicians and Proliferation*. New York: Cambridge University Press.

India Shuts Down Trishul Missile Project," *Rediff on the Net* (February).

India and Israel's Barak SAM Development Project(s). January 24, 2013. *Defense Industry Daily*, http://www.defenseindustrydaily.com/india-israel-introducing-mr-sam-03461/ (May 2013).

Ikenberry, J.G. 1992. "A World Economy Restored: Expert Consensus and the Anglo-American Post-War Settlement," *International Organization*, 46, 1: 289–321.

International Atomic Energy Agency Information Circular, INFCIRC/209. September 3, 1974. Communication Received from Members Regarding the Export of Nuclear Material and of Certain Categories of Equipment and Other Material, http://www.fas.org/nuke/control/zangger/text/inf209.htm

Iyengar, P.K. 2009. "Non-Fissile Doubts," *OutlookIndia*, http://www.outlookindia.com/article.aspx?262331.

Iyengar, P.K. (Chairman, Atomic Energy Commission/Secretary, Department of Atomic Energy:1990–1993). June 20, 2010. Interview with author. Mumbai, India

Janis, I.L. 1982. *Groupthink: Psychological Studies of Political Decisions and Fiascoes*. Boston: Wadsworth.

Jha, L.K. May 3, 1967. "Nuclear Policy," Prime Minister's Secretariat. New Delhi: P.N. Haksar Files, Sub. F. – 111, Nehru Memorial Library.

Joshi, S. 2012. "The Indian Mutiny That Wasn't," *Foreign Policy*, http://www.foreignpolicy.com/articles/2012/04/05/the_indian_mutiny_that_wasn_t?page=full.

Joshi, Y. June 2015. "The Imagined Arsenal," *Nuclear Proliferation History Project*, http://www.wilsoncenter.org/publication/the-imagined-arsenal (July 2015).

Kahneman, D., Slovic, P., and Tversky, A. 1982. *Judgment under Uncertainty: Heuristics and Biases*. Cambridge: Cambridge University Press.

Kalam, Abdul A.P.J. with Tiwari, Arun. 1999. *Wings of Fire*. Hyderabad: Universities Press.

Kampani, G. October 2013. "India: The Challenges of Nuclear Operationalization and Strategic Stability," Tellis, A.J., Denmark, A.M., and Tanner, T. eds., *Asia in the Second Nuclear Age*. National Bureau of Asian Research, p. 106.

Kampani, G. 2014a. "Is the Indian Nuclear Tiger Changing Its Stripes? Data, Interpretation and Fact," *Nonproliferation Review*, 21, 3–4: 387.

Kampani, G. Spring 2014b. "New Delhi's Long Nuclear Journey: How Secrecy and Institutional Roadblocks Delayed India's Weaponization," *International Security*, 28, 4: 79–114.

Kampani, G. June 2016. "India's Evolving Civil-Military Institutions in an Operational Nuclear Context," *Carnegie Endowment for International Peace*, http://carnegieendowment.org/2016/06/30/india-s-evolving-civil-military-institutions-in-operational-nuclear-context-pub-63910 (July 2016).

Karnad, B. 2002. *Nuclear Weapons and Indian Security: The Realist Foundations of Strategy*. New Delhi: Macmillan.

Karnad, B. 2008. *India's Nuclear Policy*. Westport: Praeger Security International.

Karpin, M. 2006. *The Bomb in the Basement: How Israel Went Nuclear and What That Means for the World*. New York: Simon & Schuster.

Katznelson, I. and Milner, H.V. (eds.) 2002. *Political Science: State of the Discipline*. New York: W.W. Norton & Company.

Kaufman, S. 2013. *Project Ploughshare: The Peaceful Use of Nuclear Explosives in Cold War America*. Ithaca: Cornell University Press.

Kelley, R.E. 1996. "The Iraqi and South African Nuclear Weapon Programs: The Importance of Management," *Security Dialogue*, 27, 1: 27–38.

Keohane, R.O. (ed.) 1986. *Neorealism and Its Critics*. New York: Columbia University Press.

Khadduri, I. 2003. *Iraq's Nuclear Mirage: Memoirs and Delusions*. Toronto: Springhead Publishers.

Khan, H.F. 2012. *Eating Grass: The Making of the Pakistani Bomb*. Stanford: Stanford University Press.

Khilnani, S. 1997. *The Idea of India*. New York: Farrar, Straus & Giroux.

Kohl, W.L. 1971. *French Nuclear Diplomacy*. Princeton: Princeton University Press.

Koithara, V. 2012. *Managing India's Nuclear Forces*. Washington, D.C: Brookings Institution Press.

Lavoy, P.R. (ed.). 2009. *Asymmetric Warfare in South Asia: The Causes and Consequences of the Kargil Conflict*. Cambridge: Cambridge University Press.

Levacic, R. March 2009. "Teacher Incentive and Performance: An Application of Principal-Agent Theory," *Oxford Development Studies*, 37, 1: 35.

Levy, J. 1994. "Learning and Foreign Policy: Sweeping a Conceptual Minefield," *International Organization*, 48, 2: 279–312.

Lindblom, C. 1959. "The Science of Muddling Through," *Public & Administration Review*, 19, 2: 79–88.

Lindblom, C. 1979. "Still Muddling, Not Yet Through, *Public Administration Review*, 39, 6: 517–526.

Lt. Gen. Nagal. June 2014. "Checks and Balances," *Force*, http://www.forceindia.net/Checks_and_Balances.aspx (September 2014).

Lt. General Nagal (retd.), C-in-C, Strategic Forces Command (2008–2010). March 2015. Interview with author, New Delhi, India.

Mahoney, J. and Rueschemeyer, D. (eds.) 2003. *Comparative Historical Analysis in the Social Sciences*. Cambridge: Cambridge University Press.

Martin, M.L. 1981. *Warriors to Managers: The French Military Establishment Since 1945*. Chapel Hill: University of North Carolina Press.

Mendl, W. 1970. *Deterrence and Persuasion: French Nuclear Armament in the Context of National Policy, 1945–1969*. New York: Praeger Publishers.

Mian, Z., Nayyar, A.H., and Ramana, M.V. 1998. "Bringing the Prithvi Down to Earth: The Capabilities and Potential Effectiveness of India's Prithvi Missile," *Science & Global Security*, 7, 3: 333–360.

Milogram, P. and Roberts, J. 1992. *Economics, Organization and Management*. Englewood Cliffs: Prentice Hall.

Miller, G.J. 2005. "The Political Evolution of Principal-Agent Models," *Annual Review of Political Science*, 8: 203–225.

Mishra, Brajesh (National Security Advisor / Principal Secretary to Prime Minister: 1998–2004). October 2009. Interview with author. New Delhi, India.

Morgenthau, H.J. 1985. *Politics among Nations*. New York: Alfred A. Knopf.

Mukherjee, A. July 2009. "The Absent Dialogue," *Seminar*, No. 509, http://www.india-seminar.com/2009/599/599_anit_mukherjee.htm (July 2015).

National Security Council. 1993. Report to Congress on Status of China, India and Pakistan Nuclear and Ballistic Missile Programs (F94-1392) (Washington, DC); retrieved from http://www.fas.org/irp/threat/930728-wmd.htm (May 2012).

Narang, V. 2009. "Posturing for Peace? Pakistan's Nuclear Postures and South Asian Stability?" *International Security*, 34, 3: 38–78.

Narang, V. 2010. Posturing for Peace? The Sources and Deterrence Consequences of Regional Power Nuclear Postures, PhD Dissertation. Cambridge: Harvard University.

Narang, V. Summer 2013. "Five Myths about India's Nuclear Posture," *Washington Quarterly*, 36.

Narang, V. 2014. *Nuclear Strategy in the Nuclear Era: Regional Powers and International Conflict*. Princeton: Princeton University Press.

Narang, V. 2016/17. "Strategies of Nuclear Proliferation: How States Purse the Bomb," *International Security*, 41, 3: 110–150.

National Security Advisory Board. 1999. *India's Draft Nuclear Doctrine*. New Delhi: Government of India.

North, D.C. 1990. *Institutions, Institutional Change and Economic Performance*. Cambridge: Cambridge University Press.

Nuclear Anxiety. May 13, 1998. "Indian's Letter to Clinton on the Nuclear Testing," *New York Times*, http://www.nytimes.com/1998/05/13/world/nuclear-anxiety-indian-s-letter-to-clinton-on-the-nuclear-testing.html (November 2012).

Nuclear Regulatory Legislation. 2013. "United States Nuclear Regulatory Commission," NUREG-0980, Vol. 3, No. 10, http://www.nrc.gov/reading-rm/doc-collections/nuregs/staff/sr0980/v3/sr0980v3.pdf (May 2013).

O'Neil, B. 2002. Nuclear Weapons and the Pursuit of Prestige, http://www.sscnet.ucla.edu/polisci/faculty/boneill/prestap5.pdf.

Obeidi, M. and Pitzer, K. 2004. *The Bomb in My Garden: The Secrets of Saddam's Nuclear Mastermind*. Hoboken: John Wiley & Sons, Inc.

Office of the Secretary of Defense. 1996. Proliferation Threat and Response, Washington, DC, http://www.fas.org/irp/threat/prolif96/.

Or Rabinowitz. 2014. *Bargaining on Nuclear Tests: Washington and Its Cold War Rivals*. Oxford University Press.

Parthasarathi, A. 2007. *Technology at the Core: Science and Technology with Indira Gandhi*. New Delhi: Pearson/Longman.

Paul, T.V. 2000. *Power Versus Prudence: Why Nations Forgo Nuclear Weapons*. Montreal: McGill-Queen's University Press.

Perform or Perish: Antony Tells DRDO. May 29, 2013, *Zee News.com*, http://zeenews.india.com/news/nation/perform-or-perish-antony-tells-drdo_851697.html (May 2013)

Perkovich, G. 1999. *India's Nuclear Bomb: The Impact on Global Proliferation*, Berkeley: University of California Press.

Perrow, C. 1986. *Complex Organizations: A Critical Essay*. New York: McGraw Hill.
Pierson, P. 2000. "Increasing Returns, Path Dependency and the Study of Politics," *American Political Science Review*, 94, 2: 251–267.
Pierson, P. 2002. "The Limits of Change: Explaining Institutional Origin and Change," *Governance: An International Journal of Policy and Administration*, 13, 4: 475–499.
Polanyi, M. 1966. *The Tacit Dimension*. Chicago: University of Chicago Press.
Pressler Amendment. 1985. "Requiring Yearly Certification That Pakistan Does Not Have Nuclear Weapons," *History Commons*, http://www.historycommons.org/context.jsp?item=a0885pressleramendment (May 2013).
Pubby, M. April 17, 2008. "Arjun Tank Fails Winter Trials, Army Chief Writes to Antony," *Indian Express*, http://www.indianexpress.com/news/arjun-tank-fails-winter-trials-army-chief-writes-to-antony/297768/ (May, 2013).
Putnam, R.D. 1988. "Diplomacy and Domestic Politics: The Logic of Two-Level Games," *International Organization*, 42, 3: 427–460.
Quester, G.H. 1992. "Nuclear Pakistan and Nuclear India: Stable Deterrent or Proliferation Challenge," Strategic Studies Institute. Carlisle: US Army War College.
Raghavan, S. 2009. "Civil-Military Relations in India: The China Crisis and after," *Journal of Strategic Studies*, 32, 1: 149–175.
Raghavan, S. 2012. "Soldiers, Statesmen and India's Security Policy," *India Review*, 11, 2: 116–133.
Ramana, M.V. 2004. "India's Uranium Enrichment Program," INESAP Information Bulletin, 2, http://www.cised.org/uraniumenrichment_INESAP.pdf.
Ramana, M.V. 2009. "The Indian Nuclear Industry: Status and Prospects," Nuclear Energy Futures, Paper No. 9, Waterloo: The Center for International Governance Innovation.
Ramanna, R. 1991. *My Years of Pilgrimage*. New Delhi: Viking.
Ranjan, A. November 27, 2006. "Arjun, Main Battle Tanked," *Indian Express*, http://www.indianexpress.com/news/arjun-main-battle-tanked/16589/1 (May 2013).
Rao, K.V. December 2004. "China Was the Real Concern: In Conversation with Gen. K.V. Rao," *Force*, p. 31.
Rear Admiral (retd.) Menon, Raja. March 2009. Interview with author. New Delhi, India.
Rear Admiral (retd.) Shankar, Vijay (C-in-C, Strategic Forces Command: 2006-08). July and August 2010. Interviews with author. New Delhi, India.
Rear Admiral (retd.) Shankar, Vijay (C-in-C, Strategic Forces Command: 2006-08). July 2015. Interview with Bharath Gopalaswamy. Wellington, India.
Reed, T.C. and Stillman, D.B. 2009. *The Nuclear Express: A Political History of the Bomb and its Proliferation*. Minneapolis: Zenith Press.
Revi, A.P. 2009. "Arihant: The Annihilator," *Indian Defense Review*, 24, 4, http://www.indiandefencereview.com/spotlights/arihant-the-annihilator.
Reynolds, R. 1996. "The Diplomatic Role of Non-Weaponized Programs," INSS Occasional Paper 7. Colorado Springs: USAF Institute for National Security Studies, https://www.fas.org/irp/threat/ocp7.htm.
Richelson, J.T. 2006. *Spying on the Bomb: American Nuclear Intelligence from Nazi Germany to Iran and North Korea*. New York: W.W. Norton Company.
Ris, W.K. 1974. "Comments – French Nuclear Testing: A Crisis for International Law," *Denver Journal of International Law and Policy*, 4,1: 112–113.

Rublee, M.R. 2009. *Nonproliferation Norms: Why States Choose Nuclear Restraint*. Athens: University of Georgia Press.

Sagan, S.D. 1996/1997. "Why Do States Build Nuclear Weapons? Three Models in Search of a Bomb," *International Security*, 21, 3: 54–86.

Sagan, S.D. 2009. *Inside Nuclear South Asia*. Stanford: Stanford Security Series.

Sagan, S.D. and Waltz, K. 2003. *The Spread of Nuclear Weapons: A Debate Renewed*. New York: W.W. Norton Company.

Santhanam, K. (Chief Technology Advisor to Science Advisor to Defense Minister). May 2009. Interview with author. New Delhi, India.

Saran, S. May 4, 2013. "Weapon That Has More Than Symbolic Value," *Hindu*, http://www.thehindu.com/opinion/lead/weapon-that-has-more-than-symbolic-value/article4681085.ece.

Sawhney, P. February 2004. "Bombed," *Force*. 8–10.

Scheinman, L. 1965. *Atomic Energy Policy in France Under the Fourth Republic*. Princeton: Princeton University Press.

Senior Air Force Officer "Z". February 2010. Non-attributable interviews with author. New Delhi, India.

Senior Army Officer "Q" (NBC Warfare Directorate: Indian Army Headquarters). May 2009. Non-attributable interview with author. New Delhi, India.

Senior Indian Air Force Officer "L". December 2009. Non-attributable interview with author. New Delhi, India.

Senior Indian Air Force Officer "M". December 2009. Non-attributable interview with author, New Delhi, India.

Senior Indian Air Force Officer "S". December 2009. Non-attributable interview with author. New Delhi, India.

Senior Indian Defense Official "A". July and August 2010. Non-attributable interviews with author. New Delhi, India.

Senior Indian Defense Official "F". December 2009. Non-attributable interview with author. New Delhi, India

Senior Indian Defense Official "X". October/November 2009. Non-attributable interviews with author. New Delhi, India.

Senior Indian National Security Official "T". May 8, 2015. Non-attributable interview with author, Cambridge, United States.

Shankman, N.A. 1999. "Reframing the Debate between Agency and Stakeholder Theories of the Firm," *Journal of Business Ethics*, 19, 4: 319–334.

Sharma, P. and Ashraf, A. October 5, 2009. "The Myth Bomber: Interview with K. Santhanam," *Outlook India*, http://www.outlookindia.com/article.aspx?262027.

Shukla, A. April 19, 2008. "Armed Forces Prefer Russian Armor," *Business Standard*, http://web.archive.org/web/20110607132933/http://www.business-standard.com/india/storypage.php?autono=320574 (May 2013).

Sidhu, M.S. September–October 1998. "Victimized by the Official Secrets Act: The Story of Dr. B.K. Subbarao," *Manushi*, 108, http://www.indiatogether.org/manushi/issue108/subbprof.htm.

Simon, H.A. "Alternative Visions of Rationality," pp. 19–23.

Simon, H.A. 1983. *Reason in Human Affairs*. Stanford: Stanford University Press.

Singh, J. (ed.). 1998a. *Nuclear India*. New Delhi: Knowledge World.

Singh, J. (ed.). 1999a. *Kargil: Pakistan's Fourth War for Kashmir*. New Delhi: South Asia Books.

Singh, J. 1999b. *Defending India*. Bangalore: Macmillan Press India.

Singh, J. 2007. *In Service of Emergent India: Call to Honor*. Bloomington: Indiana University Press.
Singh, M. September 1, 1998b. "Who Should Control India's Nuclear Button? Armed Forces Have a Proposal," *Indian Express*.
Solingen, E. 2007. *Nuclear Logics: Contrasting Paths in East Asia and the Middle East*. Princeton: Princeton University Press.
Solingen, S. 1994. "The Political Economy of Nuclear Restraint," *International Security*, 19, 2: 126–169.
Spector, L.S. 1985. *New Nuclear Nations*. New York: Vintage Books.
Spector, L.S. 1987. *Going Nuclear*. Cambridge: Ballinger Publishing Company.
Spector, Leonard S. with Smith, Jacqueline R. 1990. *Nuclear Ambitions: The Spread of Nuclear Weapons 1989–1990*. Boulder: Westview Press.
Speier, R.H., Chow, B.G., and Starr, R.S. 2001. *Nonproliferation Sanctions*. Santa Monica: Rand.
Spence, M. 1973. "Job Market Signaling," *The Quarterly Journal of Economics*, 87, 3: 355–374.
Sreedhar. 1986. *Pakistan's Bomb: A Documentary Study*. New Delhi: ABC Publishing House.
Srinivasan, M.R. 2002. *From Fission to Fusion: The Story of India's Atomic Energy Program*. New Delhi: Viking.
Srinivasan, M.R. (Chairman Atomic Energy Commission/Secretary, Department of Atomic Energy, Government of India: 1987–1990). July 8, 2010. Interview with author. Bangalore, India.
Statement by Deeply Concerned Senior Scientists. December 26, 2009. "On Thermonuclear Weapon Capability and Its Implications for Credible Minimum Deterrence," *Mainstream*, XLVIII, 1, http://www.mainstreamweekly.net/article1865.html.
Steinbruner, J.D. 1974. *The Cybernetic Theory of Decision: New Dimensions of Political Analysis*. Princeton: Princeton University Press.
Stiglitz, J.E. 1975. "The Theory of 'Screening', Education, and the Distribution of Income," *The American Economic Review*, 65, 3: 283–300.
Subbarao, K. October 5, 2009. "The Darkness Surrounding That Day in the Desert," *OutlookIndia*, http://www.outlookindia.com/article.aspx?262028.
Subrahmanyam, K. October 2009. Interviews with author. Noida, India.
Subrahmanyam, K. and Arunachalam, V.S. September 2009. "Deterrence and Explosive Yield," *Hindu*, http://www.thehindu.com/opinion/op-ed/article22870.ece.
Subrahmanyam, K. with Monteiro, Arthur. 2005. "Indian Nuclear Policy," *Shedding Shibboleths: India's Evolving Strategic Outlook*. Delhi: Wordsmiths.
Sundarji, K., "Effects of Nuclear Asymmetry on Conventional Deterrence.
Sundarji, K. 1981a. Combat Paper No. 1. Mhow: College of Combat.
Sundarji, K. 1981b. "Nuclear Weapons in a Third World Context," Combat Paper No. 2. Mhow: College of Combat.
Sundarji, K. 1993. *Blind Men of Hindoostan*. New Delhi: UBS Publishers.
Sundarji, K. 2003. *Vision 2100: A Strategy for the Twenty-First Century*. New Delhi: Konark Publishers Ltd.
Surowiecki, J. 2004. *The Wisdom of Crowds*. New York: Doubleday.
Tanham, G. 1996. *Securing India: Strategic Thought and Practice*. New Delhi: Manohar.

Tellis, A.J. 2001. *India's Emerging Nuclear Posture: Between Recessed and Ready Arsenal*. Santa Monica: Rand.

Venkataraman, R. 1994. *My Presidential Years*. New Delhi: HarperCollins Publishers India.

Walt, S.M. 1985. "Alliance Formation and the Balance of World Power," *International Security*, 9, 4: 3–43.

Waltz, K.N. 1981. "The Spread of Nuclear Weapons: More May Be Better," Adelphi Paper 171. London: IISS.

Waterman, R.W. and Meier, K.J. 1998. "Principal-Agent Models: An Expansion?" *Journal of Public Administration Research and Theory: J-PART*, 8, 2: 173–202.

Weissman, S. and Krosney, H. 1981. *The Islamic Bomb: The Nuclear Threat to Israel and the Middle East*, New York: Times Books.

Woolsey, R.J. February 24, 1993. "Testimony before the US Senate Committee on Governmental Affairs," *Proliferation Threats of the 1990s: Hearing before the Committee on Governmental Affairs: United States Senate, 102nd Cong., 1st Sess.* Washington, DC: US Government Printing Office, 14–15.

Zaitseva, M. 2011. "When Allies Go Nuclear: The Changing Nature of the American Response to 'Friendly' Nuclear Programs." PhD Dissertation. Ithaca: Cornell University.

Index

Note: Page numbers in italic indicate a figure and page numbers in bold indicate a table on the corresponding page.

adaptation 3–4, 10, 105, 137
AEC *see* Atomic Energy Commission
agent competition: inter-agent 69–75; limitations 98–104
agent monitoring: cost reduction methods for 24; impact of weak 98–104; importance of 12; open and closed decision-making system comparisons of **25**
agents: definition of 21; as knights and knaves 23; signaling 25; *see also* principal-agent model
Agni Technology Demonstrator 78n44; range of 56, **56**; testing of 57, 126
Apollo program 73
arms control community, US 14
Arunachalam, V.S. 59, 64, 90, 91, 102, 104
Atomic Energy Commission (AEC): division within 54–56; of Iraq 158; of Israel 153; oversight and critical program choices from 70; of Pakistan 66, 154–157
Atoms for Peace program 61, 161

"balance of threat" 1, 7n6
ballistic missile programs: Agni Technology Demonstrator 56, **56**, 57, 78n44, 126; canisterization for 131; Gandhi, I., establishing 49–50; Prithvi 56, **56**, 57, 75, 108n75; reliability issues of 126–127; types and ranges of **56**; Valiant 52, **56**, 77n19
BARC *see* Bhabha Atomic Research Center
Basrur, Rajesh M. 37–38

Bhabha Atomic Research Center (BARC) 27, 50; autonomy of 98–99; compartmentalization between DRDO and 57; DRDO meeting with 123–124; nuclear test of 1974 analysis by 71–72; weaponization hijacked by DRDO and 101–102
Bharatiya Janata Party (BJP) 32
Bhavnani, Ajit 127–128, 134
biases: cognitive 12, 91–98; decision-making errors from 69; psychological 18–21
BJP *see* Bharatiya Janata Party
Blue Book 129
Brasstacks Crisis 92

Cabinet Committee on Security (CCS) 94–95
Canada 61
canisterization 131
Carnegie School 20, 45n52
CCoSC *see* Chairman Chiefs of Staff Committee
CCS *see* Cabinet Committee on Security
CDS *see* Chief of Defense Staff
CEA *see* Commisariat a l'Energie Atomique
Central Intelligence Agency (CIA) 62, 84
Chairman Chiefs of Staff Committee (CCoSC): CDS as replacement option of 116–117; National Strategic Nuclear Command proposed by 115; rotation of 119
Chandra, Naresh 87–89, 95, 104
Chandra, Satish 95–96, 97

Index

Chief of Defense Staff (CDS) 116–117
Chiefs of Staff Committee (CoSC) 116–117
China: ballistic missile program for targeting 126; military leader beliefs on 134; nuclear threats from 28; Pakistan nuclear weapon assistance from 2, 68–69, 156
CIA *see* Central Intelligence Agency
CIRUS reactor 61, 73–74
closed decision-making system: agent monitoring in **25**; dilemma of 113
cognitive biases: epistemic actors helping with 12; India nuclear program/policy (1989–1998) 91–98
cognitive dissonance 96
cognitive psychology 18–20
Commisariat a l'Energie Atomique (CEA) 149–151
compartmentalization: between BARC and DRDO 57; disaggregation and 50–60, **55**; India nuclear program/policy (1989–1998) 91–98; from institutional stasis 132; Kashmir crisis impacted by 89; from secrecy 5
Comprehensive Test Ban Treaty (CTBT) 35
conflict zones 29
consensual knowledge: definition of 13; incorporation of 120–121
CoSC *see* Chiefs of Staff Committee
CTBT *see* Comprehensive Test Ban Treaty
cybernetic model 19

DAE *see* Department of Atomic Energy
damage expectancy (DE) 122
DCC *see* Defense Committee of the Cabinet
DE *see* damage expectancy
decision-making: closed system of **25**, 113; heuristics into structured, shift from 121–131; monopolist 18–21; open and decentralized systems of **22**; open system of **25**; organizational schematic of optimal and actual **55**; overview 144; revisitation of efficiency in 161–163; sequestered, downside of 60–69
deep state 35
de facto nuclear weapon power: meaning of 83; status of 1
Defense Committee of the Cabinet (DCC) 155

Defense Research & Development Organization (DRDO) 27, 50; autonomy of 98–99; BARC meeting with 123–124; compartmentalization between BARC and 57; failures of 74–75; IGMDP directed by 56; scientists and technologists of 90–91; secrecy of 99–101; Special Purchase Team of 62–63; weaponization hijacked by BARC and 101–102
Defensive Realism: assumptions 75; nuclear demand-side argument 28–30; socialization in relation to 10–11
Department of Atomic Energy (DAE): on fission and thermonuclear warhead production 140n53; power generation issues 52; reactor problems for 61, 70–71
Desai, Morarji 52–53
Dhawan, Satish 52
Dhruva reactor 73–74, 81n145
Dimona reactor 151–154, 165n51
disaggregation 50–60, **55**
DRDO *see* Defense Research & Development Organization

economy 38–40
Electromagnetic Isotope Separation (EMIS) 157, 159
electromagnetic pulse (EMP) 87, 100, 102
EMIS *see* Electromagnetic Isotope Separation
EMP *see* electromagnetic pulse
Engineering Research Labs (ERL) 66, 156–157
epistemic actors/communities: consensual knowledge of 13; constraints and limitations on 5; definition of 4; disaggregation impacting 58–60; examples of successful 14; India nuclear program/policy network of 27; institutionalization of new, deepening 114–121, *117*; institutionalization of, weak 90–91; institutional strength assessment of 16–17; mobilization of 15–16; PMO secrecy impacting 51; for policy innovation 16, 40; as "primitive group" 15; role of 13–17; state learning and 17, **18**; for uncertainty management 12
"equifinality" 6
ERL *see* Engineering Research Labs
expert communities 16–17

180 *Index*

fission warheads 126, 140n53
France nuclear weapons program: CEA and 149–151; characteristics contributing to success of 148–149; outcomes and secrecy level of 146–151, **147**
Frey, Karsten 31, 32–33

Gandhi, Indira: ballistic missile program established by 49–50; election lost by 52; nuclear tests approved by 59; return to power 53
Gandhi, Rajiv: air deliverable nuclear weapon authorization from 83; LWRs favored by 56; nuclear scientists' assurances to 73; Policy Planning Group of 54, 67; pressure on 86; as "reluctant believer" of nuclear cause 34
GDP *see* gross domestic product
goals: divergence 21–22, 23; types of 16
GoM report *see* Group of Ministers report
"grey market" 62
gross domestic product (GDP) 39
Group of Ministers (GoM) report 114, 116

Haas, Ernst 13
heuristics: in decision-making and planning structure, shift from 121–131; types of 20; vulnerability to 13
higher defense management 116–117, *117*
Hindu nationalism 32

IAEA *see* International Atomic Energy Agency
IAF *see* Indian Air Force
IDS *see* Integrated Defense Staff
IGMDP *see* Integrated Guided Missile Program
India: deep state of 35; higher defense management of 116–117, *117*; institutional capacity of 2; Kargil War between Pakistan and 85, 107n20, 115; Kashmir crisis between Pakistan and 89, 90, 93–94, 106n7; national security lagging for 1; nuclear fence sitting by 9; option strategy of 50; post-colonial modernity 31–32
Indian Air Force (IAF): on aircraft reliability 126; air delivery nuclear authorization for 83; air delivery nuclear capability completion 7n18, 107n17; air delivery nuclear capability problems 57–58, 86–87, 93, 99–101; combat aircraft purchased by 50; compartmentalization between BARC and 57; DRDO complaints from 74–75, 99–101; Jaguar aircraft of 57–58, 74; Mirage 2000 aircraft of 57–58, 74, 87, 93, 100; on Osiraq attacks 80n111; on procedure complications 103–104; rotation maneuver concern of 99–100, 110n127; on training and safety issues 102–103; on weaponization, lack of information 88–89, 115–116
Indian Space Research Organization (ISRO) 51, 52, 98–99
India nuclear program/policy: bureaucracy question on 144–145; civil-military relations question on 145; consequences of delaying 2; efforts to improve 2–3; epistemic actors network influencing 27; France nuclear weapons program compared to 146–151, **147**; Iraq nuclear weapons program compared to 146–147, **147**, 157–161; Israel nuclear weapons program compared to 146–147, **147**, 151–154; nuclear demand-side arguments 28–30; nuclear supply-side constraint arguments 28, 30–40; Pakistan nuclear weapons program compared to 146–147, **147**, 154–157; puzzlement over 10; research overview of 42–43; research questions on 3–5; secrecy and decision-making efficiency revisited in 161–163; state learning and secrecy argument specific to 25–28; US nuclear weapons program compared to 146; US pressure on 161–162; "within case" analysis approach to 5–6; as work in progress 9; *see also specific topics*
India nuclear program/policy (1980–1989): developments leading to 49–50; disaggregation and compartmentalization of 50–60, 55; principal-agent problems and inter-agent competition during 69–75; sequestered decision-making and inferences during 60–69; takeaways from 75–76
India nuclear program/policy (1989–1998): agent competition limitations

and weak monitoring during 98–104; compartmentalization, cognitive biases, and constrained optimizing during 91–98; epistemic communities weak institutionalization impacting 90–91; information sharing restrictions during 88–89; non-weaponized deterrence 84, 85; nuclear learning during 86–91; recessed deterrence 84–85, 107n16; takeaways from 104–106; US on capability of 83–84
India nuclear program/policy (1999–2010): institutionalization and socialization processes formalizing in 112–113; institutionalization of new epistemic actors during 114–21, *117*; nuclear deterrence as focus of 112; principal-agent relationship evolution and operational dilemmas during 131–137; shift from heuristics to structured decisions and planning during 121–131; takeaways from 137–138
information: access to sensitive 17; cost reduction mechanisms of obtaining 98
information asymmetries 21–22, 24
institutionalization: of epistemic actors 4; epistemic actors deepening 114–121, *117*; epistemic communities weak 90–91; process of formal 112–113; of SFC and SPS 113; of state administrative structure 16–17
institutional stasis 132
Integrated Defense Staff (IDS): proposal for creating 116; SFC in relation to 119–120
Integrated Guided Missile Program (IGMDP) 99; DRDO directing 56; Prithvi missile development as part of 108n75
inter-agent competition 69–75
International Atomic Energy Agency (IAEA): Iraq inspections from 157; NNPA and 51–52
interviewing methods 6
Iraq: nuclear weapons program 146–147, **147**, 157–161; Osiraq reactor in 67, 80n111
Israel: Dimona reactor project in 151–154, 165n51; nuclear opacity term originating in 151; Osiraq reactor attacked by 67, 80n111

Israel nuclear weapons program: outcomes and secrecy level of 146–147, **147**, 151–154; US on 154, 165n51
ISRO *see* Indian Space Research Organization
Iyengar, P.K. 72–73, 125, 132–133

Jaguar aircraft 57–58, 74
Joint Intelligence Committee (JIC) 53

Kalam, Abdul A.P.J. 7n18, 107n17, 124
Kargil Review Committee: Kalam testimony before 7n18, 107n17; report 114, 139n4
Kargil War 85; cause of 107n20; outbreak of 115
Kashmir crisis: aftermath of 90; compartmentalization prior to 89; eruption of 106n7; nuclear emergency procedures lacking during 93–94
Kelley, Robert 157–158

liberalization coalitions/agendas 38–39
light-water reactors (LWRs) 56

Malik, Ved 115, 134
Manhattan project 73, 145
Mirage 2000 aircraft 57–58, 74, 87, 93, 100
Mishra, Brajesh: on DRDO and BARC meeting 123–124; on military communication 130; on nuclear command authority 118; on Soviet Union 115; on threat of sanctions 98
mobilization: demands for 114; of epistemic actors 15–16; fractional 89; against Pakistan 128–129; by PMO 53
monopolist decision-making 18–21
moral hazard concept 22–23

Narang, Vipin 29–30
National Command Authority (NCA): SASA advising 120; SPS working with 113
national security: India's lagging 1; nuclear weapons-related risks 75–76; prestige over 31
National Security Advisor (NSA): Mishra 98, 115, 118, 123–124, 130; SASA advising 120

National Strategic Nuclear Command 115
NCA *see* National Command Authority
Neorealism 9, 105
NNPA *see* Nuclear Nonproliferation Act
non-weaponized deterrence: meaning of 84; recessed deterrence compared to 85
normative ideology 34–38
NSA *see* National Security Advisor
"Nuclear Acquisition Theory" 29–30
nuclear asymmetry 7n5, 58
nuclear demand-side arguments 28–30
nuclear deterrence: India nuclear program/policy (1999–2010) focus of 112; non-weaponized 84, 85; recessed 84–85, 107n16
nuclear device 8n25, 92
nuclear fence sitting 9
nuclear minimalism 37–38
Nuclear Nonproliferation Act (NNPA): Pressler Amendment and 79n84; US Congress passing 51–52
nuclear opacity: end of 112; origin of 151; recessed deterrence in relation to 107n16; *see also* India nuclear program/policy (1989–1998)
Nuclear Suppliers Group 51, 77n12
nuclear supply-side constraint arguments: economic 38–40; normative ideology 34–38; prestige 31–34; types of 28, 30–31
nuclear tests: BJP ordering 32; Gandhi, I., approving 59; gap between 1; of 1974 49, 71–72, 76n2, 161–162; of 1998 115, 122–124, 132–133; at Pokhran test site 63, 71–72; prime ministers opposed to 38, 52; US 126–127
nuclear threats: from China 28; from Pakistan 1–2, 3, 28; vulnerability to 92

opacity: external 69; internal 51; nuclear 107n16, 112, 151
open access policy 4
open and decentralized decision-making systems **22**
open decision-making system **25**
operational dilemmas 131–137
operationalization challenges *see* India nuclear program/policy (*1999*–2010)
operational readiness 84–85
Operation Brasstacks 67

optimization: challenges to 19; India nuclear program/policy (1989–1998) constrained 91–98; parallel processing and problem decomposition for 21; rational 18, **22**; signs of uneven 121
organizational learning 18–21
Osiraq reactor 67, 80n111
oversight: from AEC 70; avoidance of institutional 105; PMO lacking 120; SPS and SFC for management and 112; SPS functions of 135–136

PAEC *see* Pakistan Atomic Energy Commission
PAF *see* Pakistan Air Force
Pakistan: Brasstacks Crisis with 92; China nuclear weapon assistance to 2, 68–69, 156; DCC of 155; ERLs in 66, 156–157; JIC report on 53; Kargil War between India and 85, 107n20, 115; Kashmir crisis between India and 89, 90, 93–94, 106n7; military leader beliefs on 134; mobilization against 128–129; nuclear device acquisition by 50; nuclear threats from 1–2, 3, 28; revanchism 49; tacit knowledge of 66; uranium enrichment as focus of 64–65; US limited sanctions on 98; US relations with 63–64, 79n84
Pakistan Air Force (PAF) 155
Pakistan Atomic Energy Commission (PAEC) 66, 154–157
Pakistan nuclear weapons program: outcomes and secrecy level of 146–147, **147**, 154–157; skepticism toward capability of 65–68; US on capability of 83–84
panic 64
parallel processing: avoidance of 105; for optimization 21; secrecy preventing 92
Parthasarathi, Ashok 61, 71
peaceful nuclear explosion (PNE): nuclear test of 1974 as 49; US ideas on conducting 76n1
Perkovich, George 83, 84, 90
Pierson, Paul 29
Ploughshares program, US 49, 76n1
PMO *see* Prime Minister's Office
PNE *see* peaceful nuclear explosion
Pokhran test site 63, 71–72
Polar Satellite Launch Vehicle (PSLV) program 52, 77n19
policy innovation 16, 40

Prakash, Arun 119, 142n110
Pressler Amendment 79n84
prestige 31–34
prime ministers: nuclear test opposition from 38, 52; weaponization concerns of 87; weaponization mixed views from 34–35, 163; *see also specific prime ministers*
Prime Minister's Office (PMO) 27, 50; extreme caution of 67–68; fears of 63; mobilization by 53; oversight ability lacking for 120; secrecy of 51
principal-agent model/relationship: evolution of 131–137; goal divergence impacting 21–22, 23; information asymmetries impacting 21–22, 24; inter-agent competition and 69–75; moral hazard and 22–23; problem 21–25, **25**; purpose of 13; roles defined in 21; transparency benefiting 131–132
Prithvi missiles: Devil program 75; IGMDP development of 108n75; range of 56, **56**; testing of 57
problem decomposition: avoidance of 105; for optimization 21; secrecy preventing 92
process-tracing method 6
PSLV program *see* Polar Satellite Launch Vehicle program
psychological biases 18–21

Ramanna, Raja 59–60, 81n145, 90
rationality-bending effects model 40–41
rational optimization: as myth 18; open and decentralized decision-making systems compared to **22**
reactors: Canada assisting with 61; CIRUS 61, 73–74; DAE problems with 61, 70–71; Dhruva 73–74, 81n145; Dimona 151–154, 165n51; LWR 56; Osiraq 67, 80n111; US supplies for 61–62
recessed deterrence: meaning of 84–85; non-weaponized deterrence compared to 85; nuclear opacity in relation to 107n16
Red Book 129

sanctions, US: end of 38; fear of 51, 61, 95–96; Pakistan limited 98; triggering events qualifying 97
Santhanam, K. 90, 124

Sarabhai, Vikram: as ISRO founder 52; Profile 70–71
SASA *see* Strategic Armaments Safety Authority
secrecy: argument specific to India nuclear program/policy 25–28; challenges with 12; as characteristic of all nuclear weapon programs 145; compartmentalization from 5; of DRDO 99–101; from fear 24, 105–106; of PMO 51; problem decomposition and parallel processing prevented by 92; rationality-bending effects model of 40–41; regimes of moderate 147–161; revisitation of 161–163; state learning limitations from 5; structural theory expectations for 42; types and variations of 146–147, **147**; of weaponization 27, 32, 88–89
SFC *see* Strategic Forces Command
Shankar, Vijay 131, 136
Singh, Arun 90, 94, 116
Singh, Jasjit 84–85
Singh, Jaswant 36–37
socialization: Defensive Realism in relation to 10–11; process of formal 112–113
Sociological Institutionalism 35
Solingen, Etel 38–39
SOP *see* standard operating procedures
Soviet Union: LWR offer from 56; NSA on 115
SPS *see* Strategic Program Staff
Srinivasan, M.R. 65–66, 81n145, 140n53
standard operating procedures (SOP): assessment of 117–118; lack of 95; as problem 21; Red Book and Blue Book 129
state learning: adaptation compared to 3–4, 10, 105, 137; argument specific to India nuclear program/policy 25–28; definition of 11; epistemic actors and 17, **18**; secrecy limiting 5; unevenness of 11–12
Strategic Armaments Safety Authority (SASA) 120, 137
strategic autonomy 98–99
strategic culture: argument 9–10; lack of 35–36; nuclear minimalism regarding 37–38
"strategic enclave" 99

Strategic Forces Command (SFC): authority of 117; beginning of 118; coordination issues for 119, 134–135; expansion of 119; force constitution protocols from 130; IDS in relation to 119–120; institutionalization of 113; for management and oversight 112; missile reliability concerns of 126–127; optimization forced by 121; on strategic security 127–128; training for 132; war game simulations of 129

Strategic Program Staff (SPS): institutionalization of 113; for management and oversight 112; members of 120; NCA working with 113; oversight functions of 135–136; problems with 136–137

strategic security 127–128

strategic stability 85

structural theories: assumptions 18; expectations of standard 41–42

Subrahmanyam, K. 36, 59–60

Suez Crisis 151–152

Sundarji, K.: on nuclear asymmetry 7n5, 58; nuclear weapon lobbying by 67, 88

Surowiecki, James 68

Symington Amendment 98

Tanham, George 36

"Task Force on Management of Defense" report 116

technics 29

Terminal Ballistics Research Laboratory and Armament Research & Development Establishment 74

thermonuclear warheads 122–126, 132–133, 140n53

"time lengthening" mechanisms 17

transparency 131–132

trust 73

uncertainty: epistemic community for managing 12; as fundamental challenge 60; questions confronting 4

United States (US): Apollo program 73; arms control community 14; Atoms for Peace program 61, 161; CIA 62, 84; Department of Defense report 96; on France nuclear weapons program 148; on India and Pakistan nuclear capability 83–84; India nuclear program/policy compared to 146; India nuclear program/policy pressure from 161–162; on Israel nuclear weapons program 154, 165n51; JASON Committee 125, 137, 140n56; Manhattan project 73, 145; National Security Council report 96; NNPA passed in 51–52; nuclear tests 126–127; Pakistan relations with 63–64, 79n84; Ploughshares program 49, 76n1; reactor supplies from 61–62; sanctions 38, 51, 61, 95–96, 97, 98

uranium enrichment: India problems with 65; Iraq program for 157–161; Pakistan focus on 64–65

US *see* United States

Vajpayee, A.B. 123

Valiant program 52, **56**, 77n19

value judgments 60–69

Walt, Stephen 7n6

weaponization: Arunachalam as manager of 91; authorization for 2; completion of 7n18; cost reduction mechanisms of obtaining information absent from 98; definition of 8n25; delaying of 10; DRDO and BARC hijacking 101–102; fear of foreign discovery of 96–97; fission warhead 126, 140n53; IAF lacking information on 88–89, 115–116; prime ministers concerns on 87; prime ministers mixed views on 34–35, 163; secrecy of 27, 32, 88–89; thermonuclear warhead 122–126, 132–33, 140n53

weapons-grade plutonium 73–74

Wisdom of Crowds (Surowiecki) 68

"wisdom of the crowds" 4, 27

"within case" analysis 5–6

Woolsey, R. James 84

Zangger Committee 51, 77n11

Made in the USA
Coppell, TX
22 January 2025